BILL ELLIOTT

Fastest Man Alive

Al Thomy

Peachtree Publishers, Ltd.

To Aunt Alice, Evelyn, the Thomys, Johnstons, Styers, Podgornys, Sims and Mildred and George Elliott, with many thanks for their cooperation and counsel.

Published by
PEACHTRÉE PUBLISHERS, LTD.
494 Armour Circle, N. E.
Atlanta, Georgia 30324

Manufactured in the United States of America

Design by Paulette L. Lambert
Photo credits:
Dozier Mobley - Front cover, #22, 25 & 26
Jack Ackerman - 13
Other photos courtesy of:
Mel Poole/Charlotte Motor Speedway -15, 16, 17 & 20
Southern MotoRacing - 12 & 21
Nascar - 23
Mildred and George Elliott - All others

10 9 8 7 6 5 4 3 2

Library of Congress Catalog Card Number 87-80976

ISBN 0-934601-38-0

Table of Contents

1

The Fastest Man Alive

FRIDAY, APRIL 24, 1987 . . .
All is not well for the Elliotts during qualifying day at Martinsville.

Like a sick panther, the No. 9 Coors Thunderbird sits on pit road, its hood raised, with Ernie Elliott's head stuck down over racing's most famous power plant. "Dr. Elliott's" diagnosis: A complete transplant is needed, this one has gone bad.

Time and qualifying wait for no one, and as Elliott works, car after car runs its lap. Soon it is announced that Morgan Shepherd in a Buick, at 92.355 miles an hour, will be on the pole for Sunday's Sovran Bank 500. Everyone goes home but the Elliotts and ol' No. 9, which is still in surgery.

Plans are to run during the second round of qualifying on Saturday, but along with Saturday come the rains, all-day rains, and for the first time in his career Bill Elliott has to accept a provisional start, thirty-first and last.

On Sunday Dale Earnhardt wins his sixth Winston Cup race of a banner season when Geoff Bodine, who has a twenty-second lead on the field, loses it in the first turn. Lost in the unexpected finish is one of the finest efforts of the NASCAR season, Elliott's derring-do in coming from last to finish sixth, even leading at one point. It is a show in itself. By the twelfth lap he has already passed twelve cars. This is the kind of short-track performance he doesn't get enough credit for.

Thursday, April 30, 1987. . .

It is qualifying day for the annual Winston 500 at Talladega, over the world's fastest closed-course track, the 2.66-mile Alabama International Motor Speedway, built on ancient Indian burial grounds. The Coors Ford, nose down and tail defiantly up, coiled like an angry panther, shows no sign of illness as it awaits its turn on the grid.

Actually, it is not the same car. It is a twin, the marathon version of ol' No. 9.

The mood is entirely different. This is Talladega, and here Bill Elliott is king, the fastest driver alive. In 1985 he took speed into another dimension by flying low at 209.398 miles an hour. This was followed by an incredible speed of 186.288 miles an hour in the Winston 500, the fastest five-hundred-mile race ever for autos, in what is considered the greatest stock car run ever. He came from two laps down to catch and pass the field without benefit of a caution flag. The assault on speed continued the next year when the Georgia redhead pushed his red-nosed Thunderbird to 212.229 miles an hour to break his own record.

Now the racing pundits are predicting speeds in the range of 214 to 215 miles an hour, which Bill ran in January tests. Some are asking, "Where will it end?" The two fastest tracks in NASCAR are Talladega and Daytona, and Bill holds all the records. He has run 210.364 over the high banks of the 2.5-mile Daytona layout. Forecasts are interesting, but Elliott knows better. It's hot, in the high nineties, and humid, and conditions are far different from those in January, when he registered a lap of 214.600 under ideal skies.

Rivals are closing the gap at Talladega. In 1986, when he ran 212, others were at 202 or 205. Now, in the early qualifying runs, Bobby Allison has run 211.797, and his rookie son Davey has reached 210.610. Five other drivers, including the omnipresent Earnhardt, are around the 210 level.

It's time for the most exciting moment in modern-day Winston Cup racing, the spontaneous roar as the Coors Thunderbird cranks up and rolls off pit road. But first Elliott has to get ready. Slipping through the window feetfirst, he adjusts himself, and an aide straps him into the protection of the steel cage. Next, like a surgeon scrubbing down, hands up, he dons one glove and then the other. An artist is about to go to work. Once the gloves are on, he slips on the helmet and secures it while the crewman attaches the mesh barrier over the window.

A strange transformation has taken place.

The fresh-faced, Huck Finn redhead, the mountain boy with the unsophisticated ways, the most popular driver in stock car racing, by vote of the fans, is no more. He has become a masked, Cyclops-like appendage of the car, swallowed whole by a fierce-looking Thunderbird. He and the car have become one.

In *The Psychology of Motor Racing*, Raymond de Becker touches on this mystical phenomenon. He writes, "Their [drivers'] real personality remains concealed and they have to share their glory with their machines. . . . It is not the man alone that conquers glory; even in the moment of victory he is one with the machine. He is stripped of his individuality and enclosed in a sort of anonymity unknown in sports where success is due to human effort alone."

Only a race driver can fully appreciate those words. Always, throughout his career, the car has been the most important item in Bill Elliott's life. Any distractions — media interviews, etc. — are resented because they take him away from his mechanical alter ego. Critics scoff and insist it's a cop-out, but drivers and wives are aware of the strange bonds that bind man and machine.

Kathy Bodine, wife of racer Geoff Bodine, talked with veteran *Landmark* motor sport writer Randy King about it. "Let's face it, we're not No. 1 in their lives," she said. "The race car is No. 1. The woman is different. I think you try in the beginning to be No. 1, but as soon as they know they've got you, you're hooked."

Said Bill's wife, Martha: "He chooses to drive that way and there's not one thing we can do about it. You never have time for yourself. Everywhere you go, somebody wants to stop and talk racing or wants an autograph. Sure we had a good year in '85, but it took its toll. All the success came so rapidly and caused so much turmoil."

Bill's father and mother, George and Mildred Elliott, are at Talladega for qualifying, and Mildred admits to some apprehension, as any mother would. "I used to go to most races but I don't anymore," she says. "Now I go to two, Talladega and Atlanta, and watch the rest on TV. You can see much better on TV than you can in person. Quite frankly, in qualifying, my heart is pounding as fast as he's driving."

She sits at a table in the infield center and holds her head in her hands as her last-born presses his foot to the floorboard amidst the tumult and the frenzy of the faceless thousands in the stands. She is relieved when the run ends and the speed is announced: 212.809, a shade better than the old record, but still a new world closed-course standard for stocks.

"That's fast enough," she says to no one in particular. But is it? Media critics are not satisfied. They remind each other that Bill ran 214 in tests. No matter what he does, being the fastest stock car driver alive is a catch-22 for Elliott. The higher he raises the stakes, the more is expected of him.

He knows this.

He says, "When we ran here in the winter, I felt we ran as fast as we could possibly go, and it was thirty degrees then. I knew going in that as hot as it was, speeds wouldn't be what people had been expecting. I don't know if you'd ever have seen 215, even under perfect conditions. One year I'm not going to win the pole at Talladega, and everyone is going to be asking why."

That's the burden of being the world's fastest stock car driver, the Quickdraw McGraw of the fast lane. Performance rarely satisfies expectations. As the resident speed king, you're everyone's target. Get a little old or a little slow, or a little of each, and you're a goner, Tex.

Bill, Ernie and Dan Elliott know both sides. They struggled for nine years before they found room at the front. In fact, through 1987, their careers were divided into two equal parts of 116 races each. Their first 116 were a bust; their next 116 a boom.

They went this way:

One hundred sixteen races, from 1976 to 1983: one win, two poles, one outside pole, twenty-one top-five finishes, thirty-three top-ten finishes, twenty-seven finishes eleventh to thirty-first; thirty-five failures to finish or dropouts, $950,656 in prize moneys, average purse per race, $8,195.31.

One hundred sixteen races, from 1984 to 1987: twenty-two wins, twenty-seven poles, twelve outside poles, thirty-four top-five finishes, fifty-nine top-ten finishes, twenty-two finishes eleventh to thirty-first, sixteen failures to finish or dropouts, $5,761,765 in purses and awards, average purse per race, $49,670.39.

During those four seasons Elliott was racing's leading money winner, with only Dale Earnhardt ($5,016,507) close. Elliott's lifetime earnings of $6,712,330 placed him third among stock car drivers, with only Waltrip ($7,942,404) and Earnhardt ($7,064,759) ahead of him. Trailing Elliott were Bobby Allison ($6,363,112) and Richard Petty ($5,819,656), both of whom had more than twice as many racing starts.

There have been drivers who've had more productive four- or five-year periods than Elliott. For example, Petty won fifty-eight races from 1971 to 1975, but those times weren't as lucrative, and the King collected only $1,373,935 during those halcyon days. Elliott made almost that much for winning only two races in 1986.

Another comparison: Petty averaged $11,127 in winnings for his 523 races; Allison, $12,675 for 502; Waltrip, $10,467 for 426; Elliott, $29,058 for 232; and Earnhardt, $25,878 for 273.

Elliott's split career is interesting. For his first 116 races, he averaged $8,194.52; for the next 116, $49,670.39. He also had racing's biggest payoff: $240,000 for winning the 1986 Winston sprint and Daytona's biggest jackpot, $204,150, not to mention the first Winston Million for sweeping three of the Big Four — Daytona, Talladega and Darlington in 1985, and $2.4 million for the eleven-victory year.

Dollar for dollar, for the number of wins, no one has ever returned more financial rewards than the unassuming mountain boy from Dawsonville, Georgia, who since 1984 has won every third super speedway race he's entered and has sat on the pole a bit more frequently. Through 1987, only Petty's fifty-five, David Pearson's and Bobby Allison's fifty-one, Cale Yarborough's fifty and Waltrip's thirty ranked ahead of Elliott's twenty-three super speedway wins. And his twenty-seven super track poles trailed only Pearson's sixty-four, Yarborough's forty-eight and Buddy Baker's twenty-nine.

When Earnhardt matched Elliott's 1985 campaign with eleven wins in 1987, he moved ahead on total victories with thirty-one, but only fifteen of them were recorded on the big tracks.

Voted Winston Cup's most popular driver four years in a row by fans, Elliott is conceded to be the sport's favorite son since the early days of Richard Petty. However, the way racing works, it is more than personal appeal. In his case, it is also Ford, or Thunderbird. Until Elliott won eleven in 1985, Ford hadn't been in double figures since 1969. Today, he is probably Ford's greatest salesman, proving that the old saying, "What wins on Sunday sells on Monday," is true in his case.

"It goes like this," says Joe McCorquodale, a former race driver who works for a North Carolina agency. "If Bill Elliott wins, we get a lot of inquiries about the 302, V-8 Thunderbird sports series. We might pick up a sale or two. If he wins two or three in a row, business really picks up." McCorquodale, who once raced against Earnhardt in North Carolina bullrings, says the same doesn't apply to Chevrolet "because General Motors has so many cars close together, copy cars."

Ford further entrenched itself with Elliott when Motorcraft parts became an associate sponsor prior to the 1988 season. On the flip side, his major sponsor, Coors, has tied its entire Southeastern sales campaign on Bill Elliott, king of the super roads, fastest man alive and your basic, average mountaineer.

Just when everyone thought Junior Johnson was the "Last American Hero," along came Bill Elliott.

"And now, laaadeeeeees and gentlemen, driving the No.9 Coors/Motorcraft Ford, here is . . . Biiiiiilllllll Ellyot . . . from Dawsonville, Georgia."

2

Open House:
The World Comes
To Dawsonville

TIME, LIKE LIFE, can be relative and selective. Four years can mean everything or nothing, can make or break a president, can change an eighteen-year-old from a freshman to an all-American or a dropout, can witness a marriage or a divorce, can discover ways to cure or kill millions.

For twice times four years, Bill Elliott did nothing. Then, as if decreed on high, he became the chosen one.

On November 20, 1983, when he won his first race at Riverside, California, he was one of the world's most widely unknown drivers, a boyish mountaineer from Georgia who talked funny, racing's equivalent to Millard Fillmore or Rodney Dangerfield. Even that first success was bland, coming under a rain-induced caution. Favorite Darrell Waltrip spun out, was passed by Benny Parsons, who was passed by Elliott, and suddenly there it was, his first checkered flag at the end of his eighth season in NASCAR racing.

Dismounting from his Thunderbird, Elliott was almost run over by media types on their way to interview ninth-place finisher Bobby Allison, who'd just clinched his first points championship in twenty-three years, and Waltrip, who'd just lost his first in three.

Like three peas in a pod, all six feet or slightly more, trim and red-haired, the sons of Mildred and George Elliott were lost in the shuffle. It wasn't as if no one knew them. They were familiar figures in the garage areas, running in the pack, borrowing and patching up and making do, despairing at times, but more a part of the background than the scene. Dan's mountain drawl was not as pronounced as Bill's and Ernie's. Bill was the one who walked with arms swinging and toes pointed slightly outward — only he didn't really walk, he was always in a hurry, a restless flame.

His one quote after the race was along the lines of "It's about time luck came our way," not words to be ranked up there with Patrick Henry's or John Paul Jones's.

Despite appearances, this was a historic moment, the start of something big in auto racing, the birth of a star to rank with the Pettys, Waltrips, Pearsons, Allisons, Johnsons, Yarboroughs, Bakers, Jarretts, Robertses, Weatherlys, Flocks, Turners and Thomases.

There's an important point to be made here. On November 20, 1983, the Elliotts were not wild-eyed kids. Bill was twenty-eight, Dan thirty-two and Ernie thirty-six. Those who study such things have said that an athlete enjoys his peak time between the ages of twenty-eight and thirty-two, and if that be true, Bill was entering what author John Jerome called the *Sweet Spot in Time*.

November 20, 1983. Freeze that time frame and pick up the action four years later, almost to the day.

It is November 14, 1987, and all roads lead not to Rome but to Dawsonville, where the Coors/Melling team is holding its first-ever open house. As far as the eye can see, roads are clogged with vans, pickups, Thunderbirds, RVs, all makes of vehicles. From Atlanta and the south they are moving up Highway 400, old Thunder Road; from Tennessee and the west, over the mountains; from North and South Carolina, Virginia and the East Coast, off Interstate 85.

They are race fans, sure, but more than that, pilgrims drawn to the shrine of speed. Dawsonville, where backyard and shade-tree engineering began with the moonshiners, is the new high-tech and research center of automobile racing, an unlikely setting for the Holy Grail of Speed as discovered by three everyday, normal, red-blooded American boys, also known as Good Ol' Boys. It is a Horatio Alger scenario too farfetched for the most spaced-out Hollywood director. If the mountains can't go to Detroit, then, by golly, Detroit, like Mohammed, has gone to the mountains.

Riverside and four years ago seem like a century away. The old racing lords, Allison and Waltrip, have fallen on hard times, having only two wins between them.

Other old-timers have begun to fade. Richard Petty, racing's all-time winner with two hundred victories, is fiftyish and floundering without a first place since 1984; Cale Yarborough is phasing out; Buddy Baker can't win for blowing up; Benny Parsons is mulling over a broadcast career, and Bobby Allison wins only occasionally. NASCAR expected their replacements to come from the next wave —

Ricky Rudd, Geoff Bodine, Terry Labonte, Rusty Wallace, Bobby Hillin, Jr., Phil Parsons, Dale Jarrett, Ken Schrader, Rick Wilson, Greg Sacks, Lake Speed and Brett Bodine — but their progress is measured, deliberate. Most promising are Davey Allison, 1987 Rookie of the Year, and Alan Kulwicki, handicapped by limited resources. Tim Richmond made a spectacular splash in 1986 with seven wins before exiting the next year under mysterious circumstances.

Fortunately, for NASCAR, Winston Cup and race fans, the last four years produced something besides those over the hill and those not ready.That exciting period came up with Bill Elliott, the Road-runner, and Dale Earnhardt, the Coyote, far and away the dominant members of the stock car racing cast.

Elliott is a genuine racing phenomenon, an "overnight" sensation after years of struggling, winner of 23 of the last 117 Winston Cup (20 percent) races, all on super speedways. In four short years he's moved from last to sixth on the list of all-time super speedway winners, trailing only Richard Petty (fifty-five), David Pearson and Bobby Allison (fifty-one each), Yarborough (fifty) and Waltrip (thirty). Through 1987, only three drivers had won more poles on the super raceways than Elliott's twenty-seven. They were Pearson with sixty-four, Yarborough with forty-eight and Baker with twenty-nine.

The Elliotts made qualifying a fine art and added a new dimension to racing. As a result, they raised the ante on the field and pushed the sport into thrilling, uncharted waters, wherein everyone was running two hundred miles an hour, or trying to.

At Daytona, Bill Elliott shattered existing records with runs of 205.114 miles an hour in 1985 and 210.364 in 1987. Results were even more spectacular at Talladega, where he blistered the 2.66-mile stretch of asphalt for 209.398 in 1985, 212.229 in 1986 and 212.809 in 1987. In January of 1988, the Georgia redhead hit 219 in unofficial test runs.

His 1985 season will always stand as a nonpareil year in auto racing — eleven wins, eleven poles, seven consecutive super speed-way poles, four consecutive super speedway wins, the Winston Million, National Motorsport Press Association Driver of the Year, world closed-course five-hundred-mile auto racing speed record (186.288) at Talladega, $2,433,187 in race earnings and Eljer Driver of the Year (an award that includes all forms of racing).

This daring young mountaineer with the unassuming, "aw shucks" manner also did something that high-powered public rela-tions experts could not do — he brought Ford back from the land of the forgotten. Until Elliott's eleven wins in 1985, Ford had not been a factor since 1969. He also revived racing interest in the state of Georgia and had a major impact on attendance at tracks throughout the nation. If they didn't come to cheer for Elliott, they came as diehard Ford fans, and a great many of them came in shiny new Thunderbirds.

That was the Elliott factor. It was complemented by the Earnhardt explosion. During that same period, the Richard Childress Chevrolet team, featuring the guy with the gunslinger looks and disposition, won twenty-two races and two championships, the one in 1987 only the second $2 million season ever, in any form of racing.

Together, from 1984 to 1987, Elliott and Earnhardt won nearly 40 percent of all Winston Cup races.

"Take away Earnhardt and Elliott and what have you got?" said former NASCAR great Buck Baker. "They're half the field."

Two opposites.

Earnhardt, tough guy, more durable than fast, winner of only one pole all season and only eight in a career, an intimidator, a banger, an old-fashioned Saturday night racer making it work on the supers.

Elliott, Huck Finn, boy next door, smoother than silk, a strategist, quick and quicker, fastest man alive.

Racing's E&E Era.

On November 14, 1987, the Elliotts don't know exactly how many to expect for their first open house. Earlier, Junior Johnson and Earnhardt had theirs, and each drew approximately thirty-five thousand people. Whatever comes, Dawsonville, a community of 347 souls, take or give a birth or a death, is ready. Banners reading "We Welcome You to Bill Elliott Country, Coors/Melling and Motorcraft" decorate downtown buildings. Natives are out in force to help with traffic control and cleanup projects.

A time to honor the local heroes, sure, but, what the heck, also a time for free enterprise. So that no one will be confused, service-station owner Rooster Ingram posts the notice on his counter: "Everything in here is for sale." Under it are the business hours: "Open most days about 9 or 10, occasionally at 7, but some days as late as 12 or 1. Close about 5:30 or 6, sometimes as late as 11 or 12. Some days or afternoons we're not here at all. Lately I've been here all the time except when I'm someplace else."

Rooster Ingram is flexible.

On this day he's moving fast, pumping gas, posing for snapshots for the flatlanders and keeping up steady chatter with visitors and friends who have dropped by to gawk at the foreign gawkers and bumper-to-bumper traffic moving around the courthouse square on its way to the racing shop some five miles from town.

"It's unreal for Dawsonville to have this many people in it," says Ruby Jean Turner, Rooster's sister. "It's fascinating. If all the people I saw at Bill's shop were here at one time, I'd say there would be more people than were here for the three weekends of the annual fall festival. For sure, Bill's put us on the map."

Ruby Jean says she went to school with Ernie Elliott but looks about the same age as Bill, which proves that women in Dawsonville are no different from women in Atlanta.

While business is brisk for Rooster Ingram, the real crowds are across the street lining up in front of the Dawsonville Pool Room, which is reaching legendary proportions via radio and TV motor sport programs. Announcers Barney Hall, Ken Squier, Dave Despain, Dr. Jerry Punch, Eli Gold, Ned Jarrett and Dick Brooks have likened the best little billards hall in Georgia to the old town criers. When Bill wins a race, proprietor Gordon Pirkle, a virtual racing encyclopedia, announces the good news with a shrill siren.

On this perfect day in the hills, Pirkle's one-room emporium looks more like a Boy Scout camp than a pool hall. Kids, parents and visitors, most in Bill Elliott T-shirts, jackets and caps, move about checking souvenirs, pictures, everything except the two green-felt tables.

"Notice no one is playing pool," Pirkle says with an approving grin, an uncommon statement for a pool-room operator.

He explains, "This is the nicest crowd, the nicest people, I've ever seen. To have this big a crowd from all the states and all parts of the country, it's incredible that there's not a rowdy one in the crowd. I've been to a lot of races and I know the reputation of some racing crowds, but this is proof positive that racing fans aren't as bad as some people think they are.

"Bill's got the right people behind him — families, kids, older people, all well-behaved. Usually when people wait in line four and five hours they get their feelings ruffled, but everybody came through here in a good mood."

No one is more pleased with that news than George Elliott, patriarch of the family and the man who started the whole Bill Elliott craze. He never was comfortable with the moonshining and brawling image of racing, and there is a bit of irony in that Dawsonville, where it all began with stills and '39 Fords, has returned in the lap of propriety and respectability.

"Racing is a great sport and deserves to be treated with respect," says George. "Therefore, it is important to have the right image and the right people representing racing."

Any study of the Elliotts has to start with George.

Tall, gray and erect, he is the prototype of the vanishing Southern father figure. He speaks in calm, measured words without affectation, sophistry or guile. Like most mountain people, he keeps family matters to himself, but when he says something, that's what he means. Forked tongues are not part of mountain heritage.

George Elliott was successful long before racing came along. He has owned a building supply company, an Atlanta television station (with partners), a Ford agency and an auto parts firm. He built the local high school and contributed the science center. At one time or another he served as principal and teacher at two schools in the area. About a quarter of a century ago he became interested in racing, as his father Erving was before him, and made it his avocation, sponsoring cars and selling parts at backwoods tracks in Georgia.

Betty Turner, chairperson of the Democratic Party in Dawson County, knows the Elliotts well. Her husband K.K. (Kenneth) Turner, a real-estate man, is Mildred Elliott's cousin and nephew of the late and legendary Roscoe Turner, a powerful Republican committeeman who led the Eisenhower faction against the Taft faction at the historic 1952 national convention, the first to be televised. Her sons, Mike, David and Grady, were contemporaries of the Elliott boys and played major parts in getting them started by serving as volunteer pit crewmen.

Betty Turner reflects the unanimous opinion of townspeople when she says, "George Elliott is a brilliant man; he has a brilliant mind. He was my principal for a little while at Lumpkin Elementary School, and he was the best principal I ever had. This was a country school, and he built tennis courts and he had all kinds of athletic field-day events. Later he was principal over at Westside school.

"I've known George and Mildred Elliott all my life. We lived in the same community about a half mile away. His cousin Jean and I started school together, graduated together and roomed together two years in college."

As mother of three boys, Betty Turner had much in common with Mildred Elliott. "I remember them [the boys] racing down in the pasture below the house, but those boys had to work hard," she says. "I think that's why my boys and George's boys were so close. They had to work for their daddy and he was a hard taskmaster, and my boys had to work for their daddy and he was a hard taskmaster, too. The only way any of them could get off work was to play athletics. Mine were real athletic; the Elliotts were not. They just went to races and they've always raced.

"They were nice boys but they had to toe the line. Once I went to a Halloween Carnival and I saw Mildred there and I saw George at a football game and that was unusual. I said, 'Mildred, why is this? I don't usually see you here with the boys.'

"And she said, 'Oh, the boys aren't allowed to come to town unless either George or I am with them because George caught one of them throwing circles and clowning around in town. We have restricted them. They can't come to town unless one of us is with them.'

"They had come to the Halloween Carnival and Mildred was with them and they had come to the football game and George was with them. They were strict with their boys and we were strict with ours."

In both cases, Betty Turner likes the results. "Bill is such a good sports image," she says. "He's never used alcohol, never done drugs — none of those boys have, none of mine have. You couldn't smoke around George.

"I smoke but I've never let George know that I smoke because he is bitterly opposed to it. He would run those kids out of the family if they smoked. When he had that Standard Supply house up there, if you walked in smoking he'd tell you to leave. He didn't want you as a customer. He's adamant about that."

The charm of the Elliotts is that they're exceptional people who don't think they are. You wouldn't know that George Elliott is a mountain land baron and a wealthy man who, it is said, spent a million dollars on his sons' racing team before they hit the big time.

"Money didn't really mean that much," he says. "I've always had the attitude that if I had enough money to get my bills paid, that's all I wanted. I wanted to enjoy what I was doing. That's what I tried to teach the boys." Characteristically, Bill, Ernie and Dan have inherited their father's and mother's frugal ways.

"To me, money is just something necessary to live," Bill told Steve Waid of *Grand National Illustrated*. "Sure you can buy nice things with extra money. To me, I can go somewhere around home and buy the best dinner you can buy for three or four bucks. I'm not stingy, but why go out and pay a hundred dollars when you can pay much less and get what you want?

"I've tried to do things with my money. I've got CPAs helping me because I can't do it myself. I have to be ready for my future. I can't race when I'm sixty-five. I don't want to. In racing, you're only as good as your last race. You never know when it's going to end.

"To me, though, material things are irrelevant, and the American dream is to have a couple of acres of land with a house on it, a couple of dogs and cats."

Needless to say, he obtained the American dream, moving wife Martha and daughter Starr from Mama Reece's basement across the street from the shop to a spacious home in Dawsonville and later to a rustic lakeside abode in Blairsville, some forty-five minutes north of the old homestead. The others remained: Ernie, wife Sheila, children Julie, Casey and Nicki within shouting distance of his engineering shop and Dan, wife Lollie and daughter Janet down the road a piece. George and Mildred continue to live in their modest home on a ridge overlooking the Coors/Motorcraft operation and the daily activities of their offspring and across the street from Mrs. Elliott's mother, Audie (Mama) Reece, in her ninetieth year.

Like Mama Reece, George's mother, Ruby Elliott, in her eighties, remains loyal to the old homestead, still residing in the house that she and husband Erving built on the banks of Lake Lanier in 1935. Daughters Ethel and Louise, both married to Smiths, are nearby.

Living as they do, in the Blue Ridge area, racing came naturally to the Elliotts and the Reeces.

"We were all ardent race fans," George Elliott says. "Mainly, it's because Gober Sosebee lived a few miles from us and he was doing so well on the tracks around here. We went to the same church with Gober, the Methodist Church, and our tent was next to his on the church campgrounds. Some in the family — Ernie and Dan and the sisters — changed churches when they married Baptists, and Bill, he never did join the church. You know how youngest sons are, last in the pecking order."

That doesn't mean that Bill isn't religious. Eschewing attention, he worships in his own way.

"We go to the Methodist camp meeting and Bill's always gone," says Betty Turner. "He's always come in and had dinner with us and stayed some.

"Last year he came; he just kind of slips in and wants to have dinner and wants to be quiet. Well, when he came in, all those people said, 'Bill Elliott's over there' and they came running into our tent. He doesn't like that. He wants to be the same old Bill. That's the way he is. Now Dan's the jokester; he can meet people. Ernie is quiet and withdrawn, too. They're just hardworking people." Geographical loyalty is important to George Elliott. Though Dawsonville reaps most of the attention and credit for the Elliotts, the family homes and businesses are actually on the outskirts, some five miles from the town proper.

"To be precise," says pool-room operator Pirkle, "they're not from Dawsonville proper. The city limits end in a radius of a couple miles around the old courthouse. George and his family have always been natives and residents of Dawson County."

Rooster Ingram, who seldom agrees with Pirkle, defines Dawson-ville differently. "Naw," he says, "Dawsonville has a radius of eight to ten miles.That's why they call him 'Awesome Bill from Dawsonville.'"

Pirkle has come to expect that kind of argument from Rooster. When he informs his colorful business neighbor that two television crews were in his place recording interviews, Rooster comes back that four had taken pictures of his service station. It's a friendly rivalry to see who can get the most attention.

The fact is that George Elliott's geographical region covers more than Dawsonville or Dawson County. Born and raised in Dawson County, he was educated at North Georgia College in Lumpkin

County, and his Ford agency was located in Dahlonega, the county seat, thirteen miles northeast of Dawsonville.

With the exception of military service and a brief post-World War II period, when he worked for the Burroughs Machine Company in Fitzgerald, Georgia, George has never left the hills. He, Ernie and Dan earned business administration degrees from North Georgia, a respected military school. An average high-school student interested only in cars, Bill declined to further his education.

"He just positively would not go," explains George. "I think now he wishes he had. At the time he was caught up in what he was doing. Ernie, at first, didn't want to go, but we got him to go on. He almost finished, then a little later went back and finished."

Like most young men at the time, George's higher education was interrupted by service duty, in his case a four-year hitch in the Navy. He started at North Georgia in 1942 and finished with the class of 1949. A lot occurred in the interim. In 1943 with the war going full blast, he and Mildred, whom he met in the Dawsonville Agriculture Office, were married, and he enlisted in the Navy.

The war ended halfway through his enlistment, and George Elliott, not one to mark time, found more opportunities to expand his knowledge. As part of the Navy's V-7 program, he attended the University of Pennsylvania and Cornell for advanced studies in math and physics. At Penn he completed a year's course in six weeks. That sort of punches holes in the myth that the Elliotts are some sort of backwoods unsophisticates.

Upon service discharge, George and Mildred returned to Dawsonville to await the arrival of their firstborn, Ernie, on July 25, 1947, at the Mary Alice Clinic in Cumming, a wagon greasin' from Dawsonville. Dan (January 1, 1951) and Bill (October 8, 1955) were born in the same building and delivered by the same doctors, the Mashburn brothers, Jim and Mark.

Returning to complete his education at North Georgia, George Elliott made his mark with a most distinguished group, the class of 1949. This exceptional class contributed six enshrinees to the school's Hall of Fame, to wit: Eugene Patterson, publisher of *The St. Petersburg Times* and a Watergate-era managing editor of *The Washington Post*; his brother, Dr. Bill Patterson of Marietta, Georgia; Tom Murphy, longtime speaker of the Georgia Legislature; Jim Minter, a legendary journalist and editor of *The Atlanta Journal-Constitution*; Boyd McWhorter, athletic commissioner of the Southeastern Conference, now retired, and George Elliott.

Dahlonega, a Cherokee word meaning "precious yellow metal," was the scene of the nation's first gold rush in 1828. For years afterward, millions of dollars in gold were taken out of its hills and streams, and, because of the primitive methods of panning, much of the precious metal was said to be lost. When North Georgia College was founded in 1873, its administration building was located over the site of the old U.S. Mint, taken over in the Civil War by the Confederacy. Today the gold-plated steeple of the W.P. Price Memorial Building is one of the most attractive and unique landmarks on any college campus.

In addition to the distinguished class of 1949, the school has produced outstanding military and civilian leaders, including General William Livsey, Jr., a commander in Korea, Vietnam and Europe; Major General Burton D. Patrick, leader of the 101st Airborne Division; General Courtney Hodges, a World War II hero; and Lewis R. Slaton, longtime Atlanta district attorney.Once strictly military, North Georgia is now the nation's only coeducational, liberal arts military college, with nearly two thousand students. "This is a college with a special mission," says current president John H. Owen.

The picture-postcard campus is surrounded by quaint nineteenth-century souvenir shops and on the square an old courthouse converted into a gold museum. The Smith House in Dahlonega has long been one of Georgia's favorite family-style restaurants. For those still a-hankering to pan gold, there is the Crisson Gold Mine and Campground, originally opened in 1947 and located just outside of town. In the center of all this history is the Bill Elliott Ford Company.

Dawsonville means a lot to George Elliott. But then so does Dahlonega. Significantly, his auto parts and used car place sits on a huge hill halfway between the two mountain communities where he has spent his life and where his loyalties lie. He does more than talk about regional dedication. He has endowed North Georgia College with the Will D. Young and Newton Oakes scholarships, named for school deans, but they're not for just anyone.

He explains: "These scholarships are for students who will do their life's work here. It's an effort to get away from the 'born 'em and bury 'em' pattern of the past in which people are born and buried here in the hills after spending their productive years in other places. To grow as an area, we need to keep our talent and brains here."

At sixty-plus, George Elliott has accomplished many of his life's goals. He has taught his sons the virtue of hard work, and he has struggled with them in racing for years, bankrolling their apprenticeships and advising them along the way. Then he stepped back and turned the team over to Harry Melling. For many it would have been a time to retreat, retire and enjoy the fruits of labor.

For many, but not George Elliott. He's up every morning with the chickens and at work at his used car and parts business by seven o'clock. He's seldom home before eight or nine at night. He personifies Kahlil Gibran's description of work: visible love. The one theme that runs through his life and, as a heritage through the lives of his sons, is that good things happen to those who work hard.

As an erstwhile principal, it is perhaps appropriate that George located his place of business in an old schoolhouse on a huge hill, almost a mountainside, equidistant from Dawsonville and Dahlonega. Surrounding the building are rows and rows of junked and used cars. On the top row, at the crest of the hill, are dozens of twisted and scorched vehicular frames, the result of a major fire several years ago.

At one time his Ford dealership was in this building.

He recalls: "In 1969 I took on the Ford franchise mainly because I was using some thirty vehicles in the building supply business, and it was cheaper to get them through my own agency than to buy them from others. At one time the dealership was on the square [in Dahlonega], then out here on the east side of the school. On the west side we put the racing operation. In 1980, about the same time Ernie moved the racing operation back to where it is now, Dan wanted to move the dealership uptown, and we put it in the old skating rink building. The board of education closed this school in 1972, and I bought it in 1974."

Coincidentally, that was about the same time that young Bill Elliott, then nineteen, was serving his apprenticeship on the short tracks of the North Georgia hills.

The old Speed Shop, an enclosed ton-and-a-half truck that Ernie used to peddle parts at race tracks, still stands on George's lot, a relic of the past and a vivid reminder of how far the Elliotts have come. It is a stark contrast to the million-dollar racing plant on County Road 183. After seventeen years in the dealership business, George Elliott turned it over to others in May of 1987. The agency now operates under Bill's name.

Watching George Elliott at work is an adventure in frontier nostalgia. As a one-man operation, chairman of the board, president, chief clerk and mechanic, he does it all. His office, with papers strewn over chairs, radiators and floors and used auto parts everywhere, could do justice to Fibber McGee's closet.

"I've never seen the top of his desk," says Gordon Pirkle. "I don't know what color it is. But don't let that fool you. He knows where everything is at, even all that stuff spread out in the woods. Mention one tiny item and he can tell you where it's at and what material it is made of. He has a photographic memory.

"When he was in the lumber business, I've seen him sitting there behind the desk making change, talking on the phone, telling old man Stiles to check on so-and-so, he needs so much lumber and where it's at — doing five things at once and never missing a beat. He's an amazing man."

Betty Turner smiles when reminded of George's unorthodox filing system. "You know," she says, "they say highly intelligent people don't need to put everything in order to get them straightened out and that's the way George is."

Considering his background as a supply officer at the nation's largest naval blimp base, his training as a principal and his advanced studies in math and physics, George Elliott's aptitude for keeping tabs on things may not be as mysterious as it seems. And, through example, this thoroughness was passed on to Bill and his chassis setups, Ernie and his motors and Dan and his engine and crew work.

In George's case, the Beatitudes might have included this line, "Blessed are the cluttered, for they shall find order."

It is a hot and sultry day in July 1987, the week of the Talladega 500, and to attract a breeze George is sitting in the open-door foyer of the old schoolhouse under a sign reading, "Positively No Smoking." The heat is the least of the problems. While he was at Talladega for qualifying the day before, George's office was burglarized. He lost a twenty-thousand-dollar coin collection. You wouldn't expect this in the hills where there are few strangers, but it happens.

As he talks a wasp-like creature buzzes in and out of the door, upsetting the visitor more than George.

"If you don't bother him, he won't bother you," he says. Be and let be, the code of the hills, where one learns to coexist with nature.

The lazy summer day is a good time to reminisce, to talk of the beginnings of the Elliott family, and George fills in a few gaps for the visitor.

"First met Mildred in 1940 when I was sixteen," he says. "She worked in the Dawsonville Agriculture Office, and I used to go there quite often. We became good friends. Two years later I started college at North Georgia, but, with the war heating up, that lasted only through 1943 when Mildred and I got married and I enlisted in the Navy. That was a hectic time in everybody's lives.

"With the war ending in '45, I finished up my hitch at Brunswick as supply officer at the blimp base, came back in 1947 and finished college and joined the Burroughs Machine Company in Fitzgerald, where I worked in blueprints, sales and machinery. I guess I was born to tinker."

He would later retire from the Naval Reserve with the rank of commander.

All along, racing was a part of George's heritage. As he says, "In those days, with Gober Sosebee and Jim and Parker Seay doing so well, I became interested in racing, but, at that time, all I could do was watch.

"Racing is a fascinating sport; it condenses time. Sports like football, baseball and basketball, you play every day and it's one day at a time; in racing you prepare all week and race on Saturday and it makes a week feel like a day. It is also unique in that your success doesn't depend entirely on what you can do yourself. You have to rely on something mechanical, and you end up with one winner and thirty-nine losers.

"When the boys came along, they were just that, boys. They started out racing go-carts and motorcycles, but mainly they had to work in the building supply business. As soon as Ernie became old enough, he went to work. Same with the others. Not having time to participate in school sports, racing was a natural diversion for them.

"By the time Bill came along, Gober Sosebee had pretty much retired, and they had other heroes. Jody Ridley, from nearby Chatsworth, was one they admired along with the Pearsons, Pettys and Yarboroughs. Each had his own hero. It was pretty much split between Jody and the others.

"Responsibility had to be learned at an early age. That might happen earlier in the mountains because each family is an independent entity. Still, they were boys and Bill got bruised a couple of times riding his bike on trails in the woods. He and Ernie would go riding together, but Dan, he was more conservative and wouldn't risk his equipment in the woods and things like that.

"Like all kids and brothers, they'd get into scraps with each other, and it was always two against one and never the same two."

In the late 1960s George got more involved in racing, first as a provider of parts and then as a car owner and sponsor, and the boys' interest intensified. It seemed to be ordained that sooner or later there'd be a race driver in the family. But if George Elliott had anything to do with it, it would be accomplished with professionalism and class, as far removed from the old redneck image as possible.

He says, "A lot of people thought of racing as cow-pasture brawls, and we didn't need that. For many years that image kept racing from becoming the super sport it is.

"In that respect, I never thought that Bill France, Sr., got enough credit for founding NASCAR and making a respectable sport out of stock car racing. What he did reminds me of the story of the forty men who decided to go in, buy a farm and run it together. Two years later it stood there vacant in the tall weeds. There's no way forty men can run anything without a leader.

"France knew this, and he took an unwieldy group of race drivers, all going in different directions, organized them, laid out the rules and brought the whole thing together. Looking back, that was a job of staggering proportions. Whatever else he did, Bill France took care of the people who took care of him and made racing respectable. The fruits of his labor are seen each racing Sunday."

Former driver and now master chassis builder Banjo Matthews has said virtually the same thing in different words. "Who'd have ever thought that you'd see us old race drivers in black tie and tux at the Waldorf Astoria Hotel in New York every December?" he asks rhetorically. "I guess you could say racing has come a long way from moonshining and back-alley garages."

That doesn't mean the sport has reached perfection, and as he relaxes on a hot summer day in the mountains, George Elliott says that, sure, there are some things that can be improved on. "First of all, I think racing needs a more refined scoring system, one that keeps up-to-the-second track of every car, eliminating arguments and controversy. If nothing else, they have the equipment to film a race from start to finish and eliminate all doubt after the finishes.

"Otherwise, there is always the chance of human error. Other than George DeLong, who worked most of the tracks in Georgia and who could score a race all by himself and tell you which car was running where on whatever lap, I haven't known many great scorekeepers. If I could begin a race, I keep up with five or ten cars, but, beyond that I was lost."

The conversation is interrupted by two teenaged boys.

"Still got that '84 Mustang?" asks one.

"The one with the T-top and all the goodies?" asks George.

"That's the one."

"Still got it."

While George and the boys are gone to check out the Mustang with the T-top and goodies, a young mountaineer and his family arrive to close a deal on a car. The husband is bare-chested and his teen wife is attired in cut-offs and a blouse that is only half-buttoned. They're barefooted, as are their small children. They're hill people, young but responsible, unpolished but honest, Li'l Abner and Daisy Mae reincarnated.

It's obvious there is trust between George and the young customers. He goes over the terms, step by step, explaining carefully the obligations of both sides, and the papers are signed.

Like most of George's patrons, race talk is part of the deal.

"Bill done good at Talladega," says the young woman. "All that traveling and seeing the world must be nice."

Her world revolves around a couple of hills, and someone asks if she's done much traveling.

"Been to Atlanta," she says. "Twice."

Isolation is still part of the Blue Ridge and Dawsonville, but now it's the exception rather than the rule in an America of changing demographics. The big-city people and sophisticates are leaving overcrowding, overpollution and overworking for thinly populated mountainsides. On one side of Dawsonville are Springer and Burnt Mountains and the start of the Appalachian Trail, near Amicalola Falls; on the other, the tourist attraction of Dahlonega, bordered by Lake Lanier and homes of the rich and famous. Many predict that eventually Dawsonville will evolve as a resort center.

Betty Turner prefers that option. "People from the North, the South and Atlanta have found this is such a beautiful place to live," she says. "I hate that. I liked it about ten or fifteen years ago when it was kind of a laid-back community. If we wanted to take our children into Atlanta for a night at the theater, we could. We could enjoy the amenities of Atlanta and live up here in a quiet neighborhood. It's not that way anymore.

"If it goes on to become anything, I hope it's a resort area. I'd rather see that than manufacturing and pollution and all that. The only pollution we have now is the automobile."

3

From Moonshine
To Cheeseburgers:
How Stock Car
Racing Began

IF YOU'RE LOOKING FOR Waldorf salads, the Dawsonville Pool Room is not your best bet.

"We don't have no salad bars in here," says Gordon Pirkle, proprietor of the most famous pool hall in the land. "But, for Bill, we'll make an exception. He likes plenty of salad and green stuff, and when he comes in, the girls fix it up for him."

When he's home between races, Bill Elliott frequently lunches at the Dawsonville Pool Room. He is so fond of Pirkle and the place that he contributed the grill off the Thunderbird he smashed at Martinsville, and it's there for all to see, fitting nicely over the air-conditioning vent on the ceiling. A man of his financial means could develop a taste for caviar, but Pirkle's menu suits him just fine.

"He likes cheeseburgers, chicken fingers and salad, any kind of salad," says Pirkle. "During the week before the 1987 Firecracker 400, we'd closed up and stacked the chairs on the tables, planning to give everyone a break and close up for a few days. Everyone around here goes down to Daytona anyway.

"Well, just before we were to leave, here came Bill trying the front door. He saw we were closed and just threw up his hands like we'd left him out there starving. I opened the door and told him there wasn't any problem. We'd make him a cheeseburger and fix a salad. We sat in there and had a real good time talking about things. He's more relaxed with small groups that he knows."

Friends like to tell about the time Bill went to New York for the

NASCAR awards banquet at the Waldorf, and, instead of dining at one of those expensive Gotham restaurants, he slipped into a deli, grabbed a hamburger and smuggled it back to his room for a solitary meal. If he had his choice, he'd pick a Dawsonville Pool Room burger over steak and lobster at Sardi's.

If nothing else, the Elliotts are frugal. Brother Ernie seldom makes the luncheon scene at the pool room. "Lord, no," says Pirkle with a smile. "Ernie goes home for lunch. He lives right next to the shop, and if Sheila's not there, he'll go and make a sandwich for himself. And George thinks eating out is too extravagant."

Pool rooms, in general, have an unsavory connotation, attracting undesirables, hustlers and loiterers, but Pirkle's emporium is not your basic room of game and chance. Though modest in appearance, it is the social center of Dawsonville, the country club, civic hall, confessional and unofficial archives and museum of the Elliott racing team.

From baseboard to ceiling, from corner to corner, walls are plastered with newspaper clippings and pictures chronicling the hometown boy's career from its start in the mid-1970s to the latest Winston Cup race. What information can't be found in the pool room proper is available in the rest room, which is papered in early and contemporary Elliott.

It's all there: the first taste of success at Riverside in 1983, the three wins and thirteen top-five finishes a year later and the explosive season of 1985 when "Just Plain Bill" became "Awesome Bill From Dawsonville" with eleven super speedway victories, a like number of poles, sixteen top-five finishes, the Winston Million and $2,433,287 in prize moneys and awards — the most incomparable auto racing year ever. No one, not A. J. Foyt, Richard Petty, Mario Andretti, Darrell Waltrip, Cale Yarborough, Bobby Allison nor Dale Earnhardt ever attained such a plateau in a single season.

The rise was so stunning and meteoric that the next year when Elliott won only two races and more than a million dollars, the media described the season as a failure.

The story, from the beginning to the most current accomplishment, is there on Pirkle's walls, which received national exposure on the night of February 21, 1987, when Elliott's most recent win, the Daytona 500, was celebrated in the Dawsonville Pool Room and televised nationally by WTBS, the Superstation.

The next morning, Pirkle, self-appointed town historian, mountain philosopher and sports buff extraordinaire, took a visitor on a guided tour through the clippings, old scrapbooks and pictures and challenged him with a rhetorical question.

"Bill Elliott is the first race driver from Dawsonville to win at Daytona, right?"

"Right."

"Wrong."

Pirkle was enjoying the game.

"He's the sixth."

"You mean Dawsonville has had six Daytona winners?"

"That's right. That's not bad for a county with less than 5,000 people and a town with less than 350. Another thing, a lot of people are unaware that stock car racing was born right here in Dawson County.

"Our people were racing long before NASCAR was founded and long before super speedways. In fact, the founder of NASCAR, Bill France, drove for two Dawsonville car owners, Andrew Bearden and Raymond Parks, before he ever thought of the sanctioning business. The ultimate in those days was the Daytona Beach course — I'm talking the thirties and forties — and five of our citizens won down there. They were Lloyd Seay, Roy Hall, Gober Sosebee, Bernard G. Long and Carleen Rouse.

"Mrs. Rouse, whose son Greg works for me in the pool hall, won two races in Daytona, both against outstanding men drivers. It wasn't the Daytona 500, of course, but there was some precedent when Bill Elliott first won there in 1985."

"There was also some precedent when Ernie Elliott built his super engines in 1985. Dawson County's Raymond Parks was the foremost NASCAR pioneer in putting super-swift cars on the racetracks. He was the first major car owner, the ultimate sportsman. For some strange reason, Parks's name was omitted when annual balloting for Racing's Hall of Fame was held.

A Ford man, like the Elliotts, Parks provided first-class rides for drivers such as Atlantan Red Byron, first Winston Cup (or Grand National) winner; Fonty Flock, who won a pre-NASCAR national championship in 1947; France; and Curtis Turner, the most daring and reckless dirt track driver of them all. His engines were built by the two best in the business, Red Vogt and Buckshot Morris of Atlanta.

Crusty Joe Littlejohn of Spartanburg, South Carolina, who sat in on the founding of NASCAR after an early driving career, agrees that no one contributed more to stock car racing than Parks, now a highly successful Atlanta businessman.

"Without the good cars, you'd have no racing, and Raymond had the good cars," Littlejohn says. "He was the money man, the sponsor and the confidante of France. If anyone belongs in the Hall of Fame, he does." Parks usually left the driving to others, but Littlejohn, who promoted at the nation's first half-mile track in Spartanburg for thirty years, recalls two occasions on which Parks took the wheel. "Once was at Langhorne," he remembers. "Raymond didn't think the driver was getting the most out of the car, and he jerked the guy out and drove half the race himself. The other time was at Daytona when I kept needling him about his driving. He called Bob Flock in, jumped in the car and outran everyone on the track. When he figured he'd taught me a lesson, he turned the car back over to Bob.

"He proved he could drive, but the overriding thing about Parks is that in those pioneer days he had the best cars on the tracks."

It's an old story that stock car racing started with the trippers and moonshiners in the Blue Ridge Mountains during the Prohibition days of the 1930s and 1940s. By their nature, beginnings can be difficult to trace. What appears to be the horizon can be just another starting point. Likewise, looking for the genesis of stock car racing can end in a maze of hills and cow pastures.

This, however, we know: Street, or stock, car racing was born somewhere, or perhaps everywhere, in a square outlined by Dawson County, Wilkes County, North Carolina; Franklin County, Virginia; Corbin, Kentucky, and the eastern counties of Tennessee, from the start of the Appalachian Trail near Dawsonville to points bordering the Blue Ridge Parkway.

Not coincidentally, this was moonshine, or white lightning, country, the isolated land of stills, winding mountain roads, souped-up cars, good ol' boys and Treasury agents or revenuers. As an interesting twist, it has been said that many moonshiners became church deacons and led campaigns to keep their counties dry. It was simply a free-enterprising case of supply and demand, and when demand gave way to legalized sale of alcoholic beverages, moonshiners joined dinosaurs in extinction.

Millionaire race-car owner Junior Johnson, formerly one of great drivers of the sport, freely admits his moonshining days, which cost him eleven months in the Atlanta Federal Penitentiary.

"It was a way of life," he says. "Not so much a crime as a failure to tax on whiskey. The problem was if you paid tax you couldn't make any money. There was rarely any violence; moonshiners and revenuers had a lot of respect for each other. It was not like the Hatfields and the McCoys shooting at each other."

A native of Ronda, North Carolina, just outside North Wilkesboro, Johnson was familiar with Dawson County long before Bill Elliott came on the scene. When things got tight at home, he'd make trips to pick up loads in Dawson County, and he still regards his favorite tripping vehicle, a 1939 Ford coupe, with much affection.

"That was my pride and joy," he says. "It would run two hundred miles an hour, not at Daytona but on the back roads of North Carolina; not in 1987 but in 1951."

Amusingly enough, the moonshiners had their own rating system provided by the U.S. Government.

"At one time or another both Dawson and Wilkes Counties claimed the honor — if you'd call it an honor — of being the moonshine capital of the world," Johnson says. "That was determined by government statistics on the number of stills busted."

Johnson is not just making idle talk when he speaks of implied honor between moonshiners and revenuers. This was more than brought home several years ago in a remarkable convention at Dahlonega, thirteen miles from Dawsonville, where retired trippers and revenuers gathered to feast and swap stories from their adversarial days. It was like a family reunion. Often the hunters and the hunted were relatives or close friends.

Johnson recalls a personal incident from his past:

Barreling around a mountain curve, his Ford coupe's rear end dragging the road with 180 gallons of 'shine, he spotted a revenuer parked on a side road.

The chase began. Souped-up engines screaming, tires screeching, through dangerous hairpin curves, up and down hills, until Johnson was forced to the side of the road by unexpected traffic.

Getting out of his car, the revenuer walked up to Johnson's window, picked his teeth and said, "Gotcha again, Junior."

Johnson shrugged.

"Yep, Joe, sure did."

That was it. The game had been played out, and the hunter had won this time. There would be other times when he'd lose, and that, too, was part of the game.

More often than not, the difference was the car. And more often than not, it was the tripper and not the Treasury agent who had the high-production engine. In those days most of the powerful engines were coming out of Atlanta, being built by such master mechanics as Red Vogt and Buckshot Morris.

Johnson acknowledges the Atlanta connection. "In the area of high-performance engines, there was more accomplished in Atlanta in the 1940s than there ever has been in any other place, in any other period of time," he says.

Even before Johnson, however, Lloyd Seay was a legendary tripper and tracker in Dawsonville, the southern leg of 'shine country. At the tender age of eighteen, he won the first one-hundred-mile race run over the Lakewood mile track in Atlanta. Traveling the loosely run racing circuit, he also won at Allentown, Pennsylvania, High Point and Greensboro, North Carolina, and Daytona. Most of the time he was only slightly faster than his cousin, Roy Hall, who shared both his vocation and his avocation.

On the dusty roads or on the racetracks, few could keep up with the lanky, blond and handsome Seay, a charismatic figure.

Says one revenuer, "I caught him eight times, and each time I had to shoot out his tires."

Alas, the brief song of Lloyd Seay has a sad ending. At age twenty-one, a day after winning the National Stock Car Racing Championship at Lakewood on September 1, 1941, Seay was shot through the heart by a relative over a load of sugar meant for moonshine. His funeral in Dawsonville was attended by hundreds of relatives, friends and fans, and flowers were delivered by the truckload.

Jack Smith, a Georgian and one of the greats of early Winston Cup racing, recalls that day. "I was eighteen at the time and working at a shop in Roswell, a little town between Atlanta and Dawsonville," he says. "That had to be the weirdest day I ever spent. Every two or three minutes, like clockwork, cars would screech around the curve in front of the shop on their way to the funeral. They all came down that road, and they knew nothing was going to catch them. Obviously, Lloyd Seay was well-liked."

From the newspaper account of the death and funeral of Seay, it is interesting to note how the tone of journalism has changed over the years.

The Atlanta Constitution reported:

"Lloyd Seay was well known in Atlanta and all along the highways in the mountains. Federal, state and county law officers knew him as the most daring of all the daredevil crew that hauled liquor from mountain stills to Atlanta. They had many a wild chase when they hit his trail, but had caught him only rarely, for he hurled his car down the twisting blacktop hill country roads at a pace few of them cared to follow.

"He will be missed by racetrack fans as well. Fifteen thousand people saw him hurl his souped-up Ford around the track at Lakewood Monday, running the hundred miles in 89 minutes to win more than $450 in cash. He drove a careful race, unlike his usual headlong recklessness, lying back off the pace while the leaders burned out or came to the pits for service. He then took the lead and held it, sputtering across the finish line with a dying motor."

Fans and the media found irony in Seay's decision to change his car number from 7 to 13 just prior to the Lakewood race.

If the newspaper eulogy seems lenient, or even laudatory, it must be realized this was another place, another time and another attitude. One of the mistakes of history is the insistence on placing events or postures of the past in the context of the present. In the post-Depression period, making a living was paramount, and derring-do, even bootlegging derring-do, was understood, if not admired.

Jack Smith understands those days. "Until [raising] chickens came along, Dawsonville was an economically depressed area," he says. "The forests had been topped, there was little pasture land and the soil was too poor to raise anything. Moonshine was the only product. Later, when the chicken industry boomed in nearby Gainesville, stills began to fade out."

During the peak of the moonshine days, from Prohibition to the late forties, the industry in Dawsonville was centralized in a downtown service station.

"A lot of people don't want to talk about it, but I tell them it's history," says Gordon Pirkle. "Everyone knew that station and what was going on. It was open twenty-four hours a day, and it had the only pay phone in town. That was a mighty busy phone.

"Moonshining was a way to make a living. The Kennedys made theirs [in Scotch] behind a big, shiny desk. The guys here made theirs on the dusty back roads."

In between deliveries to Atlanta the moonshiners would sit around and argue about who had the faster car or who was the most skilled driver, and as Pirkle says, "They'd get to betting, find a pasture out there somewhere and get to racing. It was all unorganized, spur-of-the-moment things."

That was the beginning of stock car racing in Dawsonville and throughout the country.

Soon the locals were joined by the visiting trippers, guys from Atlanta and points in between. Fonty and Bob Flock came up from the big city to load their sturdy cars with 'shine, and they'd stay around to try their racing acumen with locals such as Roy Hall, Legs Law, Lloyd Seay and others. Usually the Flocks brought their little brother Tim along with them.

Fonty and Bob are gone now, victims of heart attacks, and Tim, who has had bypass surgery, works in the front office of the Charlotte Motor Speedway. No one did more in the founding of organized stock car racing, or NASCAR, than the Flock brothers. In all, Tim won forty Winston Cup races and two Winston Cup (then called Grand National) championships in a Hudson Hornet and a Chrysler 300. Fonty won nineteen races, and although Bob was credited with only four, he might have been the best of all, as Jack Smith tells it.

Smith says, "I've always insisted that Bob was the race driver in the family, and I'd tell Tim that right now. It's just that NASCAR came along later in his career."

The articulate Tim wouldn't argue the point. Suffice to say that all three are enshrined in the National Motorsport Press Hall of Fame at Darlington, the first time three brothers have achieved that honor in any hall of fame. Additionally, Tim is in the State of Georgia Hall of Fame.

Though he quit racing years ago, Tim Flock is still recognized and sought out by autograph-seeking race fans. And he takes a lot of ribbing from callers from North Georgia.

"I get a lot of calls from Elliott fans in Dahlonega and Dawsonville asking if I remember the winding roads up there," he says. "One guy asked for tickets and then added, 'How many gallons of liquor did you haul out of here?'

"I told him, well, I never did haul, but I rode with Fonty and Bob up in the mountains when they did. We'd get in that '34 Ford with all the seats out and stack it with 180 gallons up to the windows and right out the back.

"Lot of times, before loading up, we'd go out in the pasture and race with the locals, and that's exactly where stock car racing began. The first modified cars that ran at the old Lakewood track in Atlanta were nothing but liquor cars, down from North Georgia. Those North Carolina trippers didn't know nothing about racing 'til they opened up some tracks and we Georgia boys went up there and put on some shows. It just kind of spread around."

There are legendary stories about trippers and racing, and the most famous involves Bob Flock at Lakewood. Over the years the the tale has been repeated many times, with the featured role changing with each telling, but the man involved was definitely Bob Flock.

As an eyewitness, Tim Flock knows the details firsthand. "At the time, the city of Atlanta said that if you had any kind of record you couldn't race at Lakewood, which was city property," he says. "And, of course, Bob had a record for hauling booze.

"Nonetheless, he had gone to Lakewood and qualified Red Vogt's car for the pole position, and there he was, sitting at the front with a handkerchief tied around his face to conceal his identity.

"That didn't fool Captain Jenkins of the Atlanta Police Department, who later became chief. Walking up with his aides, Jenkins put his hand on Bob's arm and said, 'Bob, get out of the car. You're not going to run in this race today.'

"So Bob put it in low gear and, honestly, this is the way it happened because I was there. He went through the first and second turns and parked on the backstretch, just sitting there. Seeing what happened, Jenkins sent motorcycle patrolmen each way on the track to block Bob.

"Waiting until the motorcycle cops were near, Bob suddenly spun around, gunned it toward the second turn and crashed through the big, wooden fence and onto Pryor Street with the cop right behind him. There was no way that motorcycle could keep up with that high-performance engine, and Bob just lost 'em.

"I've got the article and picture on the whole incident. Three days later Bob and Fonty went uptown to court and were charged $173.

The newspaper picture shows Fonty standing there in court with Bob and Bob looking so pitiful paying that money out."

Despite his daring in the hills and on the tracks, Bob Flock was the kindest and the gentlest of the brothers. On his trips to race at Darlington, he'd load up his Cadillac with friends, and his wife, Ruby, would pack the trunk with fried chicken, potato salad and beans, and they'd stop every fifty miles or so to feast and socialize.

An extremely colorful and active family, the Flocks lived life to its fullest.

Consider . . .

— Papa Carl, who moved his family from Fort Payne, Alabama, to Atlanta, was an accomplished tightrope walker.

— Son Carl, Jr., who in his time made a few hauls to North Georgia, was one of the nation's leading boat racers and winner of the prestigious Chicago World's Fair race.

— Bob and Fonty, in addition to being race drivers, were also promoters and track owners, and Fonty was one of the founders of NASCAR, along with Bill France, Sr.

— Daughter Reo, named after an early car, was a parachutist and an air daredevil who rode the plane's wings and dangled by the axle. In those days the parachute rip cord had to be cut by a knife in midair.

— Daughter Ethel, named after a fuel, was one of the outstanding women race drivers in the nation, ranking up there with Sara Christian and Louise Smith.

— Overseeing this adventurous family was Big Mama, as everyone knew her. She would sit in the stands, cross fingers on her left hand for Fonty, on her right for Bob and her arms for Tim. Only an earthquake or the sight of revenuers would budge her from her "good luck" position.

There was another, an adopted, member of the family, at least briefly. A monkey. Jocko Flocko.

Tim Flock recalls this hilarious chapter of Grand National racing. "In 1952, the year I won the championship in a Hudson Hornet, Ted Chester, my car owner, got this idea of buying a monkey to ride with me," he reminisces.

"I'm the only driver in history that's ever run eight races with a monkey as my copilot, and the only driver who ever had to make a pit stop to let a monkey out.

"After picking out this cute little monkey, we made a uniform for him and painted his name, Jocko Flocko, on his side of the car. In those days we ran fullseat backs, and we built him a perch on the passenger side so he could look out the window. We didn't tell the other drivers, so you can imagine the expressions on their faces when I passed them with this monkey staring . . . at them.

"All went well but in the eighth race of the season, at Raleigh, North Carolina, the monkey got out from under the safety belts, jumped around the car and then hopped on my back and started screaming. I was running behind Fonty and Speedy Thompson was running third, and I had to reach back and hold the monkey down to keep from wrecking.

"Next, I had to come into the pits and real carefully hand him to one of the pit crew. I got back in second gear and went back out, but Speedy had passed me.

"That monkey cost me second place and $750.

"After the race everybody came out of the stands to see the monkey, and I told them I had to fire him because I couldn't teach him to sign autographs. The poor guy was so shaken up he died a few weeks later."

Perhaps there is some significance to Flock's racing with a monkey in those days, for he also raced for peanuts. "I was the Richard Petty of my time," he said. "In 1955, driving the Chrysler, I won eighteen Grand National Races and, until now, Richard's the only one to win more in a single season (twenty-one in 1971, twenty-seven in 1967).

"I won forty races, two national championships and no money. The championship paid $2,800 in 1952, and three years later, when I won again, I got a raise to $2,950. Know what it's worth now? A cool million. Know what forty wins are worth now? Five or six million. I was like Joe Louis and Sam Snead and those early guys who played for peanuts."

Jack Smith, a native of Cherokee County, adjacent to Dawson County, another of the NASCAR pioneers, also collected peanuts for his twenty-one Winston Cup wins. "I didn't run much NASCAR," he says. "It didn't make much sense to go a thousand miles and run for a thousand dollars when I could run the Peach Bowl [a half-mile paved track in Atlanta] and win five hundred dollars.

"You could run twice a week there if you had a good car and they'd pay you lap money once in a while. It was poorer running NASCAR because if you were running hard you were not going to finish races. It was the strokers — what I called strokers — that backed in and won races. I just never enjoyed it.

"Sometimes I'd run eight times in a week. Many times I'd run Birmingham in the afternoon and come back and run the Peach Bowl that night. I'd run Martinsville, fly back, they'd pick me up, and I'd run the Peach Bowl that night. It wasn't until 1955 that I ran some regular races on the Grand National circuit."

It was three years later, in 1958, that Smith was involved in one of the most spectacular accidents ever in Winston Cup, at Darlington. Those in the old open press box, at the first turn, well remember the horror of seeing Smith's car literally take wings and fly some fifty yards over the first-turn guardrail, crashing to the earth nose-first.

"I had just built a '55 Chevrolet," says Smith, "and I felt it was very competitive. I was doing well in the race until Jim Reed, driving one of Lee Petty's Oldsmobiles, spilled oil on the track. Next thing I knew I was flying."

Thereafter, it was said that every time Smith drove to that spot on the track appropriately named "The Lady in Black," his right foot would involuntarily lighten up on the gas pedal.

If Smith had opted to drive the NASCAR circuit from the beginning of his career, there is little doubt he would have been among the all-time winners. He was one of the sport's hardest chargers. Since his retirement, Smith has operated a successful garage in Spartanburg, South Carolina.

Dawsonville's Gober Sosebee is another who likely would have hit the big time had he had the equipment and finances. Still, he merited attention in 1950-1951 when he put together back-to-back victories in the modified Speed Week races at Daytona. In contrast to his two hundred or more wins on out-of-the-way tracks, his only Winston Cup victory came at Augusta, Georgia, June 1, 1952, in a Chrysler. His son, David, is currently a second-generation driver on the Winston Cup circuit.

After the Flocks and Smith, however, the state of Georgia suffered a real drought in stock car racing success. Until Bill Elliott won at Riverside in 1983, only two Georgians in thirty years had driven into victory lane. Sam McQuagg of Columbus won the 1966 Daytona Firecracker 400 and Jody Ridley of Chatsworth prevailed in the 1981 Delaware 500.

Then came the red-haired thunderbolt in a Thunderbird.

Until late 1983, Dawsonville hadn't had much to celebrate about anything except its resort-like proximity to Amicalola Falls and the start of the Appalachian Trail. Neighboring towns such as Cornelia and Demorest could claim connections to baseball immortals Ty Cobb and Johnny Mize, but Dawsonville hadn't had a hero since the trippers of Prohibition days.

Then Elliott had his breakthrough at Riverside.

It was a time for civic rejoicing. "On December 18, 1983, we held 'Bill Elliott Day' in Dawsonville," says Gordon Pirkle. "There were only about 350 people in the whole town, but more than two thousand showed up for a parade that lasted three hours. It was more people than we usually had for the Dawson County Fall Festival that runs the last three Sundays of October."

The best was yet to come.

In 1984, with Coors joining car owner Harry Melling as sponsor,

Elliott recorded three victories, thirteen top-five finishes and more than a half-million dollars in earnings.

Then, the blockbusting 1985 season, and everyone was checking Georgia maps to locate Dawsonville. The national media took notice, and suddenly there were about as many reporters in town as natives.

"It was something new to them," says Gordon Pirkle. "This was a small town and these were just mountain boys who'd built from scratch, boys who'd hardly been to any big-time races before they started running in the mid-seventies. The media saw a good story in that."

Martha Elliott, Bill's wife, took over the phones in the trailer-office at the racing compound and tried to keep all the visitors happy. Elliott needed a buffer and she was it.

In the midst of the media rush, she told veteran racing writer Clyde Bolton of *The Birmingham News*, "Last Tuesday we had *People* magazine, *The New Yorker* and *USA Today*. We've got two TV crews coming today. I don't think *The New Yorker* has ever covered anything about racing before."

Every visiting photographer was taking pictures of the battered old red brick courthouse on the town square, and there were stops to interview citizens in such emporiums as the Dawsonville Pool Room, Looper's Food Mart, Ace Hardware, Mark Heard Fuel Company, Dawson County Bank, Eva Bendley Realty, Cain's Auto Parts, Dairy Queen, Betty's Country Store, Dawson County Library, *The Dawson County Advertiser*, Shenandoah Kountry Store and B&B Service Station. True to Andy Warhol's prophecy, everyone, at least in Dawsonville, became a celebrity for fifteen minutes.

This thought was not lost on Cathy Puckett, managing editor of *The Dawson County Advertiser*, a weekly. She says, "I would say that Bill Elliott has put Dawson County and Dawsonville on the map. The whole family is great, and I've personally enjoyed getting to know and write about them."

Unintentionally, through his success, Bill Elliott was responsible for reviving the legend of Lloyd Seay, who died fourteen years before Bill was born. Seay's tombstone, located in a square-block cemetery less than three blocks from the old courthouse, is now the shrine for racing fans' and writers' pilgrimages. The stone's front had been shaved away to leave the clear outline of a 1939 Ford, and Seay's picture, transferred to porcelain, is glued to the window. Below is an inscription reading, "Lloyd Seay, Winner National Stock Car Championship, Sept. 1, 1941, Lakewood Speedway."

The stone rests there as a historical monument. And, for all anybody knows, it could be on the very spot where stock car racing was born.

4

The Early Years: The Origins of Greatness

HIS NAME IS Grady Clinton Ingram. When he pronounces his given name, it comes out something like "Gwa-dee." But never mind. No one calls him Grady Clinton. He's Rooster. In Mayberry, RFD, he'd be Gomer or Goober. Every mountain town has a Rooster or a Gomer. Dawsonville comes close to having with Rooster Ingram and retired race driver Gober Sosebee.

Ingram likes to tell how he got his name. "When they started growing chickens here, I was what was known as a chicken catcher," he reports. "I'd catch them to vaccinate them, and I'd hand them over to Spec Burns and he'd hold them and give them a shot. I found if I caught the roosters first, they'd get to flopping and get away and Spec'd have to run them down and I'd get time to rest.

"One day I caught all the roosters in the pen and didn't have nothing but hens left, and Spec, he commence a-hollering, 'Rooster, give me another rooster.' There wasn't no more to give him. Ever since that's been my name, Rooster."

Ingram, who operates the service station across the street from the Dawsonville Pool Room, was a frequent companion of the Elliott boys when they were growing up. Mostly he did odd jobs for George Elliott at the building supply company and later the Ford agency in Dahlonega, but he also found time to share in the mischief of the active sons.

Though his words plod out as thick as Gomer Pyle's, there is keen insight in what he says about racing's most famous redhead and his brothers.

On a brisk March morning, Ingram sits in his service station, beneath a banner reading "Welcome To Dawsonville, Home of Million Dollar Bill," and offers a colloquial interpretation of what early life was like in Dawsonville. It was from this same frame building that the moonshine business was conducted in the thirties and forties, and the pay phone on the wall is another vivid reminder.

In his colorful way, Ingram describes the Elliotts in childhood. "Me and Ernie, we run more together because we was closer in age," he begins. "There's lots of difference in them boys' personalities. Ernie, he's always had kind of an ambitious personality, like he's going to grow up smart. Dan, the middle one, he just kinda growed up like everyone else, and Bill, he growed up like he's going to be just the quiet one."

Quiet.

Quiet, but still 100 percent boy.

Asked if his boys were good Christians, George Elliott smiles and replies, "They were just boys."

Tommy Stowers, owner of the Amicalola Florist Shop, agrees. "I was just about seventeen at the time, trying to make a living on my own, and I was working for George at the building supply business. It was red and muddy around the building, and they'd get handfuls out of a mudhole and throw mudballs at me. Bill was very mischievous . . . 100 percent boy. He and Dan would just try to see what they could hunt up to aggravate somebody. They were characters.

"At that time no one would have ever thought they'd be as famous as they are now, but it's not surprising because they have one of the finest mothers and daddies that's ever been."

George's sister Ethel and her husband, Tommie Gene Smith, have returned to the family homestead after years in Gainesville, Monroe and Athens. They're proprietors of the only barber shop in Dawsonville.

She has fond memories of her nephew's early years. "We lived away for a long time," she says. "When Ernie and Dan were growing up, I saw more of them, but I do remember one amusing incident concerning Bill.

"Once, many, many years ago, when he was about five or six, were down at Mama's. It was Christmastime and all the family had gathered, and all the boys had gone down to the lake. The next thing we knew we had this rip- roaring fire going on down at the house. It got so we had to call the fire department to put it out.

"When they drove in, little Bill looked up at the firemen and said, 'I don't know how it happened. I didn't shoot a firecracker!' He had the most innocent look you've ever seen.

"The boys were named for relatives. George has stuck with family names: Ernest George after his father and an uncle Ernie, who had a daughter and no sons; Daniel Loy for Mildred's father; and William Clyde for our cousins, two brothers now deceased.

"William Elliott was a prisoner of war in World War II. He came home, but he was never the same. If I remember correctly, he was in a VA hospital most of the time until his death. Clyde Elliott was killed in an automobile accident when he was about fourteen. I was about six when he was killed and I remember it to this day. He was one of those people who brightened the day for you. I really loved him and was so happy when he would walk over to our house. I would watch his approach with great joy.

"William was older — he was a 'grown-up' — and I didn't know him as well as I did Clyde.

"When Bill came along, Mildred had already had Ernie and Dan and she thought, 'Surely this one's going to be a girl.' They had the name already picked out, Nancy Louise. Well, you know who Nancy Louise turned out to be. It was three years before Mildred would have his hair cut.

"They've always been hardworking boys. George never tolerated any hanky-panky, and when they were old enough to pick up lumber, that's what they did. Dan would drive the forklift, and they'd pick up lumber."

From earliest childhood, the Elliott boys had one passion, cars, inherited from their environment. Fast cars came with moonshiners, and when the 'shiners left, they stayed. Wheels were status.

There was another heritage. Papa George Elliott had been one of the race car owner pioneers from the early sixties. Sponsoring several drivers, among them Jody Ridley of Chatsworth, Georgia, Winston Cup Rookie of the Year in 1980, he was a familiar participant at Lakewood in Atlanta, Daytona, Rockingham and other NASCAR stops. Racing, and more specifically racing Fords, came naturally for George since he was in the Ford agency business.

The Elliotts did more than race. Operating out of a mobile Speed Shop, they made the short track circuit providing parts for other teams and race drivers. In George's priorities, racing was number two. Learning the value of work was first. If there is one word that weaves, like a golden thread, through the lives of the Elliotts, it is *work*.

Says Gordon Pirkle, "George was raised down near where my family was raised, and when he came back from the Navy he went into different businesses. First was the building supply business, and we traded with him. When he got the Ford dealership, I always bought my vehicles from him.

"We saw Bill and the other kids grow up, but, believe me, we didn't see them in this pool room. They were too busy working all the time, and they didn't have time to loaf. Ever since they were big enough to load a truck, they've worked."

A thought occurred to Pirkle and he smiled.

"Once in a while there was a distraction," he said. "Like the story told by a man who hangs out in here. The story appeared in *USA Today*.

"George had asked him to go out and get the boys to help load up an order he had. Well, this fellow goes down behind the building and finds all three boys with their heads stuck under a car hood. After calling several times with no response, he gave up and loaded the truck himself.

"When he saw George later, he said, 'I hope those boys make good in racing. If they don't, they're going to starve to death.'

"I'd have to say that was an exception. They were good boys, never no trouble. Bill was so quiet you hardly knew he was there. Quiet and mannerly."

Across the street, at the B&B Service Station, Ingram tells a similar story of respect for George Elliott's guidance. He says, "My daddy died when I was five, and by the time I was thirteen I was doing jobs all around. George, he was real nice about working me and the other school kids. He'd let us come in after school and get up orders and stuff for the next day. And Mildred, she's got one of the nicest personalities. She always treated me nice.

"I worked for George at the lumberyard and later at the Ford company. And Ernie, Dan and Bill, they always worked as long as I can remember. When he was only seven or eight, Bill would drive trucks and forklifts.

"George taught me a lot of things and helped me out a lot. He let me brick houses for him, showed me [how to use] a cement mixer, and he let me buy some land from him and didn't even cost me no interest."

Being older, Ingram more or less babysat Bill, but his relationship with Ernie was on a more competitive peer level, made more intense in that he drove a Chevrolet and Ernie a Ford.

"Even then Ernie didn't like to lose," says Ingram. "I'd outrun him and he'd get upset and go home and work all week on another motor, and then he'd come back and want to run again, sure did.

"One night over there at the pine tree next to the supermarket, he wanted to drag race. I told him, naw, I couldn't do it because mine was skipping. He kept on. I finally got in my car and he was going to carry me a ride.

"Up there on the perimeter road, he went to first and second gear. When he went to third and started to come back to fourth, something stuck. I tried to get him to come back and get my Chevrolet to pull him, but he wouldn't hear of it. He said he was going home to get a Ford to pull him.

"He knowed if I got hooked up to him in that Chevrolet I'd pull him 'round and 'round the courthouse out here. He wasn't going to be pulled by no Chevrolet.

"The town was full, and if I had got a-hold of him, I'd have pulled him around the square all night . . . and he knowed it.

"In all our funning, only once did we almost get into trouble. We were drag racing on old Highway 36, and when we got to the end, there was the sheriff just sitting there. We'd done slowed down and all, but he pretty well knowed what we'd done.

"Lucky for us, he didn't make no case at all."

Sound familiar? Change a few names and the location, and instead of the *Dukes of Hazzard*, you'd have the *Elliotts of Dawsonville*. The scenario is similar: a harried sheriff and his lone deputy trying to curb the exhuberance of youth, plus plenty of fast car chases.

When the Elliotts and Ingram were growing up, the weekend recreation for kids was not painting the town, but, rather, "oiling the town." To get things started, the kids first had to divert the sheriff and his deputy. A call reporting a burglary at an outlying country store usually did the trick. If not, a couple of fast cars would bait the officers with a fake drag race, then run off and leave them in a cloud of fumes.

With the law out of the way, says Ingram, "Someone would come along in a pickup truck and dump a barrel of oil on the street near the square, and we'd get out there in souped-up cars and do 360-degree spins and clown around. I've seen it so crowded on Friday and Saturday nights that you couldn't find a place to park."

There is no record that the Elliott boys ever oiled the town. But, as he reached his teens, Bill did find ways of testing his driving prowess in more private ways. And usually Rooster Ingram was an accomplice.

He remembers. "When I went to work for George at the Ford place, Bill, he was about thirteen and he'd come around on Saturday and say, 'Rooster, clean my car.' Then he'd say, 'Let's go eat dinner,' and I knowed what he meant.

"I'd get in with him, and we'd go up to Crown Mountain and clown around for thirty minutes. He'd lay flags and throw figure-eights, circles and things like that. There is a big ole drop-off cliff there, and, Bill, he'd come near to the end before he'd swing it left and miss the cliff, then he'd just laugh. Well as I remember, we was in a '63 Fairlane Ford.

"After thirty minutes of clowning, we'd run down to Muncho's, grab a hamburger and be back on Crown Mountain for thirty more minutes of clowning."

Bill was getting to the age when he needed to flex his muscles, and his parents knew it. So did his maternal grandparents. A plan of supervision was devised.

Says Audie (Mama) Reece, now 90: "My husband was living then and he had the field up over the hill past the fish pond, and he told Bill, 'If you want to clown, instead of getting on the highway where you might hurt somebody, you come here on that field. You can clown all you please over there and you won't hurt anybody.'

"And that's what he did. They just had them a perfect road and that was a sight over there. You could just hear them a-whooping and a-hollering. You could hear them from the house. I didn't go over there, but my husband did and he enjoyed it."

George and Mildred Elliott gave their blessings to the project, which allowed young Bill to exercise his adventurous spirit while limiting the risks.

"Out in the country here there wasn't much recreation for kids," George recalls. "Since the boys didn't play sports in school, racing was the other sport we had. If not supervised, they're going to wander and race in the streets."

George Elliott frowned on racing in the streets, but he didn't frown on racing. Heavily involved in the sport himself, he had always hoped for a driver in the family. Ernie was first to give it a shot, but he decided to stick to building engines, a field in which he was already showing great aptitude. Dan was going to school and never showed that much interest in driving. And then Bill came along.

"He fell right in," George Elliott remembers.

Still, there was a test to be faced under racing conditions at a nearby track.

"I've never forgotten that day," says George. "After only a lap or two, Ernie turned to me and said, 'He's a race driver.'"

The next step was to get Bill in a real race against real race drivers. In early 1972, when he was not yet seventeen, it was decided that he would enter a Sportsman race at the Middle Georgia Raceway in Byron, just outside Macon. His first car, a 1965 Mustang with only primer and no paint, was a far cry from the menacing red-and-white Thunderbird of the Coors/Motorcraft team.

The Elliotts, with Mustang in tow, pulled into the Middle Georgia Raceway and prepared to go racing. It wasn't that simple. Raceway officials took one look at the young kid, checked his age and denied admission to the garage area.

Persisting, George asked attendants to summon Jimmy Mosteller, the promoter and a legendary track public address announcer. If anyone was destined to play a role in Bill Elliott's debut, it was Mosteller, a cigar-chomping little guy who traveled the backwoods racing circuit preaching the gospel of belching motors and screeching tires with evangelic zeal. Racing to him was only marginally less important than Hav-A-Tampa cigars, his long-time employer, and he never passed up the opportunity to promote both with a high-pitched staccato delivery. He might have been the first to slap a commercial sticker on a sport now gagging with patches, banners, flags and billboards.

Moreover, Mosteller never announced a boring race. A lousy race only raised the level of his vivid imagination. He was a legend at the old Peach Bowl in Atlanta. Just when fans began to nod off, Mosteller would scream into the mike, "Trouble in turn three! Trouble in turn three!" Prodded from their slumber, spectators would jump to their feet to see what was happening in turn three, only to discover that nothing was happening. That's when Mosteller would add, "What a beautiful piece of driving! Everything's fine now." Everything had been fine all along; little Jimmy was only exercising broadcasting poetic license.

Calling races was just one of his talents. He mingled with fans, calling most by name, and, by sheer persistence, forced newspapers to carry results of every small out-of-way track by making thousands of paid telephone calls. Sometimes the two-paragraph stories made the morning editions, often they didn't. That didn't deter Mosteller from calling in the next race, and he never complained about the reports that weren't published.

With that kind of missionary zeal, it wouldn't figure that Mosteller would decline a helping hand to a kid trying to break into the racing game. He didn't.

But first there had to be talk.

Mosteller recalls, "I went over and talked with George and I talked with Bill. I asked George if he would sign a minor's release so the track would be cleared if anything should happen. George did sign the release and, needless to say, before he went on the track I saw Bill and I said, 'Let me tell you something, son. This track is fast, and these cars are going to be flying. You're a good driver, but you're young and this is your first time here, so I'm going to ask you to do one thing for me. Do not get in anyone's way. If you get in anyone's way I'm going to ask that you be black-flagged.'

"He agreed to that. And I told him, 'Another thing, I don't want to see you getting over your head. Don't let your foot feed get larger than your steering wheel. If so, we're going to black-flag you.'

"With that understanding, Bill Elliott went in there and drove a beautiful race, finishing third, I believe. Even then, in his first race, there were signs that he was going to be something special."

The finish is unimportant. At long last, the Elliotts were in the racing business. It was about that same time that brother Ernie began getting involved in building engines for short-track car owners.

"If I'm not mistaken," says Jody Ridley, " my engine was the first one Ernie worked on. We sort of learned together. When Ernie got out of school, George got him that little Speed Shop, and he learned his way working on those 311 and 302 motors.

"George sponsored me for a year. I ran his advertisement on my car, and he helped me with motors and other equipment. There were times Ernie and I would work two or three days in a row to get a car ready. In '73 we went to Rockingham and lost a clutch.

"On one of my racing trips, to Odessa, Missouri, I took Bill with me. It was his first trip away from home and his mother didn't want him to go. My recollection of the time is that Bill was just a kid, a sort of a roustabout at the Speed Shop, doing everything. You know, they give kids the worst end of it."

Ridley was one of Bill Elliott's early heroes. Another was Winston Cup superstar David Pearson. In 1973, Ridley and Elliott would run on the same track, but in different classes. At the Dixie Speedway in Woodstock, Ridley won most of the A-Class races, and Elliott, in his first semiregular season, dominated the B-Class.

One mission had been accomplished. Elliott had run his first race. Still to come was his first taste of success. Although he'd run tracks at Rome, Macon and Chattanooga, most of his attention was focused on the Dixie Speedway at Woodstock.

Elliott wasted little time in getting over his first-win hurdle. He won his first race there.

Appropriately enough, Jimmy Mosteller was there. He saw it this way: "Bill came in there with a car that just had primer paint on it. It did not even have a number, if I remember correctly. George had said, 'I told him if he'd ever win a race, then we'd get the car painted.'

"Needless to say, Bill started in the back of the pack and from the announcing booth I picked him up immediately coming off turns three and four and onto the front straightaway. He was flying.

"He was moving toward the front, and picking this up real quick and getting the spectators as excited as I was. Would you believe that when the checkered flag went down there must have been four or five thousand people standing up cheering for Bill Elliott?

"He brought that kind of excitement into racing. It's even more intensified today."

Thereafter, for the remainder of B-Class season, young Bill Elliott, still a high-school junior, showed amazing consistency and progress. The next week he was fourth, then first, then third, then first, then second, then first for the rest of the schedule. Of thirteen races entered, he won ten.

A key to that initial success was the paving of the Dixie Speedway. "Bill had to have total control, and he never felt he had control on dirt," says George Elliott. "The car was too much out of control. If he had his choice, he'd never, never drive dirt."

With ten wins, it was stage three of Bill's career, as choreographed by his father. Stage one was entering a race. In stage two he got to paint his car when he won. And stage three called for moving up a class after ten wins.

"He had won ten races that first season, and I told him he'd have to move up to A-Class," says George. "You stagnate if you stay in one place too long."

Hal Hamrick, Dixie Speedway track manager at the time, says young Bill Elliott wasn't overjoyed about moving up, "but he went along."

Elevated to A-Class in August, or mid-season, Elliott managed to win a race in that division before the schedule ran out.

"The impressive thing about Elliott," says Hamrick, "is that at even so young an age he was a smart driver who knew where he was on the track."

Having completed that maiden year, Bill Elliott found a lot of things happening to him in 1974. He graduated from high school, he continued to win races and he got married.

Oddly enough, he and Martha Welchel had been senior classmates at Dahlonega but had never met until they were introduced at a roller skating rink in Suches, Georgia, a tiny community with only a post office and a couple of stores. As Bill tells it, his first call for a date was turned down. The second was accepted, and in less than a year they were wed. His nineteenth birthday and their marriage came about the same time in that October.

Those early marriage years were no bed of roses. Like thousands of other young couples, the Elliotts struggled to make ends meet. First, they moved in with her folks; then they accepted George's offer of a rental house that he owned.

Small-track winnings were hardly lucrative and Martha, who washed cars at the Ford agency, took in sewing and worked with retarded children in Dahlonega, brought home more money than he did. Neither had a lot of loose change.

On the racing circuit, Bill Elliott was doing very well. The wins came regularly. The major victory of those years came in a two-hundred-mile Memorial Day race in 1975. After both the 1974 and 1975 seasons, he had tried and failed to qualify in Sportsman races at the Charlotte Motor Speedway.

All along, Papa George was anticipating stage four, the move up to the major leagues of stock car racing, the Winston Cup. A longtime family friend, Bill Gazaway, technical inspector and racing director of NASCAR, had indicated he thought Bill was ready to run with the big boys.

To do that, however, Bill needed a car, so George shopped around. The best prospect he found was a 1975 Ford Torino.

"It originally belonged to Richie Panch," George says. "I think he wrecked it at Daytona, and I know he wrecked it at Darlington, where he really smacked the wall. They just sort of patched it up, and I think Panch ended up taking bankruptcy. He owed Bobby Allison some money, and Bobby took the car as settlement of the debt."

How did it run?

George can smile now.

"Bill said not worth a flip," he says. "We had several people work on it, trying to get the frame back straight, and we never did get it where it was comfortable driving. And Bill was never comfortable in it.

"In those days I used to kid him that he knew he had to fix it if he wrecked it. So he tried hard not to wreck. That extreme carefulness carried over even after he started driving for Harry [Melling]. He was extremely careful for a long, long time. Of course, you still get wrecked, I don't care how careful you are. The risks increase when you're around people you've never driven with before.

"If you've driven with them, you sort of know what to expect, the way they drive, how they react to certain situations, how they handle passing you and how they handle letting you pass them. There's just no substitute for experience."

Likewise, no substitute for equipment.

Late in the fall of 1975, the Elliotts previewed their new racer at Atlanta and found little to be encouraged about. Bill got the Torino up to only about 147 miles an hour and failed to qualify.

He ran only a limited, eight-race schedule in 1976, his first season in the Winston Cup, passing up the Daytona 500 for obvious reasons. The Bill Elliott major league career was launched at Rockingham.

The team consisted primarily of the Elliott brothers and the Turner brothers, Mike, David and Grady, sons of Kenneth and Betty Turner, lifelong neighbors and friends.

Betty Turner recalls that beginning: "They rode up to the races in a pickup truck and slept in sleeping bags. Mike filled the gas, David acted as carrier and Grady, the youngest, acted as sort of bodyguard and PR helper, going with Bill when he was introduced.

"Once when Bill was interviewed he said, 'When I first got into racing we had my brothers and the Turner brothers, and we were a motley-looking bunch.'"

Hardly anyone at Rockingham noticed the new kid on the block.

The big news concerned Dave Marcis, who beat Buddy Baker for the pole at the Carolina 500, and A. J. Foyt, who unleashed an attack on NASCAR for what he charged were unfair fines at Daytona. The Daytona 500 pole and its five-thousand-dollar prize were taken away from Foyt and car owner Hoss Ellington after his car was declared illegal. Adding insult to injury, NASCAR then subtracted another one-thousand-dollar fine from Foyt's race earnings. The livid Foyt said he might never run Daytona again and he was running Rockingham only because he and Ellington had committed to the promoter.

Neither he nor Elliott was around very long in the race. Bill qualified thirty-fourth and finished thirty-third, just behind Foyt and ahead of Cecil Gordon, when he lost his oil pump after only thirty-two laps. His first Winston Cup purse was $640. Foyt lasted fifty-seven laps and finished thirty-second. The race winner was Richard Petty, who had a two-lap margin over Darrell Waltrip despite two late pit stops for four tires under the green.

Elliott's other attempts in 1976 went like this:

Winston 500 at Talladega — Started thirty-ninth, finished thirty-eighth, completed twenty-three laps, engine failure.

Atlanta 500 — Started thirty-third, finished thirty-sixth, twenty-one laps, broken drive shaft.

Firecracker 400 at Daytona — Started thirty-eighth, finished nineteenth, running at the finish.

Cam2 400 in Michigan — Started twenty-first, finished twenty-eighth, forty-six laps, engine failure.

Purolator 500 at Pocono — Started thirty-third, finished thirty-second, fifty-five laps, engine failure.

Nashville 420 — Started eighteenth, finished fourteenth, running at finish.

Significantly, the respectable finishes Elliott had in 1976 were run in a Ford belonging to Bill Champion, not the Panch Torino. In a temporary agreement, he ran the Champion car at Daytona, Nashville, Pocono and Michigan, if nothing else proving that given the right equipment, he could complete.

Although the payoffs beat the purses at Woodstock, his first Winston Cup season returned only $11,635. To put that figure in perspective, that was the year that Cale Yarborough, in Junior Johnson's Holly Farms Chevrolet, banked $387,173 and won the first of his three straight Winston Cup championships, the only driver to score a triple. During that stretch, Yarborough won twenty-eight races, a career for most drivers.

It was also the year a young driver by the name of Dale Earnhardt ran two races and didn't finish either.

Meanwhile, a situation was developing that was to add another dimension to the Elliotts' future. Bobby Allison, who'd won twenty-seven races during his first five years in Winston Cup, was shut out for the first time and, in disgust, quit the Roger Penske Mercury team. Allison did not agree with Penske's decision to run only selected tracks, omitting some on which Allison traditionally fared well.

So once more the Allison connection was to have a bearing on what was happening in Dawsonville, Georgia. Allison recalls that chain of events. "Penske decided to step away from NASCAR because he found conditions here were different from what he was used to in his other racing life," he says. "I'm talking about Indianapolis and Formula One.

"I wanted to run all the Winston Cup races and several others besides. I didn't mind the Indy races, but I just didn't want to run a handful of Indy races and not be able to run anything else."

In running Indy for Penske, Allison became one of a select few NASCAR drivers to make the transition. His brother Donnie was Indy Rookie of The Year in 1970, and Cale and LeeRoy Yarborough also tried their hands at the open cockpit cars. More drivers have crossed over from Indy to NASCAR than the other way around.

Nonetheless, Allison's decision to leave Penske proved a step up for the Elliotts. "I guess I was involved in their start," Allison says. "The first car they had in Winston Cup racing was the Torino I sold them, and they went on from there and bought the Penske car. That Mercury, I guess, was one of the cars I drove because the following year Penske changed over to Chevrolet."

5

What's in a Number?

"WHAT'S IN A NAME?" the bard once asked. If he were living today, the question could well be, "What's in a number?"

People live by the numbers, and each person has his or her own. You're either a credit card number, a Social Security number, a prison number or an athletic team number. In a lottery there are winning and losing numbers. Thirteen is unlucky, and seven and eleven are lucky. Look out for "snake eyes."

CBS football analyst John Madden, a gregarious bear of a man, entertains by assigning numbers to people according to their appearance. For example, Ronald Reagan might be a "42" and Hulk Hogan an "85." Not so strangely, their numerological brand corresponds to a position on a football team.

At a dinner a few years ago, a writer asked for a reading.

"What is my number?" he asked.

Madden sized him up.

"I'd say you're a nine."

"What's a nine?"

"A Hungarian placekicker."

That seemed so neutral, even bland.

Not around Dawsonville and Dahlonega, it isn't.

Nine is the number on Bill Elliott's Coors/Motorcraft Thunderbird.

It is the number on the highway that links Dawsonville with Dahlonega, a thirteen-mile roller coaster that used to be negotiated in nine minutes by whiskey trippers and drag racers. It is also the number of years it took Elliott to win more than one race on the Winston Cup trail.

Perhaps significantly, there's an extension of Highway 9 leading from Georgia to Talladega, where in 1985 Elliott set the world's closed-course qualifying record with 209.398 miles an hour.

On that occasion, just before the Winston 500, the second leg of Elliott's Million Dollar year, Dawsonville Pool Room operator Gordon Pirkle made a serious numerological error. After Elliott ran a 206-plus in practice, Pirkle hung big yellow letters on his shop window reading, "206 Ain't Bad." Then he attended qualifying and watched the Dawsonville redhead fly low for an amazing 209.398, a world record at the time.

He rushed to a phone and called his pool room attendant.

"Go out to the window and turn that six upside down," he instructed his aide.

He should have known better. In Dawsonville, everything comes up nines.

In his sixty-plus years, George Elliott has seldom been far away from Highway 9. His father Erving helped build it. He was born and raised on one end, in Dawson County; educated on the other end, in in Dahlonega; and split the difference by conducting his business halfway between, six and one-half miles from each town.

His whole life has involved Highway 9. "I can remember when the section from the bridge to Dahlonega was the only paved road in Georgia," he reminisces.

Although Highway 9 has played a major part in the lives of the Elliotts, it is not, as many believe, the reason Bill drives No. 9.

"The car number has nothing to do with the highway," says George. "The No. 9 goes back to Jody and Biddle Ridley, who were two of the idols the boys had. Like the rest of us at the time, they were operating on a shoestring. When Ernie was working at the Speed Shop that we had, he and Biddle got together and used No. 9.

"In races in which both Bill and Biddle ran, Bill used No. 97 on his car, and there were times when he used No. 98. In two races in which he and Biddle ran, he was No. 97, and there were other races in which he was No. 98."

It turns out that No. 9 did not originate with the Ridleys, but, instead, it was lifted from a most unusual source, an Indianapolis car.

"That's where I got it," says Jody Ridley. "I was partial to No. 98 because I really liked Parnelli Jones and his shiny blue-and-white racer. And because I used No. 98, my brother Biddle started using No. 9. All sort of went together."

So scratch off one mystery. The No. 9 Thunderbird comes from Parnelli Jones through Jody and Biddle Ridley through Ernie Elliott to Bill Elliott and the Coors/Motorcraft team.

Bill Elliott has come a long way, literally, from that first car that had neither paint nor identifying number. In a few short years, it has taken its place with Fred Lorenzen's No. 28 as the most recognizable Ford in stock car racing.

Intense research did turn up some "Nines" of the world who made it big — Ted Williams, Jim McMahon and Tommy Kramer. And one Hungarian, or otherwise, placekicker, Matt Bahr. So John Madden wasn't all wrong.

6

1977-1982: Fast, But Not Reckless or Dumb

THE SCENARIO IS familiar to Bill Elliott watchers.

It is late in a race and Elliott, who has gotten behind, steadily moves up on the leaders, making up lost ground in a hurry. When he reaches the fourth or fifth position, he camps in and rides out the laps. Sometimes he drops back a notch or two.

Some observers are perplexed.

They ask, "Why didn't he go for it? He had the jets turned on, then cut them off."

Bill might be fast, but he ain't reckless or dumb. Papa George knows him better than anyone else.

"Bill is a student of the sport," he says, "with total concentration, catlike reflexes and an uncanny feel for things. What you have to know about him is that he has to have a car absolutely under control or he won't drive it. He'll either back off where it's comfortable or he'll park it.

"If it's the least bit out of shape he won't try to make it do something it can't. That's why he wouldn't drive dirt; you don't have control on dirt. Part of that comes from the way we came up. We started with one car and one engine and if we broke either we were out of luck. Taking care of equipment was a big item. I used to kid him that he had to fix it if he wrecked it, so he tried not to wreck it.

"If you go back and watch some of the race videos over the years, you'll find that he does what I call rooting himself out a hole and running by himself. Of course, you couldn't do that at Daytona and

Talladega, where if you got out of the drafts you went backwards in a hurry. So on those tracks you had to stay with a pack, whichever pack you could run with, whichever you felt comfortable with and could latch onto.

"A lot of times when you run in a pack you get in trouble. His power of concentration is beyond imagination. I remember once he backed off, and we asked what happened. He said, 'There's a wreck fixing to happen up ahead.' And sure enough three or four cars got into it and got torn up pretty good.

"He has that sixth sense. At Macon, in those early days, there was a six-car pileup, and he was the only one who got through it. I'm not saying there won't be wrecks. No matter how careful you are, there will be wrecks in racing. But it's foolish to go out looking for them.

"If everything is not working right, Bill waits for attrition to take care of him. One of the prime rules of racing is to be there at the finish."

With the Panch car, which was never comfortable, Bill was seldom around at the finish. Going nowhere fast, George Elliott decided a step up was in order and opened negotiations with Roger Penske, who was closing down his operation after the split with Bobby Allison. In mid-season 1977 the deal was consummated, and Penske turned over the "whole works," including a 1976 Mercury Cougar.

Still, 1977 was a confused sort of year. Bill started in the Ford Torino, shared in the driving of Roger Hamby's 1977 Chevrolet Monte Carlo, of all things, and finished in the Cougar. The Elliotts took the Mercury to the fall race at Talladega, where Bill made an impression before falling out. He picked up a tenth in the NAPA 500 at Charlotte and an eleventh in the Dixie 500 at Atlanta. Before making the switch, he'd managed a tenth in the Ford in the Southern 500.

"I remember when I first associated with them," says veteran chassis builder Banjo Matthews. "They had the Penske car, and they learned a lot of their engine stuff from that."

The boys and George were encouraged by the performance of the new equipment. "We were running pretty good and it gave them great impetus," Matthews says.

The financial returns were also better, though far from enough to take care of expenses. Still, $19,925 almost doubled the income of 1976.

The third year was even better, $42,065 in prize moneys, five top-ten places in ten races and attention-grabbing runs on the super speedways. It all started at Daytona, where Bill qualified eleventh, ran fifth in the 125-mile qualifying race and then eighth in the 500. A few weeks later he improved on that, claiming a sixth-place finish in the Winston 500 at Talladega, the Autobahn of race tracks, and causing a stir among rivals in the garage area. He also had a sixth and a ninth at Darlington and another ninth in the Firecracker 400.

A reputation for high speeds and big tracks was beginning to germinate.

With 1979 came two milestones, or a milestone and a millstone, depending on which side of the fence you sit on.

For the first time in an infant career, Bill Elliott broke into the top five. He placed a strong second in the Southern 500, trailing only his boyhood hero, David Pearson, in a Chevy, and gave the Ford crowd something to cheer about. Behind him, all in Chevys, were Terry Labonte, Buddy Baker and Benny Parsons. For that day, at least, second place was like winning the World Series.

"He probably did his best racing at Darlington in the early days," says his father, "though he was probably noticed for the first time at Daytona in 1978 when he got in the draft of the lead two or three cars in the qualifying race and held onto the checkered flag for a fifth place."

Equally important as the showing at Darlington is the fact that for the only time in his "pure" Ford career, Elliott had a top-ten finish in a Chevrolet, horror of all horrors. He took over for an injured Roger Hamby and wheeled the 1977 Monte Carlo in races at Richmond, Rockingham and Bristol. He was tenth in the Volunteer 500 at Bristol, eleventh at Richmond and twenty-third at Rockingham.

He also had more than a modicum of success in the Cougar, a sixth in the Winston 500 at Talladega and a pair of sevens in the fall events at Darlington and Charlotte.

Along with the respectable finishes came a substantial hike in earnings, to $57,330. Better, but not enough to avert destitution. The Elliott team had one fairly competitive car, but having one car in Winston Cup racing is akin to having one horse in a polo match. Rivals overwhelm you with horsepower. Some teams helped with parts and advice, but not many. The exceptions were driver Benny Parsons and Ford legend Bud Moore,who at the time were sponsored by Michigan industrialist Harry Melling.

A pleasant, articulate and successful Winston Cup driver since 1970, Parsons came from a background similar to the Elliotts' and identified with them. Wilkes County, North Carolina, his birthplace, was the Dawson County of the Tarheel state, even down to its moonshine reputation. His own driving apprenticeship was spent working for his father's taxicab company in Detroit. Later, he returned to the South to become a racing millionaire and the leading citizen of tiny Ellerbe, just a left turn from the North Carolina Motor Speedway.

When Elliott broke in, there was very little rookie schooling or indoctrination, so Parsons was a godsend. With most of his brilliant racing career, including two ARCA titles and the 1973 Winston Cup, behind him, Parsons did not feel threatened by the shy kid from the Georgia hills. His advice on track nuances and strategies was invaluable.

Moore, a Hall-of-Famer and one of the greatest wrench turners, worked with Ernie Elliott on some engine problems.

Driver and mechanical support was eagerly embraced, but the Elliotts had a greater need. Sponsorship. George, by no means a pauper, was being drained financially.

"I didn't have that kind of money," he says. "Each time we raced I was down ten thousand dollars. At that time Bobby Allison was spending seventy thousand a race, and I could only dream of seventy thousand. I remember when Pete Hamilton left Petty Engineering, he got $135,000 for a year's sponsorship and blew the whole wad during Speed Week at Daytona. To make it in racing, especially in a small operation, you've got to watch your pennies and budget your time.

"One of the ways we raised money when we started was through the efforts of friends such as Jim Knudsen, a distant relative of Bunkie Knudsen [NASCAR commissioner], of Michigan City, Michigan. The boys got to be friendly with him, and he came up with mini-sponsors at one hundred dollars apiece. We'd put their names on the deck of the car. Picking up thirty or forty of those sponsors kept us going for a long time."

As the eighties got under way, the Elliotts found themselves on the razor's edge once more. When they could run full bore, they were competitive, but it had to be a sometimes thing. They had to concentrate on either the spring or fall races. For example, in the spring they were twenty-first at Talladega, forty-second at Charlotte and thirty-third at Darlington. The fall finishes, respectively, were seventh, sixth and eleventh.

Ernie always thought it was important to run well at Daytona and Michigan, home of the automakers, and he and Bill were ready for all four races in 1980. They rolled two twelves at Daytona and two nines at Michigan.

Bill won more than sixth place and $6,300 in the fall race at Charlotte. As it turned out, the National 500 was the beginning of the rest of his racing life. Appropriately enough, Benny Parsons played a featured role. Another assist goes to H. A. (Humpy) Wheeler, president and general manager of Charlotte Motor Speedway.

Wheeler had come up with another of his intriguing promotions, a challenge race with a winner teaming with a non-winner, to be sponsored by the Buck Stove Company. The two teams would average out their finishes with the best overall finish winning, sort of like a best-ball golf tournament.

George Elliott picks up the story.

"Bill was running strong that fall. As I said many times, Ernie always had consistency as his main consideration, and he'd gotten the Cougar where it was really humming. So Bill was running very consistently and finishing races and about six or seven other drivers asked him to team up with them.

"Benny also asked, and because he'd been such a friend in the past, Bill chose him. Bill just asked Benny if he could get him some help, and Benny called Harry Melling, who was sponsoring the car that Benny drove."

Melling, president and chairman of the Melling Tool Company of Jackson, Michigan, had long supplied oil pumps to the automotive industry, and the pumps were well publicized on Parsons's car. He had another product, Mell-Gear timing components, which wasn't as well known, and it struck him that painting a Mell-Gear advertisement on the quarter panel of the Elliott Thunderbird would be a good investment.

He offered five hundred dollars.

Parsons, who also works as a sales representative for Melling Tool, adds a touch of humor to his version of the story. "I had Melling Oil Pumps on the side of my car, and Harry wanted to know if someone would carry Mell-Gear on theirs," Parsons says. "He said, 'I've got five hundred dollars,' and I said, 'Harry!'

"So I went out in the garage area, and Bill Elliott was the only guy I could find that I could get for five hundred dollars."

For maximum exposure, Parsons certainly picked the right car. Not only did "Mell-Gear" get top play on the No. 9 T-Bird; it also got the only play on an otherwise bare quarter panel. And, in return, the Elliotts received a nice raise over their usual one-hundred-dollar fee.

George Elliott completes the story.

"In the race, Benny ended up wrecking. He had a flat tire and got a lap down, and he was trying to pass the lead car and make up the lap when he was involved in an accident with Darrell Waltrip, I believe it was. Bill finished sixth in the race.

"If Benny had won or finished ahead of Bill, I think they would have won the Buck Stove Challenge part of the race. Nonetheless, the Buck Stove was the start of something good for the team."

But nobody knew it. The five hundred dollars was a help in a specific race, but not enough to build a future on, and Bill's future appeared behind him when he arrived at the 1.522-mile Atlanta International Raceway, a high-banked layout with deep turns and short straights. Oddly enough, some of Bill's poorest showings had come at his home track, where he hoped to impress the most.

His finishes, up to that *Atlanta Journal* 500 in 1980, had been thirty-sixth, thirty-second, eleventh, thirty-eighth, thirty-seventh, thirty-sixth and twenty-ninth. Lack of success at AIR can be attributed to its emphasis on handling and tires and not strictly on driving skill. A one-car operation has a hard time meeting those criteria.

It was not general knowledge at the time, but George Elliott had made an agonizing decision to pack it in after Atlanta. The race with the bank had won out over the race on the track. This was to be the team's swan song.

He recalls that period in the life of the racing Elliotts: "We didn't have a sponsor for the car. It was going to cost us to take Harry's name off, or repaint the car, so we just left 'Mell-Gear' there. It's pretty expensive to repaint a car.

"NASCAR had already decided to downsize the cars — this was the last race for the big cars — and we couldn't afford a new one. When we went to that race, the boys were already talking. Although the automobile business was bad, we still had the dealership and Dan was working there. We felt we could put the other two boys there and make a living, but, really, we had no immediate plans.

"In other words, we were sort of going out of the racing business." Then, a funny thing happened on the way to the poorhouse. In what was regarded as a last gasp, Bill Elliott, with Mell-Gear bigger than life on the quarter panel of the Cougar, won the outside pole position, his first front-row seat ever. The home-boy angle played well with the local media and, naturally, Elliott got a lot of attention in the pit area, not the least of which came from Harry Melling, Mr. Mell-Gear himself.

Nothing pumps a businessman like seeing his product out front.

Alas, the race didn't go as well as the qualifying. The clutch went out early and the laps sped by as Elliott waited restlessly for repairs. Once back on the track, he put on a vintage Elliott finish and came in eighteenth for a seventeen-hundred-dollar payoff. The race was won by Cale Yarborough in a Chevy. For Elliott, however, it was a gutty performance in a hopeless situation.

The moment is vivid in George's memory.

"With the race over, we were just sitting there dreading to go home. We knew it was all over. We had given it everything we had. After the clutch burned out, it took us like sixty laps to change clutches. When he went back in, he just fell in with the leaders, and he stayed with the lead pack for the whole rest of the race.

"Considering the circumstances, Bill couldn't have done better. Luck had just run against us."

Or had it?

As they sat there delaying the inevitable, they saw Gary Cross, Melling's racing liaison man, come out of the stands, through the gate and across the track. He walked to their garage stall with a piece of paper in his hand.

Approaching George, he handed him the slip of paper.

"That's your budget for twelve races next year," he said.

In a matter of hours, the Elliotts had ridden a complete emotional roller coaster, from elation at the start to dejection at a faulty clutch to excitement over a courageous finish to resignation toward finality. Now there was the hope of resurrection. The governor had called at 11:59 with a reprieve.

By giving Mell-Gear one free ride, they'd earned a twelve-race ride in 1981.

"I didn't know until much later, but that's what really tilted Harry toward sponsoring our car," George Elliott says. "He was so happy to have his name on the car that he gave us a limited sponsorship for the next year. That just shows you never know. It didn't cost us anything to leave Mell-Gear on the car.

"Also, I think what impressed Harry was the determination of the effort. Though we had a major problem in the race, we had the car running competitively at the end."

The fate and furies of racing, it seems, work in mysterious ways. In the case of the mountain boy from Dawsonville, they always seem to involve paint. He ran his first race in an unpainted car. He was allowed to paint after he won his first race. And he gained his first sponsor when he didn't paint over an advertisement.

Melling's agreement called for an investment of between twenty-five and thirty-five thousand dollars, and it didn't take the red-topped boys long to spend it. The day after the Atlanta race, Bill and Ernie were up in Asheville, North Carolina, ordering a chassis from expert builder Banjo Matthews.

"We spent the whole wad on a new car," says George. "They went up to Banjo's place and picked out what they wanted. That gave us two cars to operate with, the Cougar, which we downsized and put an '80 or '81 Thunderbird body on, and the new car, a Merc-Bird, which also was downsized."

For the first time, Bill Elliott, age twenty-five, had a new, custom-built car to go racing with. Not only that, but for twelve races at least, he and the brothers knew they wouldn't have to beg, borrow or scrape for parts and equipment. Like the devoted father he is, George had gone the limit in getting his sons started, but, in modern stock racing, it takes more than one father or one businessman and often more than one sponsor to keep those cars running.

They weren't home free by any means. But with Melling's limited sponsorship, George's resources and Bill's winnings, it meant they were assured of short-term survival. So in 1981 they ran Melling's twelve races and one on their own. Though they reached a team high in prize money, $70,320, money was still coming out of George's pockets. It was still a productive year in many ways. Of the thirteen races, Bill was running at the finish in seven and six in the top ten.

One important goal was reached when, with the help of Jake Elder, hired on a one-race deal after he'd left the Ricky Rudd team, Bill recorded his first pole in the spring race at Darlington with a run of 153.896. Elder did the chassis work and relieved Bill of that chore.

Elliott was pleased to be over that hurdle. "So many times last year we were close," he said in 1981, reflecting on the 1980 season. "We thought about it last winter and really dedicated ourselves to racing. I've worked hard and paid my dues, and it's about time some things started coming my way.

"I'm not sure what it is, but I really like this track, I really do. I finished ninth in my first race here. I just seem to be able to adapt to the track."

He bettered that finish in the CRC Rebel 500, run on Sunday, placing fourth behind winner Darrell Waltrip, Harry Gant and Dave Marcis, but it wasn't easy, as George Elliott remembers it.

"The radio went out," he says. "When that happens, you have to switch to a private channel, but we didn't have one. We had to go to the pit boards, and Jake was a little bit upset. He preached my funeral that day."

Still, Elder was impressed. "Here's a guy who would probably be better off if he didn't build his own cars," he said. "But he's consistent and really seems to like Darlington, which is unusual for a young driver."

Daytona and Talladega were mixed bags. At the former, Bill had a sixth in the 500 and a thirty-fourth in the Firecracker; at the 2.66-mile Alabama International Motor Speedway, he was fortieth and eleventh. There was no luck at all at Charlotte with a fortieth and a thirty-third.

But, even at that early date, the Elliotts were beginning to reel in the four-wide, two-mile Michigan International Speedway, which was to become their patsy. After wrecking early in the first race, they returned to start sixth and finish eighth.

The real progress came at the home track in Atlanta, where, for the first time, Bill broke into the top ten with a ninth and a sixth.

The extra race was run at Rockingham, where the Dawsonville Kid wheeled in eighth from a twenty-second start.

All things considered, as the season came to an end, the signs were unmistakable. Given the horses, the Kid could handle them.

The year of reprieve had been successful, but it was just that, a reprieve. In NASCAR racing funds last about as long as fuel, and once more the Melling team faced a crossroads. Once more they lived a charmed life.

This time paint didn't come to the rescue. Instead, they found themselves squarely in the perennial NASCAR game of musical chairs. Dale Earnhardt, the only driver to win Rookie-of-the-Year and the points title in consecutive years (1979-1980), was leaving the Jim Stacy team, and Benny Parsons, now forty, was mulling retirement and a broadcasting career or a limited schedule with the Melling/Moore team. It followed logically that Earnhardt and Moore, good friends, would team up.

After much thought, Parsons stepped aside on the Melling team and recommended Elliott to succeed him. Earnhardt, taking his Wrangler sponsorship with him, went with Moore, and on December 1, 1981, Melling bought the Dawsonville operation from George Elliott. Deciding to ease out gradually, Parsons then signed with Harry Ranier in what was to be an abbreviated schedule.

In light of Bill's tremendous success later, George was asked if he ever regretted selling the team. His answer: "Absolutely not. There was no way I could handle it from a money standpoint. I knew the team had potential. The best thing I could have done at the time was just step out of the way. I'm just glad it all worked out."

While no one denies the importance of drivers and cars, the name of the racing game is money, sponsorship and state-of-the-art equipment that only megabucks will buy. For example, during his first three seasons, with Wrangler backing, Dale Earnhardt won six races with six seconds, ten thirds, nine fourths and eight fifths, plus eighteen other top-ten purses.

He was a millionaire in three years.

Conversely, in six years of limited, out-of-pocket racing, Elliott had one top-five finish and $201,755 in winnings.

The difference was money. Unlike the old days of racing, an independent or limited-sponsored racer courts Chapter 11 bankruptcy. Even a wealthy team owner such as Harry Melling couldn't get over the major hurdle until Coors added its huge resources in 1984.

Probably the wisest marketing move Melling ever made was attaching his Mell-Pro and later his Melling Oil Pumps to the No. 9 Thunderbird. For an original investment of five hundred dollars, he's received millions of dollars of exposure.

His involvement with racing, first with Parsons and now with Elliott, was strictly a business deal, though he did have some racing experience in go-carts and sailboats.

"Getting more business was the whole idea behind getting into the sport," he says. "In some states, largely the Southeast, our sales have increased 300 percent. Our product is designed for name recognition, and NASCAR people are more loyal to products on the cars."

Not that Melling Tool, a relatively small family-founded operation, wasn't successful before. Started in 1944, the year Harry Melling was born, by his father Ben and his grandfather, George Melling, the company first prospered in making war materials and later turned to oil pumps and automotive products. Today Melling Automotive Products is said to be the largest U.S. supplier of pumps and associated parts.

Short, compact and mustachioed, Melling attends races when he's not tied to his duties as president and chairman of the company. He also owns a ski lodge and a golf course.

Both Melling and the Elliotts profited from their first full season in Winston Cup, 1982. In the twenty-one-race schedule, Bill made his first appearance at the one-mile Dover and the 2.62-mile Riverside tracks, and only his second at the .596-mile Nashville, .533-mile Bristol and the 2.5-mile Pocono raceways.

Much has been made of Elliott's weak short-track record, but overlooked is the fact he is a mountain boy who came out of almost complete isolation and had never seen many of the Winston Cup tracks before he raced on them.

As late as 1982, he'd never been to North Wilkesboro or Martinsville, and his lone trip to Bristol was in Roger Hamby's Chevrolet. The first time he saw Daytona International Speedway, in 1976, he raced on it.

It wasn't until 1983 that he made the complete Winston Cup circuit, and it was two years later, in the midst of the Million Dollar season, that critics began to ridicule his short-track program. He did have a short-track program . . . and it was a full two years old!

As in other years, 1982, with Melling backing, resulted in another step forward. For the first time, Elliott's name popped up more than once in the top five. Still missing was a visit to victory lane, but the consistency George Elliott spoke of was evident in three seconds, a like number of thirds, a fourth and a fifth, eight top-five rides in twenty-one races.

He was runner-up twice at Charlotte, to Neil Bonnett in the World 600 and to Harry Gant in the National 500.

His gutty run in the 600 won a lot of admirers and stamped him for future stardom. He tried to take Bonnett as the laps wound down but failed. He cites inexperience. "If I had it to do over, I'd make my move on Neil earlier," he says. "I made it on the last lap and didn't get it. I should have tried on the next-to-last lap. I had a better chance then. I might not have taken him then, but I should have tried. Who knows?

"I went high coming into the fourth turn hoping he'd come up there with me and then I could beat him back to the bottom of the track. But he didn't go up there with me. If he had, I'm sure I should have beaten him back to the bottom and, who knows, I might have beat him to the checkered flag.

"That was just my inexperience showing. I'm learning, though."

Because of the oppressive heat, which reached 135 degrees in the car, Bill said he considered turning the driving over to Benny Parsons, who had fallen out of the race. Having to get to the track at 6 a.m. and work on his own car, Elliott was not only overheated. He was fatigued, dead tired.

But as he mulled wheeling into the pits, leader Bobby Allison went out of the race, and quite unexpectedly Elliott found himself leading.

"You don't get that chance too often," he said after the race. "So I just forgot about being tired. But the edge had been taken off. I really had trouble even holding up my hand for the last hundred laps. When you're leading, though, you don't want to get out of the car."

After finishing second and wheeling into the garage area, he collapsed of heat prostration and had to be attended to by medical personnel, who administered oxygen.

When he recovered sufficiently, he could talk only of regrets.

"That was the best race I've ever run," he said. "I worked my butt off. But I finished second and I can think of a million things I should have done."

The long day, the many duties had taken their toll.

"It's hard to do it all by yourself," Elliott added.

His efforts and his team's handicaps weren't lost on Leonard Wood, crew chief of the winning Ford. He saw something special that afternoon.

"I guess the thing I remember most about that win was that we wound up racing Elliott to the wire," he says. "At that time he hadn't won a race and a lot of people were surprised that he was up front at the finish — everybody but us.

"We knew he was strong, and as the day wore on it became clear to us that Elliott would have to be reckoned with."

That was the Woods brothers' third 600 win. It was to be five years before they were to mark up No. 4, with Kyle Petty in 1987.

Clearly, the full backing of Melling in 1982 was paying off at the finish line and the pay window.

Bill's first victory could have come at Daytona had he not spent the entire race dodging bullets. Starting twentieth, the obstacles came early. On the fourth lap, Bobby Allison lost a rear bumper that hit Joe Millikan. Bill's catlike reflexes saved him. He slipped through untouched.

Later, Elliott and Jody Ridley were drafting with Richard Petty when a blown engine by Bobby Warwack started a chain reaction that took out Petty, Benny Parsons and Neil Bonnett. Petty had taken the low road. Bill and Jody took the high road and escaped to race again.

The No. 9 Ford was not exactly trouble-free. Cut tires and a runaway wheel that hit the car and knocked it out of alignment kept the pit crew of Johnny Brown, Bill Brookhart, Clinton Chumley, Nick Gazaway, Wayne Hamby, Michael Hill, Steve Reagan, Lewis Smith, Mike and Grady Turner, Gerald Swafford, Ricky and Loyal Wilson and the Elliotts busy making repairs. Considering the circumstances, a fifth-place finish was outstanding. He was to return on July 4 and make his best showing ever at Daytona, second to Bobby Allison.

There were third-place finishes in the Rebel 500 at Darlington, at Michigan and Dover and a fourth in the Southern 500. As in 1981, all the drivers were having trouble keeping Waltrip in their sights. He and the Junior Johnson Chevrolet were on their way to their second straight driver's championship and an amazing twenty-four wins in two seasons. Waltrip was second at Michigan and the winner at Dover.

The highlight, for Elliott, had to be his second pole, which came in the fall race at Michigan. His fast lap of 162.995 edged Waltrip, whose Buick turned a 162.859. The race didn't go so smoothly, however, and Elliott finished twenty-seventh.

Nineteen eighty-two had been a good year. Elliott felt he should have won both Charlotte races, but he didn't. Baseball great Paul Richards used to say when you're close and you don't win, you're a glove, a bat, a step or a pitch short. The Elliotts were a wrench, a tire or a car short. Whereas others had a fleet of vehicles, they went through the year with only two. The good news was they were running near the front, for the first time they were in six figures, $226,780, and Ernie's pit direction had resulted in the Ingersoll-Rand Pit Crew championship.

Although not yet fully in sync, for the first time they ended a season with the security of knowing they could come back and take up where they left off.

7

Janie Turner and the Bill Elliott Fan Club

H E'D QUALIFIED FIFTH, but he wasn't satisfied.
Not that the Bill, Ernie and Dan Elliott of October 8, 1982, were expected to sit on the pole in the fall race at the Charlotte Motor Speedway; they weren't. But even then, before they'd won a single Winston Cup race, they had the confidence that they could do better, and on this dark, dank day Bill was under his car, in his hands-on style, looking for that little bit extra.

Outside of their garage peers, few took them seriously in those days. The main topic of conversation revolved around glib and quotable Darrell Waltrip, on his way to twelve victories and a second straight points championship.

Bill Elliott, completing his first year under the sponsorship of Harry Melling, was beginning to make muffled and unobstrusive noises, and his work ethic then was no less than it is now, which means total dedication. He had arrived at the track at 5 A.M. to begin setting up his Thunderbird, and he was still at it when a crewman suggested they take a break in the pit cafeteria.

Reluctantly, Bill joined his friend, only to discover he was the victim of a conspiracy. Janie Turner, president of the Bill Elliott Fan Club, takes up the story.

"Bill, greasy fingers and all, walked into the cafeteria to find all these people gathered around a birthday cake. I guess he'd forgotten it was his twenty-seventh birthday, but Humpy Wheeler [Speedway president and general manager] hadn't. Humpy had always liked

Bill, and he had arranged with Monkey Business to put on a show. After we sang 'Happy Birthday,' a belly dancer popped into the room, went up to Bill and threw her arms around him.

"Being as bashful as he is, he took on a red glow and gave me a look like I was the one responsible. He was really embarrassed by the attention, and it got worse.

"The dancer grabbed his hand and said she was going to read his palms. Seeing only a handful of grease, she said it might be better to read his hair and started running her fingers through his curls. Bill looked like he wanted to go right through the floor.

"Pretending to be a fortune teller, the dancer said, 'I see you are married,' and Bill stuttered and stammered and said, 'I *was* married.'

"When he got back to his motel room, he locked his door and wouldn't let anyone in. Later he said, 'I'm supposed to race, not do all that stuff. At least you could have told me so I could have washed my hands.'

"That illustrates how totally dedicated to racing Bill is. As far as he's concerned, he's part of the car and everything else is a distraction, even a birthday celebration."

Incidentally, Bill went on to finish second to Harry Gant in the National 500 that year.

The Turners, Janie and her husband, Melvin, have sort of grown in the racing business with the Elliotts. Melvin is the Coors/Motorcraft team's paint and body man. Even before the team hit the big time, he handled those chores for Bill in his Suches, Georgia, shop.

Janie remembers the fun and informality of those days.

"Because of our higher elevation, it snows in Suches before it does in Dawsonville, and when it did we'd call Bill and he'd come up," she said. "We had this 440 high-performance car that once belonged to George, and it was a lot of fun clowning in that old junker. When it got stuck in a ditch, we'd pull it out with a tractor and clown some more."

Janie Turner, a graduate of Brenau College in Gainesville, Georgia, and an elementary schoolteacher, was one of the first to recognize the talent and the vast potential in the unassuming Dawsonville redhead, and she was to play a major role in his future promotions.

For openers, she knew that any driver worth his car number had a fan club. It's a fact of life in Winston Cup and NASCAR, where fan loyalty and allegiance are unwavering, whether the drivers are the King, Richard Petty, or such nonwinners as Buddy Arrington and J. D. McDuffie.

In 1984 Janie Turner approached Bill with the idea. "Bill," she said, "one of these days you've got to start thinking about a fan club."

Shortly thereafter she received a call from Martha Elliott, who asked if she'd handle Bill's club.

The decision wasn't difficult. Janie Turner had all the credentials. She'd been Bill's secretary at one time, and as a mountain neighbor she understood the Elliotts and could protect their interests. At the same time, as a teacher and mother with gracious and patient Southern ways, she related to families, parents and children.

There was another plus. Blessed with artistic talents, she was able to design her own logos, T-shirts, sweatshirts and caps and offer club members mementos and items not available elsewhere.

Under Janie Turner's leadership, the Bill Elliott Fan Club has grown to more than five thousand members in all fifty states and Canada and, most recently, Australia. Originally, membership fees were ten dollars, but they had to be raised to twelve dollars because of increased postage expenses.

During that first year, Janie found herself faced with another golden opportunity to promote the team. For the first time in twenty-seven years, NASCAR got out of the Most Popular Driver business and turned the contest over to the National Motorsports Press Association, which changed the format and added a twenty-thousand-dollar cash award. Instead of restricting the balloting to NASCAR members, as had been the case, the NMPA opened it up to the general public.

That provided a challenge, and once more Janie Turner approached Bill. "I can get that for you," she said. "Do you want me to work on it?"

Bill left it up to her, and she went to work.

She got in touch with every state where the Elliotts had a fan club and asked members to send in ballots. She organized a group in Dawsonville and placed a ballot box in Gordon Pirkle's pool room. Having organized the driver side of the contest, she knew there was another vast group of voters across the country: loyal Ford drivers and dealers. She made ballots available at dealerships and even worked the Thunderbird assembly plant in Atlanta for votes.

At that time, Bobby Allison had won the Most Popular Driver accolade four years in a row and, with exception of David Pearson in 1979, either Allison or Richard Petty had won every year since 1970. Overall, Petty was the all-time leader with nine awards and Allison runner-up with seven.

Race fans welcomed a new face as its most popular driver of 1984, Bill Elliott, and the balloting wasn't even close. With some Chevrolet people crossing over because they liked Bill personally, he compiled 23,539 votes, easily outdistancing points champion Terry Labonte, with 14,460, and Geoff Bodine, with 14,357.

That wasn't bad for a young driver who'd won only three races.

Naturally, Bill was pleased by the show of fan support, and his gratitude was conveyed by the way of the Melling Press Guide.

"This award really means a lot to me," he said. "I haven't been on the Winston Cup circuit very long compared to a lot of people and to win this award is really something. It is hard to put in words how much this means to me.

"There are a lot of people I need to thank for this award, but especially Janie Turner. She really did a lot of work to help me win . . . . She and the people of Dawsonville really got the vote out for me."

Dawsonville Pool Room operator Gordon Pirkle was another impressed by the efforts. "When you remember that we have only four hundred or less people in Dawsonville proper, it's amazing that thousands in the area — and visitors — turned out to vote," he says. "Everybody really got behind Bill."

As it turned out, 1984 was only the beginning, the first of four straight years as Most Popular Driver for Bill Elliott. Janie Turner sees something special in the people who support him.

"To see the type of people in our club is to know the type of people Bill attracts," she says. "They are families and kids — kids love him — the real salt-of-the-earth type of people. A patrolman who worked traffic at the team's first open house said he'd never seen such a big crowd so well-behaved with no drinking, no fighting, no problems at all.

"Bill has a magnetism that draws kids to him. I get letters from fans asking to enroll children four, six and twelve years old, and I write them back and tell them their children couldn't have a better role model. He doesn't drink, smoke or do drugs; he doesn't even drink coffee, none of the Elliott boys do. They believe in clean bodies for good purposes.

"It may be irony that, as nondrinkers, they drive for Coors, and some letters from people who say they're Christians ask how he could do that. I tell them that Mr. Melling pays the bills, and we have no control over the sponsors."

In his revealing interview with Bill, *Grand National Illustrated* executive editor Steve Waid asked the same question and got a logical answer.

The question was: "You had any qualms about having a beer sponsor?"

And the answer:

"None whatsoever. I hear that from a lot of people. It's a product like anything else. I think it gets misused a lot of times, but as far as people getting onto beer as the cause of a lot of problems, I think it's up to the individual person. He has to know what his limits are. I have no problems with it. It's just a product and Coors is a company trying to promote that product. I am used as a tool for promotion. That's the way I look at it."

In addition to the serious inquiries, Janie Turner receives some unusual and interesting requests from fans.

One wanted a spark plug off Bill's car, and she managed to get one for him.

She has to laugh about another question. "The fan wanted to know how race drivers go to the bathroom," she says. "I wrote back and told him they don't. Racing causes dehydration and quiets the urge to go to the bathroom."

For one fan, at least, a great mystery had been solved.

Everyone knows about the professional side of Bill Elliott. There is another side, involving consideration, compassion and sensitivity, that few are aware of. The Turners know that side from firsthand experience.

In 1984 when their home in Suches was struck by lightning and burned to the ground, they found themselves without insurance or a place to live. Bill asked what they planned to do, and they said they were looking at trailers in Gainesville. He said he knew a dealer who'd help out.

"Then," says Janie Turner, "he wrote out a check for the whole amount and told us to pay him back when we could. That's the kind of person Bill Elliott is."

Joe Locke, his skiing partner, is another who knows the private Elliott. He says, "A few years ago, just before the NASCAR banquet in New York, Bill got word that the wife of a close friend had passed away. He didn't hesitate a moment. Here it was the night before the big event and all, and he quickly packed a suitcase, went out in the freezing weather and boarded a flight to be at the funeral.

"He felt compelled to be with his friend, and, even more, to be with the surviving child, a young boy. He is a very loyal and considerate person.

"If I could sum up Bill, I'd say he's a good, ol' country boy, proud to be where he's from, a private person who doesn't try to be somebody famous and important even though he is."

Strangers, as well as friends, are drawn to the Elliott mystique. Terry Graham, a railroader from Birmingham, one of the fifty thousand who attended the first Coors Open House, says there is no secret to Bill's popularity.

"I'm a Ford fan mainly," he says, "but I like the Elliotts. They're just like the rest of us, country boys, and you relate to them, feel like they're the same class of people.

"You can talk to them. Now take Bobby Allison. He's from Birmingham. He's friendly but you can't carry on a conversation with him."

Pretty, young Brandi Black, in her teens, had another reason: "I like him because he wins all the races, he's from Georgia and my daddy, Harold Black, has two Thunderbirds."

One of the most conspicuous groups of Elliott fans are familiar to most infield race fans. Tony Cooper, David Bailey, Jeff Tanner and their friends of Louisville, Georgia, always arrive in a huge former church bus painted in team colors.

"We're Ford fans and Elliott fans," says Bailey, the driver. "This bus used to belong to the First Baptist Church, and we wanted to make sure it was painted in the right colors. So we talked to Melvin Turner, the team body and paint man, and we wrote to the Melling Tool Company. They gave us the exact colors.

"Janie Turner was real nice. She sent us a club kit and was very helpful. Bill came over and talked to us for about thirty minutes once. He was as nice as he could be. We sent him some pictures of the bus."

Cindy Leonard, whose father Charlie Leonard once worked for Bobby Allison and is credited with coining the "Alabama Gang" tag, says the same thing in a different way: "Bill's a good ol' country boy not affected by wealth."

One of the most aggravating thing racing wives have to put up with is the attention their husbands receive from groupies or just your ordinary female fans. Professional sports figures, like entertainers, are surrounded by girls drawn to celebrities. In the old days, drivers used to party and drink away most of the nights, then meet the noon starting time, though not always in the best of shape.

Times are tamer, but the groupies will always be there.

Janie Turner has to smile when she recalls one incident that happened during the week of the *Atlanta Journal* 500. "We were at this party," she says, "and this lady, I'd say about fifty, went up to Bill, threw her arms around him and gave him a big kiss.

"Then she turned to Martha and said, 'Honey, why don't you get some sugar?'

"Martha looked at her and said, 'I'll get mine tonight.' I thought she handled the situation with a lot of class, just perfectly."

8

1983-1984:
On the Brink
of Greatness

UNLIKE BOBBY ALLISON, Bill Elliott is not a race-a-holic, but from time to time, schedule permitting, he gets the itch to get away from the Talladegas and Daytonas and return to his roots, the informality of the small tracks, the off-Broadway shows. There are two benefits. It is relaxing, and it keeps the instincts sharp for the ones that count.

When the 1982 season ended, Bill wasn't through racing. The urge was still there, so he hopped into his personal Thunderbird and motored up I-85 to the Jefco Speedway in Jefferson, Georgia, where old friend Hal Hamrick was running things.

"Want a ride?" asked Hamrick.

"Yup."

Hamrick went shopping for an available car.

In recalling the occasion, he says, "You've got to remember that although Bill had already signed with Harry Melling, he wasn't the renowned Bill Elliott we know today."

Not to "Big Daddy" he wasn't. That was his name, "Big Daddy." Few knew him by any other. Out of Greenville, South Carolina, he was a racetrack regular who always showed up with three cars, some of them competitive. Hamrick sought him out.

"Bill Elliott is a friend of mine, and he needs a ride," he said. "Can he drive one of yours, Big Daddy?"

Big Daddy cast a skeptical eye.

"Can he drive?"

"Oh, yes."

"Well, maybe . . . I'll let him have my No. 3 car, my worst car. That way I won't have to worry about it."

That was fine with Elliott, who strapped himself in and started at the back of the pack because he hadn't qualified the car. "Those who criticize Bill's short-track record should have seen him on that half-mile clay oval," says Hamrick. "From his position at the tail end of the field, he swept by everyone and won the race handily. I nudged Big Daddy and said, 'You think he can drive now?'

"Three years later, after Elliott's great 1985 season, I reminded him again. 'You think that boy's a driver?' I said. Big Daddy laughed and said, 'He can drive my car — my No. 1 car — any damn time.'"

As 1983 approached, Melling and the Elliotts had serious discussions about how many races they should run. Melling was reluctant to run a full schedule but listened to the reasons put forth and consented to making all of the thirty stops on the circuit. Progress had been made in 1982, but they were still running on the fringes. To pick up moneys available from the Winner's Circle and Unocal, they desperately need a win. That was the one obstacle they hadn't been able to clear, though it wasn't always the driver's or the car's fault.

Bill came close in the opener at Daytona.

Ricky Rudd, then in a Chevrolet, won the pole with a record 198.864 miles an hour, but fellow GM driver Cale Yarborough captured the Daytona 500 with Elliott on his exhaust in second place.

Close, but no Unocal or Winner's Circle.

Riverside was a repeat.

Making only his second trip to the West Coast, Bill worked his way from a nineteenth starting post to finish as runner-up to Rudd, an omen of things to come later in the season.

He also played second banana to Bobby Allison in the Southern 500 and Richard Petty in the Hodgdon Carolina 500 at Rockingham, the King's 196th visit to victory lane.

He was almost there, but not quite.

Petty was again his nemesis in the Winston 500 at Talladega on May 1. The King had taken the lead when an early wreck sidelined pole-sitter Yarborough, Darrell Waltrip, Tim Richmond, A. J. Foyt and David Pearson. Elliott had narrowly escaped by scooting under an airborne car.

In the late stages, Elliott made a move on Petty, couldn't quite make it and was kicked back in the draft to eighth. He had to settle for fifth.

For Petty, then forty-five, it was his second victory of the season and the 197th of a brilliant career.

The World 600 on Memorial Day was another missed golden opportunity for both Elliott and hot-running Bobby Allison, both innocent victims of someone else's accident.

With sixty laps to go, Elliott was running a strong second to Allison when Sterling Marlin cut a tire and spun out. As trailing drivers hit the brakes, both Elliott and Allison crashed into Slick Johnson's car and spun to the infield. Allison, with steering damage, returned to place third, while Elliott, who lost fifteen laps in repairs, managed a sixteenth.

Taking advantages of others' misfortunes, Neil Bonnett, in a Chevy, captured his second straight World 600. A year earlier he'd won in a Wood brothers Ford.

During the week of the World 600, Elliott wrote a daily diary for *The Greensboro Daily News.* In it he made some insightful observations.

On his routine: "I got here at 7 A.M. Getting up early isn't easy for me, but it's part of this business and you've got to get used to it. My brother Ernie came in this morning with a brand-new engine we'll use in the race. For qualifying, though, we decided to stick with an old engine we used at Daytona. I spent the morning changing things around and finding out what the car liked and didn't like. Then I went out on the track to find the best line in the race. We decided if we could get a good set of tires, we'd at least be in the ballpark.

"We kept moving things around trying to find some speed but we weren't having any luck. Sometimes you can go places and every move you make is right; other times, no matter what you do, you can't pick up a thing. Then it's better if you quit and think about something else.

"When it comes time to qualify, all we seem to do is hurry up and wait. To me, waiting is the toughest part of all, and since I qualified fifty-second I had to wait a long time. I tried to think about what I wanted to do and the way I wanted to run each lap. But really there isn't any strategy when you get to this point. You just go out and run as fast as you can."

On qualifying second to Buddy Baker: "Now I wish I was a lot farther off instead of being so close. Now I'll go back to the motel and wonder what I could have done differently to have beat him."

On conditioning: "For the first time I think I'm in shape to run six hundred miles. Last year I couldn't have done it. I wasn't running that many races and because of that I never got into condition. If a football player only plays once a month, he can't get very strong and that was my problem. But I've raced every week this year so I think I can handle it.

"The main thing to be concerned about is the heat because it takes so much out of you. I keep a can of water and try to drink a lot during the race. The suits we wear are pretty thick and it's like putting on a rain suit, and it gets pretty steamy inside.

"First thing I do when the race starts is learn the capabilities of the car. I've got to find out if it can run up front or not."

On mental preparation: "I'm usually pretty moody the morning of a race, depending on how everything is going. It's hard not to be because we're in a sport where you think you have everything under control one minute and it's out of control the next. There's nothing you can do about it and it wears on you sometimes. I used to have a lot of trouble sleeping the night before a race. But now I sleep pretty well. It's not that I'm excited about the race. After a few years out here you realize there's no need to worry because you won't change what's already been done.

". . . I've really changed my attitude about the minutes before a race. Used to be I'd walk around in a daze and only think about what I was going to do once I got going. Now I just walk around and talk to people and wait my turn to be introduced. When I get in the car, though, I start thinking about the first few laps — the line I want to take around the track. When the race starts, I put everything else out of my mind. That's when you've got your hands full.

"Before the race, you check and double-check everything except the engine. You can put that together only once. You just hope you got good parts. All of the final decisions about what changes we make on the car are up to me, except for the engine. My brother Ernie has control over that.

". . . Everyone thinks the engine is everything, but someone has to know when to hit the gas and when to back off. I'm no different from any other professional. You've got to have a little bit of pride in what you do. You've got to have your ups and downs or you're not worth anything."

From those early words, when he hadn't won a race, it is obvious that Elliott has a winner's temperament. In 1982, when he was runner-up to Bonnett and collapsed of exhaustion after the race, he knew he had to be in better condition, and you get better by racing.

There was another problem. He had practically no short-track program, and skeptics were anxious to see how he fared in his first full run. In almost every case, his fall run was better than his spring. At Martinsville, he was twenty-first and fourteenth; at Wilkesboro, twenty-first and fourth; at Richmond, sixth and fourth. Only Nashville, where he'd run before, was an exception. He slipped two places from fifth to seventh. At North Wilkesboro he led for more than one hundred laps, not exactly a shabby performance.

As the finale at Riverside neared, one ingredient remained missing and elusive. A win. But his record to that week — twenty-one top-ten finishes in twenty-nine races — had attracted the attention of important people, primarily potential sponsors, specifically the Adolph Coors Company.

Steve Saunders of the Coors Sports Marketing Department made contact and expressed interest, and the Elliotts countered with their terms. A deal was struck, to begin with the 1984 season.

Coors, a conservative Americana-type business, shops for a certain image, the outdoorsy, clean-cut All-American projection. Low-key. Actor Mark Harmon, a former quarterback at UCLA and son of Michigan All-American Tom Harmon, fit the image for their TV commercials with a brief spiel against a backdrop of clean lakes and the outdoors and topped off with a soft-sell, "Coors is the one." Elliott became his Southern counterpart, uncomplicated, sincere.

In retrospect, Saunders pulled a real coup by having the foresight to spot the vast potential in a winless mountain boy from Georgia. Elliott made him look good in the very next race, at Riverside, but hardly anyone outside of Coors, Melling and team members noticed.

The big story at Riverside was the points race between leader Bobby Allison and Darrell Waltrip, going for his third straight Winston Cup title. With a sixty-four-point lead, Allison needed only a thirteenth place finish for his first driver's championship in twenty-three years, but Waltrip, as per custom, had the war of words going.

He talked about how it was against Allison's nature to run a conservative race and how much championship experience meant in a tight situation.

Then he turned the screws a little tighter, saying, "Every time he shifts the gears he'll do it in slow motion, making sure he does it right. Every time he wants to pass a car, he'll think twice. When you start thinking about every little thing you do, that's when you foul up."

Vintage Waltrip.

With most of the pre-race attention on Waltrip, from the pole, and Allison, from the sixth position, Elliott, in tenth, was just another face in the lineup.

This time, however, the fates smiled on him.

Waltrip, in the lead with eight laps to go, spun out with Tim Richmond in turn nine, and Benny Parsons jumped out in front, only to give way to a hurrying Elliott, who cruised to his first win, under a rain-forced caution flag, at what was for him a snail's pace of 95.859 miles an hour, about half his usual speed on the supers. Allison finished ninth and claimed his first driver's championship by forty-seven comfortable points.

Elliott's first Winston Cup victory came in his seventh year, on his 116th attempt, and was a welcome relief. "All the bad luck that had kept me out of victory lane previously seemed to turn around for me today," he sighed after the race. This was one that someone else had within his grasp and lost. Bill had had a few like that himself.

At long last the breakthrough had been made, the last hurdle cleared, and the Elliotts were up there with the big boys, the gravy-collectors, in a league with solid ownership and corporate mega-bucks. With Coors in the wings, the timing was perfect. They'd come from one sick car that had been wrecked to a fleet of ten or more, from good ol' boys from the hills who pitched in on Sundays to a large staff of professionals who were paid big money to get the job done.

Melling had to confess that the Elliotts were right; the full schedule had paid off in twelve top-ten finishes, $479,965 in purses and extras and third place in the point standings behind winner Allison and runner-up Waltrip.

There was another plus: Having made all the stops, Ernie was learning how to put more oomph into the engine while Bill was mastering the best way to set up the car. They were falling into the right combinations. The only regret was the absence of a pole that season, the last time they've been shut out.

As 1984 rolled around, Bill was not yet "Awesome Bill from Dawsonville." Instead, he was, in the tradition of all Bills since "Wild Bill" Hickok, "Wild Bill" Elliott, a misnomer. The handle didn't fit the Kid from Dawsonville. If there's a trait he's never owned, it's being wild in comportment, dress, actions or racing. Shy and retiring would have been more in line.

That the media was beginning to discover him brought a measure of discomfort. But, as usual, his timing was right. Most of the attention at the start of the 1984 season was focused on the King, Richard Petty, who, at forty-seven, was just two wins away from the magical plateau of two hundred. Also, Bobby Allison was back to defend his title, Waltrip was running strong and Terry Labonte, a transplanted Texan, was beginning to come on.

If he had his way, Elliott would walk in the service entrance, race and leave out the back door.

Having accomplished some goals, the game plan in 1984 was to put more numbers in the win column. This objective was accomplished in the fifteenth race at Michigan, the twenty-sixth at Charlotte and the twenty-eighth at Rockingham. He also swept to four poles, seven outside poles, thirteen top-fives, twenty-four top-tens, picked up $660,226 in racing loot and failed to finish only two races, neither involving a blown engine.

On a lesser scale, the season was almost as amazing as the 1985 season.

As the campaign opened, Bill qualified third and ran fifth in the Daytona 500. That week belonged to Cale Yarborough and his

Hardee's Chevrolet. He made hamburger meat out of the field by sweeping the pole, a 125-mile qualifying race, and the 500 for a grand slam. A compact, rugged former football player, Yarborough came from behind to nip Waltrip on the last lap and pocket $160,300, to that point the largest payoff in NASCAR history.

Nevertheless, Elliott was there with the lead pack in a sprint for the checkers. His fifth-place check of $58,700 more than doubled his earnings from his win at Riverside.

The nine races after Daytona were rather bizarre. In those he had eight top-tens, yet in none was he in the same lap as the winner.

His third-place finish in the TranSouth 500 at Darlington was even stranger. When his T-Bird locked up two laps from the finish, he hopped out of the window and physically pushed No. 9 over the line. That physical exertion was worth $17,775.

Elliott really wanted to win the Coors 420 at Nashville on May 12, for the dear old sponsor and all, but, unfortunately, he had mechanical problems and finished twentieth, ten laps off the pace.

Two weeks later, at Pocono, the difference between Elliott and Richard Petty's 199th career win was a cut tire. Harry Gant had dominated the race before exiting with a busted oil pan. Then it was Elliott, Tim Richmond and Petty going head-to-head. The King was in luck. Richmond had suspension problems, and Elliott had to pit under green for a flat.

Gant admitted Elliott was the fastest in the race. "I was about a half-second quicker than anyone except Bill," he says.

With the pressure mounting for number two hundred, Petty said he was anxious to get it over with as soon as possible and preferably at Charlotte "where all that stuff happened last year," a reference to the thirty-five-thousand-dollar fine he paid for running an oversized engine and illegal tires.

While he was looking for two hundred, Elliott, on a more modest scale, was aching for win number two. Three weeks later, their wins came back-to-back, Bill's first, at the four-wide, two-mile Michigan International Speedway, a track seemingly built with him in mind.

Pole day at MIS was an occasion for celebration. Turning the asphalt at 164.339 miles an hour and bettering David Pearson's old mark of 164.073, Elliott earned his third inside front position and his second at Michigan.

He met the media afterward and said, "I just feel I get around the race track better here. The track seems to fit my style, which is a little conservative. We made some changes in the car prior to Pocono, but we didn't think they would have made so much difference as they did. We've found that what usually works well at Pocono, it works well at Michigan — I guess because of the banking and so forth."

Following the press conference, Elliott returned to join his team and change clothes, only to discover that Ernie, Dan and the rest had been so elated about winning the pole they had locked up and left, taking the keys with them.

Not only did they leave without Bill — they'd locked him out.

It was then that he probably learned where drivers stand on the totem pole of life.

"I could only laugh," he said later.

Though he'd led the qualifying, most of the attention at Michigan was on the King, Richard Petty, who had failed the first day and come back for twenty-first position on the second. Quizzed as to whether he planned to retire after number two hundred, Petty, then forty-seven, was emphatic with a *no*.

"I feel better now than I did ten years ago," he replied. "After two hundred, I'd like to go for a national championship."

Race day, June 16, Father's Day, came, and Elliott must have had that outnumbered feeling as his Thunderbird led eight Monte Carlos, headed by Geoff Bodine, on the parade laps.

Once the race started, the Monte Carlos raced each other while Elliott as in another time zone. He led seven times, quickly moving to the head of the class each time he came out of the pits. Only a caution with eleven laps left made the finish relatively close. He beat Dale Earnhardt by a full two seconds, averaging 134.706 miles an hour.

"I was hoping to run away from them," he said. "I didn't want to run with those other guys in a pack. I hated to see that last caution flag come out. I knew that might prolong the agony. When I got the lead back with six laps to go, I just hung on and kept digging."

The week was significant for Elliott. It marked his first oval track win. Riverside had been the icebreaker, but it was a road course. Also, it was his first pole since the fall Michigan race of 1982. His first had been in the TranSouth 500 at Darlington in 1981.

Michigan was his show. Two weeks later, the Firecracker 400 was to belong to the King.

It was a day that was to be dominated by high-profile politics, fender-bending, a finish on caution and a charge of conspiracy. Not involved in any of those was Elliott, who crossed the line sixth, collected his $14,500 and headed back for Dawsonville.

Two Republicans, President Ronald Reagan, in the midst of reelection, and Randleman, North Carolina, City Councilman Richard Petty were the marquee stars on that hot, humid afternoon.

Duly inspired, Petty drove a furious race and was leading when a caution came out with only a few laps remaining. He and Cale Yarborough raced for the flag because each knew the race would end on caution. On the way to the start-finish line, they gave each other a couple of whacks for good measure. Petty won the race to the flag and the Firecracker. An addled Yarborough, thinking the race had ended, drove into the pits a lap too soon and was dropped from second to third.

The macho finish excited the president, who said, "I can't believe they were bumping each other like that at two hundred miles an hour."

Not so impressed was fourth-place finisher Bobby Allison, who suggested there was something fishy about a Republican campaigner winning in front of the candidate. "I had the best finish of any car that would pass inspection," he bristled.

Predictably, NASCAR ignored the outburst and its PR people scurried about lining up a victory picture of Petty and the president, posed chatting about whatever Republicans chat about.

Reagan had gone one-up on his predecessor, Jimmy Carter, the first U.S. president to offer his benediction to a young sport as American as grandma, apple pie and Chevrolet. He came to the race *ex cathedra*, the only president to attend a Winston Cup event while in office. Carter, an unabashed fan whose roots are in backwoods racing country, had the drivers come to him, first at the governor's mansion in Atlanta for an evening of chamber music and feasting and later on the South Lawn of the White House for a Willie Nelson concert.

One of the memorable sights of the mansion visit was watching Neil (Soapy) Castles, a lean, lank North Carolinian who walked and talked funny, squirm and fidget as he listened to a male-female duet warble " Sweethearts, Sweethearts." Later, at the White House, he was infinitely more at home to Willie Nelson's "Blue Eyes Crying in the Rain."

Carter took special delight in introducing Castles and inviting him to the podium to take a bow. If he was looking for the common man, there was no driver any more common than Soapy Castles, who went four hundred races without a win and once said, "They race, I ride."

The PR difference in the two presidents was glaring. Carter had Soapy, and Reagan had Richard Petty, flags and fireworks.

The glitz of July 4 over, Elliott went on a tear. Between Independence Day and Labor Day, he recorded two poles, at Pocono and Michigan, five top-ten finishes and many valuable driver's points. He got a third at Michigan and would have won had he not run out of gas.

Then came Black September.

Beginning with the Southern 500, he hit a disastrous three-race streak in which innocent involvement in accidents cost him dearly and virtually ended his championship hopes. He was fifteenth at

Darlington, twenty-fourth at Richmond and thirty-second at Delaware. His only DNFs came at Darlington and Delaware.

One trait that returns again and again in the Elliott career is that of resiliency. Just when you think he's down, he lands on his feet again. And, ironically, considering what critics say about his short-track ability, his recovery started the week after Delaware when he ran a strong third in the Goody's 500 at Martinsville.

Thereafter, he was almost as spectacular as he was in 1985. Starting from the outside pole in both instances, he won the Miller High Life 500 at Charlotte and the Hodgdon American 500 at Rockingham. He was eighth in the Holly Farms 400 at North Wilkesboro and fourth in the Winston Western 500 at Riverside. At Atlanta, he took his fourth pole of the year and finished second.

His win at Charlotte, the third of his career, was accomplished the hard way. A chassis problem, making the T-Bird loose, dropped him a lap behind the leaders early. A caution enabled him to unlap himself, and he led the last sixty turns of the 1.5-mile CMS, beating Benny Parsons to the checkered flag by 14.5 seconds. In all, he led 128 of the 334 laps.

"Once we got the caution flag and got the tires and chassis setup worked out, we started running better," he said. "Earlier, I just couldn't get through turns three and four. We were unbelievably loose."

The fall race at Charlotte was an exorcism of the past rotten luck. He'd been runner-up twice in 1982, and only a wreck kept him from having a real shot at the 1983 World 600. Earlier, in the spring of 1984, he'd had one problem after another and finished sixty-six laps off the pace.

So far, in his three wins, Elliott hadn't had to race anyone hub-to-hub to the flag. That changed two weeks later at Rockingham, where he and Harry Gant staged a classic and memorable duel under dark, dank October skies. The race was twice delayed by rain, and the winner was announced six hours after the green flag.

But the long afternoon was worth it.

Elliott, having run strong all week, dominated most of the afternoon, but gave up the lead to Gant two laps from the finish. Then it became a sixty-second shootout. Coming off the fourth turn on the last lap, Gant slipped up a little too high and allowed Elliott to stick the nose of the Thunderbird inside.

Side-by-side, they turned on the jets and let it all out for the finish line. Elliott was first by twelve inches.

"Coming off turn two of the final lap, I wouldn't have given you two cents for my chances of winning," said Elliott later. "Harry kind of slipped in turn three, and my only chance was to beat him on the accelerator coming off four.

"I stomped the accelerator as hard as I could, took the bottom line and just managed to beat him back to the line.

"I don't think I'll ever forget this one. You're not likely to forget a race where for the first time I won when it was just me and another car headed to the flag. The last few laps of that race, my heart was in my throat wondering if I could pull it off."

For Gant, it was another heartbreak chapter, another second place, his sixth of the season and the nineteenth of his career.

He said he was confident he could win the race.

"I still don't believe he came out of that fourth turn hole that strong," he said. "I said to myself, 'Hey, guy, you're going to win this thing.' I still don't believe I didn't."

For the third win of the season and the fourth of his career, Elliott pocketed a check of $30,400, an improvement over eight years earlier when he had launched his Winston Cup career with a thirty-third place and a $640 check over the 1.017-mile very same North Carolina Motor Speedway.

While Bill was reluctantly taking the bows, brother Ernie was already planning for the next year and building better and stronger power plants. As Rooster Ingram has said, when Ernie Elliott doesn't win a race, he goes home and builds a better motor and comes back at you. Racing people are convinced he discovered the Fountain of Power during that incredible stretch at the shank of the 1984 season. They call it the racer's edge or the winning edge. Whatever it is called, the Elliotts had it in the last six races.

As Dale Earnhardt put it after the fall run at Michigan, "Bill had it dialed in."

In 1985, they were to have all rivals dialed out.

Ernie Elliott was to come up with his blockbuster.

9

Aunt Ethel, the Reporter

"HAVE YOU HEARD THIS ONE?" asked Tommie Gene Smith.

A big, good-natured, gregarious man, Smith operates the Dawsonville Barber Shop along with his wife, Ethel, George Elliott's sister and aunt of the racing Elliotts. She's a stately, attractive lady with a keen sense of humor that matches her husband's.

Unlike many of the other natives, Tommie Gene and Ethel have experienced living outside of the hills. "For eight years we lived in Gainesville," says Ethel. "Then we moved to Monroe for fifteen months and Athens for thirteen years. We came back to Dawsonville because it got so hectic in Athens. Everywhere you went you had to wait in line. Go out to eat, wait in line; go to buy something, wait in line; go through town, wait in line.

"Here it's so nice and peaceful, no waiting in line."

In the early days of Bill's Winston Cup career, Ethel Smith, a talented and published writer, served as the team's official reporter, preparing features and race stories for magazines and *The Dawson County Advertiser* and *The Dawson County News* ("Your Hometown Newspaper"). If you were looking for criticism or dirt, you didn't read the *The Advertiser* or Ethel.

She recalls those days fondly. "We went to several of the races, and I would get my interviews on the way home if a member of the team happened to be traveling with our party," she says. "Otherwise, I would have to call them up on Monday morning for info. They [Ernie and Bill] came to regard me as the number-one pest in the family. I was always given the red carpet treatment by George, though.

"George is one of the finest men I know (even if he is my brother and I may sound prejudiced — as I am — I still say it) and one of the smartest men I know. He has been very successful in his quiet, unassuming way, in business, in service and as a student at North Georgia College and the Emory University Graduate School.

"George was never too busy to tell me what he knew, and he knew a lot because he financed the whole operation and worked every race until Melling bought the team [in 1982].

"Getting back to the subject of writing, I found it was very enjoyable but totally unprofitable. There are articles in the local paper and one in a neighboring county. Their budgets were very, very limited, so I did the articles gratis for the most part."

Ethel Smith said she was pleased when Harry Melling's publicist, Alexis Leras, said she'd be responsible for media releases.

"Actually, I was relieved because Tommie Gene had been called as pastor of the First Baptist Church here in town and I, of course, became extremely involved in the activities of the church," she says. "Time was at a premium, and racing got a much lower rating on my list of priorities then."

Aunt Ethel was one of a host of volunteers, both kin and friend, who kept the race team afloat during those winless and lonely days before the moneyed people decided Bill would be worth investing in. She wrote the stories, Martha Elliott and Janie Turner worked the office, and Nick Gazaway, Ricky Wilson, Lewis Smith, Wayne Hamby, Clinton Chumley, Michael Hill, Charlie Martin, Steve Reagan, Johnny Brown, Chris Gillespie and Melvin Turner handled the pits with George, Ernie and Dan. Before them, of course, there were the Turner brothers, Mike, David and Grady.

Because most did it for love and friendship, not financial rewards, their contributions to the Elliott success story cannot be minimized. As a measure of the volunteers' dedication, in 1981 the pit crew, under Ernie and Dan, won first place in the Sears Craftsman's NASCAR Pit Crew Competition over the professionals handling the Pettys, Allisons and Yarboroughs.

Ethel Smith reported the award in *The Dawson County Advertiser* and quoted Dan Elliott on his program for success: "Do the job right, do it fast and don't get run over."

That year Bill finished sixth in the Daytona 500 and, in the words of Aunt Ethel, he'd "put the pedal to the metal." She also announced that despite Harry Melling's limited sponsorship there was advertising space available for sale on the deck lid of the No. 9 Thunderbird, which started out being bright red but was repainted in Melling blue.

She was there for Bill's first pole win at Darlington CRC Chemical 500 in 1981 and described it this way:

"The events of the past week were real morale boosters for Dawsonville's Bill Elliott and his fine crew. This past Thursday, Bill took first place in qualifying trials at Darlington International Raceway as he turned the track in the '81 Thunderbird at 153.896 miles an hour to earn the pole position for Sunday's CRC Chemical Grand National 500 NASCAR race.

"Then in the sweltering heat of Sunday's race he ran in the lead lap from the very beginning until his last pit stop — just twenty laps from the end of the 367-lap marathon — completing 366 laps, finishing fourth and running what many consider the best race yet of his career.

"Master chassis man Jake Elder, who is now between jobs, set the car up for the qualifying trials and called the shots for the pit crew during Sunday's race.

"'I should have finished third,' Bill said, 'but my radio went out and I lost control with the pit crew. That probably cost me third place.'

"Martha, Bill's wife, was extremely happy with the way things went. Always enthusiastic about Bill's career and the family's contribution toward it, she commented, 'Ernie builds some good engines. We haven't lost one this year. They've all run good — no trouble at all.'"

That about told the story.

From the Atlanta 500, Ethel Smith wrote that Bill had never had a trouble-free race on his home track and the 1981 appearance was no different. His T-Bird suffered extensive damage trying to avoid an out-of-control car and he was fortunate to finish ninth.

"If it hadn't been for the accident, I think he would have finished no further back than third," said George Elliott.

Ethel Smith had an interesting observation from the Talladega 500, where unscheduled pit stops, cut tires, a faulty ignition and a pitted windshield dropped Bill to eleventh.

She wrote: "After being snakebit (struck in the side by another racer) at Daytona in July, the Elliotts convinced Mell-Gear, their sponsor, that red was a better color for use on the racetrack than the shade of blue being used (which blended right in with the color of the track), so the car was painted a vivid red and lettered in white for the Talladega run.

"Red is a highly visible color, and, obviously, the sooner a car is sighted, the easier it is to avoid. Evidently, the color change paid off."

How many other writers noticed that important change? Now we know why the Coors Ford is red, not blue.

Bill's seventh-place finish in the Southern 500 at Darlington brought this description from his aunt:

"Dawsonville's Bill Elliott and team again proved they're no slouches in NASCAR competition even though they're competing with teams with virtually unlimited financing. Bill qualified the red-and-white Mell-Gear-sponsored 1981 in Thunderbird in four-teenth position with the sixth-highest speed (161.367), again earning the local pit crew a berth in Sears Craftsman Pit Crew Competition.

"At the very beginning of the race a light rain began falling, creating possible slick conditions on the track. Bill did not chance pushing into the pack at that point and dropped back to sixteenth, but he was still in the lead lap.

"He was soon on the move, however, continuing in the lead lap for the majority of the race and pulling up to fifth at one time before a flat tire dropped him back one lap and put him in seventh place and lap 366 at the finish of the 367-lap endurance contest."

In November, the *Atlanta Journal* 500 was a rocky time for Bill and the crew. Among other problems, the No. 9 T-Bird went through cut tires, a broken valve rocker arm, a broken push rod, a dropped cylinder and a blown engine on the final laps, yet finished sixth to winner Neil Bonnett.

All was not gloom, however, as Ethel reported:

"He [Bill] was informed that he and three other racing teams using Fords would be receiving aid from Ford Motor Company and that he would be fully sponsored next year by Melling Tool and Dye Company of Jackson, Michigan.

"Bill and the team have had to operate on a very limited budget, comparatively speaking. This season they have had only one completely new engine — the one used at Darlington in the spring where Bill won first place in qualifying, and they have had new tires for only two races. For the others, they bought used tires from other racing teams. The new sponsorship will provide a much-needed transfusion.

"Ford Motor Company will be making available the Australian block 351 Cleveland engine (which Bill already uses) and aluminum cylinder heads to begin with. Then, if NASCAR approves, they will provide a 1983 Thunderbird aerodynamically designed for racing.

"Melling has purchased the Elliotts' entire racing operation and will immediately begin improvements that will put Bill in the same league as the leading NASCAR drivers. Dan Elliott will be joining Bill and Ernie and good friend Ricky Wilson as full-time members of the staff.

"Additional equipment will be purchased for the shop and a third Thunderbird (a second one was readied a few weeks ago) has already been received.

"Bill has been fortunate to have had an excellent all-volunteer pit crew during his entire NASCAR career. These fellows have faithfully worked the races, receiving no pay — and often paying their own expenses. The new sponsorship has made provisions for them, also.

"Current plans for the newly sponsored team are for participation in at least eighteen races next year, then they will run the full circuit the following year and go for the championship."

That report captures the most significant moment in the history of Elliott racing, the turning point, the birth of a new challenger in NASCAR, and Ethel Smith captured it all in *The Dawson County Advertiser.*

Now the chores of chronicling the Elliotts' careers have been turned over to others, and Ethel and Tommie Gene Smith follow the results from the casual comfort of their barber shop, enjoying the chatter, jokes and one-liners.

"Have you heard the one about . . . . ?"

10

1985: No One Said
It Would Be Easy

With doubt and dismay you are smitten,
You think there's no chance for you, son?
Why, the best books haven't been written,
The best race hasn't been run.

— *Berton Braley*

BILL KISER CALLED HIS REGIMENT together. This was it, an attack mode, and every detail had to be reviewed.

"Okay, men," said Kiser, "synchronize your watches. It is now 10:46 A.M., September 1, 1985. Let's go over the plans one more time."

This wasn't World War III, a military operation of major import, but it had to go off like one. What it was, was the last segment of the Winston Million, the Southern 500, and Darlington International Raceway public relations director Kiser and his collaborators were preparing for the singularly most important race in the history of NASCAR and Winston Cup, the best race in terms of megabucks. It wouldn't be easy for Bill Elliott to win a million dollars; on the the other hand, it wasn't easy for Kiser and his associates to set the scene for that potential occurrence.

Kiser conferred with his brain trust, Winston Special Events director Wayne Robertson, publicist Bob Moore, series director Bob Masten, Daytona publicist Larry Balewski, members of the Darlington Jaycees and Jaycettes, highway patrol and sheriff's department.

Then he called the army of workers together.

"First," he said, "let's review Plan A.

"If Elliott is leading with five laps to go, Plan A will be immediately activated. The two hidden Winston Million Pontiacs will be manned and cranked up to come out at precisely the moment the checkered flag goes down. If they come out a second too soon and are spotted by the Ford people, there's going to be heck to pay. Elliott is to be transferred from his car to the first Pontiac, along with network announcer Ned Jarrett, and the second Pontiac will carry network cameramen and photographers. Jarrett will interview Elliott as the cars circle the track.

"Once the hero laps begin, Jaycees and Jaycettes are to start handing out ten thousand bills of Winston Million fake money. Originally, we'd planned to drop them by helicopter, but this idea was scratched for two reasons, (1) the roof on the grandstand and (2) an FAA law forbidding low-flying aircraft over large crowds. Unfortunately, Elliott's name on the fake money was spelled with one T, but it's too late to change that now.

"Also at the checkered flag, radio contact must be made promptly with fireworks people stationed on a pontoon in the nearby lake. We're out there because there is a Darlington County law against shooting off fireworks within a few hundred yards of the raceway.

"Then we must double-check to make sure downtown businesses and factories are quickly informed of the outcome so they can sound their whistles and horns.

"I cannot emphasize enough that all of this — the Pontiacs, the fake money distribution, the fireworks and the whistles and horns — must be triggered simultaneously."

Turning to a local police officer, Kiser said, "And you, of course, must be ready to escort the *Sports Illustrated* photographer to the airport posthaste. If he wins, Elliott will be on next week's *SI* cover. The magazine has a jet waiting at the airport."

Folding a sheet over his clipboard, Kiser came to Plan B.

"You never know, of course, and if Elliott doesn't win, we go to Plan B," he said.

"Say Elliott doesn't win and Richard Petty does. Okay, then right after the race, Petty goes to victory circle and Elliott to the press box to talk to reporters about his feelings. Then we flip-flop them, with Elliott going to victory circle to be presented a $100,000 check for winning two of the Big Four and Petty goes to the press box as the race winner."

Plan B was much less complicated than Plan A.

Kiser then dismissed the group, and they returned to their stations to await the plan.

It had been a long week for Elliott, with two security men always at his side to limit distractions and allow him to concentrate on his work and the Winston Million. He had won the first two of the Big Four, the Daytona 500 and the Winston 500, failed in the third, the Coca-Cola World 600, and this was it, the Last Gulch Corral, the shootout before seventy-thousand screaming fans. The boy was hotter than a Saturday-night special.

Like a knight in racing armor, he'd come riding out of the gray February skies over the North Georgia hills, in his red-and-white Ford chariot with its futuristic, air-resisting design, and swooped down over the super speedways like a T-Bird of prey. Already he'd won nine races, the Daytona 500, the Coca-Cola 500 in Atlanta, the TranSouth 500 over this very same Darlington track, the Winston 500, the Budweiser 500 at Dover, the Van Scoy and Summer 500s at Pocono and the Miller and Champion 400s at Michigan. His winnings were fast approaching the magic million dollar mark, and he held a 138-point lead over Darrell Waltrip in the Winston Cup Series.

The season hadn't been easy. Elliott's driving ability had been more advanced than his communicative and public relations skills, and there had been tense moments with the media. Then, too, the racing establishment doesn't take kindly to being left far behind in the exhausts of a newcomer. There were charges that Ernie, the engine genius, was doing something illegal, and the very isolation of Dawsonville, away from the major racing shops in North Carolina, only added to suspicions.

No car was broken down and inspected more than the No. 9 Coors/Melling Thunderbird, and never was anything illegal found. "We're the most legal car in the garage area," George Elliott had said.

Ol' No. 9 just *looked* illegal when it sped around the Alabama International Motor Speedway at 209.398 miles an hour to win the Winston 500 pole and set a new world closed-course speed record in early May. And its 186.288 miles an hour in the race itself, the fastest-ever five hundred miles, would have earned a summons on I-20, which leads into Talladega.

By golly, if the car wasn't illegal, it was illogical. At Daytona, in the first race, it had run 205.114. The two hundred-plus had come to Winston Cup. And Bill Elliott, whose early career was filled with doubt and dismay, in the words of the poet, had become the fastest stock car man alive.

Still, the best race hadn't been run.

He was about to run it.

What made the 1985 season different was not Elliott's eleven wins, eleven poles, speed records and nearly a million dollars in regular-season earnings. The one thing that set it apart from any other Winston Cup year was a stroke of brilliance from R. J. Reynolds Tobacco Company president and chief executive officer, Gerald H. Long, and his brain trust.

It all started, quite unexpectedly, at the December, 1984, NASCAR Winston Cup Awards Banquet at the Waldorf-Astoria Hotel in New York City, a time when good ol' boys dress out in tails and mingle with peers and corporate types.

Taking his turn at the podium, Long dropped the bombshell.

He said, "If one driver, competing in the Daytona 500, the Winston 500, the World 600 and the Southern 500 is good enough, and lucky enough, to win three of the four races, we're going to make him a millionaire. It's not easy, but it can be done."

After a stunned silence, the hall erupted into enthusiastic applause. If there is one thing drivers and owners would rather win than big races, it's big-money races.

Long's announcement went much deeper than that, however. It added a new dimension, a third dimension, to the racing season. On the lowest level, a team strives for the individual race. Then there is the ongoing points battle for the overall season. And now Long gave them a third incentive, a big-stakes quartet within the framework of the other two goals. While it was a bonanza for the four high-speed tracks, the spillover was sure to benefit the others.

The challenge got the attention of the Elliotts, among others. True, their record to that point, four wins in nine years, didn't beg for overconfidence, but they were strategically and psychologically suited for this kind of project. Though he'd won only at Charlotte, Bill had run well at the involved tracks. He'd been runner-up twice at both Daytona and Darlington, and his fifth at Talladega didn't tell the whole story.

There were other pluses. The team, in its second year of sponsorship by Coors, was beginning to put it all together, as the strong finish in 1984 indicated. Given equal footing, no team targets a specific goal with more dedication and zeal than the mountain boys from Georgia. They'll sacrifice where it doesn't hurt as much, in smaller-paying events, to attain a higher goal.

Back home in Dawsonville, they rolled up their sleeves, consulted with Ford engineers and went to work.

"Our whole winter, including Christmas Day, was devoted to trying to get into position to win the Winston Million," says Bill.

The ingredients were there . . . the driver, the master engine builder, and, as if in perfect harmony, Ford had come up with the most aerodynamically superior car in racing, the keys being its pointed nose and its sloped rear windows.

The chase was on, beginning in Daytona. As George Elliott remembers, "I'd say we approached the season with grim determination. We were confident. I know I've said it before, but I can't emphasize enough Ernie's insistence on consistency and scaled improvement. The plan was coming to fruition. A year earlier we'd run up front and won. Now we were ready for the next step.

"In January we went to Daytona for tests in a primer car (that paint connection again) and ran a half-second better than anyone else. When everybody got there, we were still a half-second better.

We were faster then, but we figured they'd catch up in three or four races, but they never did."

The only driver to come close to Bill's 205.114 qualifying speed was Cale Yarborough, then in another Ford, but at 203.814 he was more than a mile an hour slower. The Chevy drivers could only moan and groan.

Monte Carlo driver Neil Bonnett, who was almost three miles an hour slower, wasn't convinced. He said he wanted to see the Fords under race conditions. He said his Chevy "can flat chew the chrome off their rear bumper."

Some began to grumble about rules allowing Fords to be an inch lower than the Chevys. That was okay when Fords couldn't keep up, they said, but that day was past.

Richard Childress, owner of Dale Earnhardt's Chevy, said he'd be sitting in NASCAR's office when it opened the day after the race if Fords proved to have an unfair advantage. He said the Fords' lower profile allowed them to stick to the track better than GM products.

In Bill Elliott's eyes, turnabout was fair play.

"We used to go home to Dawsonville after being outrun by those Chevrolets and say there was no way those cars should be that much faster than Fords," he says. "It just didn't seem fair."

Elliott and Yarborough won the 125-mile qualifying races, as expected. The Georgian beat Waltrip by thirty-seven seconds, and Yarborough slingshotted past David Pearson on the last lap. In his segment, Bill led for forty-eight of the fifty laps.

Then came the first leg of the Winston Million, the Daytona 500. It was no contest.

When his car was healthy, Yarborough ran well with the wiry redhead, but he departed the race early with engine problems and left the way clear for Bill, who led 136 of the 200 laps.

A late caution made the finish closer than it actually was. His thirty-second lead over Lake Speed was reduced to eight car lengths as they sped across the start-finish line. Elliott collected $147,000, hiking his week's take to a record $185,500, and his winning speed of 172.265 was the second fastest ever for the 2.5-mile track.

Winning was vindication of sorts for Elliott, who'd failed to qualify in 1977 and 1979 and, on other occasions, had regularly been in the top ten. But, in retrospect, it was the hardest week of his career because of the pressure.

"I didn't want to put myself in a situation where I would let myself get beat," he sighed after the race. "If that had happened, I probably would have never lived it down."

By winning, he joined Fireball Roberts and Yarborough as the only drivers who had swept the pole, a qualifying race and the 500.

Rivals were duly warned.

Said Waltrip, "Boys, the handwriting is on the wall."

Said Benny Parsons, "One thing we learned is that Bill Elliott is as strong as green onions."

And said Neil Bonnett, "He pulled away from me like there's no such thing as a draft."

The chase was on.

Or was it?

In the next two races, at Richmond and Rockingham, he couldn't win for wrecking.

At Richmond, starting thirteenth, he cut a tire and crashed sixty-eight laps from the finish to place twenty-second. The Miller 400 proved to be a preview of what was to come under scrutiny soon thereafter, Dale Earnhardt's driving style. In that one, Earnhardt outbanged Tim Richmond to take the lead thirteen laps from the checkers and win.

Richmond said he wasn't surprised.

"I expected that from Earnhardt, that's his style."

If Richmond was unlucky, Rockingham and the Carolina 500 were even more serious. An argument with the wall on lap 281 relegated Elliott to twenty-ninth place and left him with a split fibula bone in his left leg. There was some question about whether he'd be able to make the Coca-Cola 500 in Atlanta two weeks away, and as a precautionary measure the Elliotts had fellow Georgian Jody Ridley stand by. The Winston Cup Rookie of the Year in 1980, Ridley had become disenchanted with the musical chairs of big-time racing and returned to the security of the small tracks, where he was a master.

Quite a bit shorter than Elliott, Ridley worried about reaching the accelerator in the Thunderbird. He need not have.

Gimpy leg and all, Bill took the wheel, started third and stuck it out to the end to record his second victory of the season and his first on his home track. He thought about coming out of the car, but when Cale Yarborough, who'd diced with him for the lead, went out with a blown engine, Elliott's competitive nature overcame his pain. He edged Geoff Bodine at the finish.

At long last, the homeboy had won at home, and that was important to him. "Atlanta is a special race to me since all our fans are here," he says. "The first race I won was all the way across the country in California. I finally made it home, I guess."

Brother Dan knew that once Bill saw a chance to win, he wouldn't be able to get him out of the car.

"I've known he's been a scrapper since we used to tangle as kids," he says with a smile.

The two-week break between Atlanta and Bristol allowed ample time for recuperation, and Bill was once more ready to go racing. He started eighth in the Valleydale 500, exchanged some metal and posted an eleventh-place finish. It was not that he wasn't trying on the short tracks; it was simply that his program was geared for the super speedways and something had to be sacrificed.

Up next was the TranSouth 500 at Darlington, and a whole new attitude had to be adopted for that. The race was important for two reasons, (1) traditionally, Bill did well there and (2) it would set the table for the last leg of the Winston Million, the Southern 500.

First objective: Go after the pole.

This Elliott did with a speed of 157.454. "If it's your day, it's your day," he said.

Sunday was also his day. In a race in which only three cars finished on the lead lap, he was almost two seconds ahead of Waltrip and much further ahead of Richmond. The payoff was $42,900.

As a matter of perspective, the win was his first at Darlington and only the seventh of his career. Where he'd run close before, he was now going that extra mile, so to speak. There was also sentiment attached to Darlington.

"This is the first place I ever sat on the pole, and it meant a lot for me to win," he said after his victory.

Richmond brought up an interesting observation. He said he chased down Earnhardt, who ran well until a broken control arm ended his chances, and unlapped himself, adding that he knew Earnhardt was going all-out because that's all he ever did.

"But I don't know about No. 9," Richmond said. "I think he's gotten smarter since Daytona."

There are those who thought Elliott made a tactical mistake by running away and hiding from the field at Daytona, ignoring the time-honored Winston Cup tradition of sandbagging. David Pearson has said that when he had the fastest car he always held something in reserve, not showing all his cards. For Elliott, however, sandbagging could present some problems. He does not do as well in packs as he does in clean air, or the lead, and holding back might interfere with his tempo. He tries to stretch a lead until it is insurmountable. Rivals would naturally prefer that he not.

Of course.

Following Darlington, the Winston Cup traveling show moved into the hills of North Carolina and Virginia for runs at North Wilkesboro and Martinsville, the only charter members of NASCAR racing's premier series, which began in 1949.

Historically, Elliott has done better at North Wilkesboro because it is longer, .625-mile to .526-mile, and has more passing lanes. The oval-shaped track has relatively long, sweeping turns which are banked fourteen degrees and connected by two straights, which average fifty and forty feet in width. An unusual characteristic is that the front straight goes downhill, the back uphill. Thirty of

Richard Petty's two hundred wins came at North Wilkesboro and Martinsville, fifteen at each, and Waltrip has always been strong on both.

The two tracks have another similarity. H. Clay Earles, the CEO of Martinsville, and Enoch Staley, his counterpart at North Wilkesboro, were associates of NASCAR founder Bill France, Sr., and among the pioneers of the sport. Earles takes special pride in the beauty of his compact racing plant, which because of its narrow asphalt is the closest thing to the nostalgic dirt tracks of the past.

On the spring visits to North Wilkesboro and Martinsville, Elliott didn't set any records, but he didn't do that badly either. At the former he started tenth and finished sixth, at the latter, eighth and thirteenth.

Most of the questions asked of winner Harry Gant at the post-race press conference at Martinsville involved the upcoming Winston 500, the second leg of the Winston Million. He offered his prediction on the pole speed. "It'll be 209 and it'll be Bill Elliott," he said. "That's assuming it's a cool day; otherwise, he'll be 208 or 207."

Before Talladega, however, there was a surprise, or maybe not. In an effort to slow down the Fords, meaning one Ford, NASCAR announced that henceforth the height of all cars would be equalized at 50½ inches, thereby raising Ford and lowering Chevrolet by ½ inch.

What that did was make a prophet of Gant.

Instead of qualifying at 211-plus, as Ernie Elliott had expected, the Coors/Melling No.9 was "held" to a world record of 209.398, breaking Yarborough's old record of 202.692 by almost seven miles an hour. Yarborough's 205.079 was good enough for the outside pole.

The rules change had lowered speeds, as NASCAR wanted, but it lowered everyone's speed proportionately. Elliott was slower, but he was still the fastest, by far. Back to the drawing board went the NASCAR officials, who mulled changes in the carburetor and/or rear spoiler. Since the other Fords were lagging behind with the Chevys, rivals were now certain the Elliotts had discovered the Great Secret, and Bill Elliott almost admitted as much when he said, "We figured it out once. Surely we can figure it out again."

Surmising that anything that fast had to be illegal, the cry again went up from the other drivers.

"There's something that shouldn't be there," charged Geoff Bodine. "There's no way they're that much smarter than the Wood brothers or Bud Moore."

Waltrip moaned, "Two or three miles an hour slower, that's acceptable. But seven, that's unreasonable."

One of the few dissenters was Yarborough, who said he had suspected something illegal at first but had changed his mind and concluded the Elliotts had gained the edge by hard work.

Qualifying may have been discouraging for rivals, but the race itself brought total futility.

In what is regarded as the best race he's ever run — the best, not the most lucrative — "Awesome Bill from Dawsonsville" made up almost a two-lap deficit under green conditions, without a single caution, to overtake the field and win at a mind-boggling 186.288 miles an hour, a world closed-course record. That there were only two caution periods, totaling eight laps, was a major factor in the race speed, of course.

An early problem, a loose oil line, repaired in a sixty-nine-second pit stop, had put Elliott behind, but fortunately it was early, on lap forty-nine, and allowed him ample time to catch up.

"That was the greatest race Bill ever ran," says George Elliott. "After he got back on the track, he began making up about a half-second a lap. You know how far a second is at Talladega? About five hundred yards. It can't be done easily. At over two hundred miles an hour, it took some eighty or ninety laps to catch up."

On lap 145 of the 188-lap race, Bill caught up with and passed Yarborough to take the lead. A quick pit stop enabled Cale to jump back out front, but five laps later Elliott took the lead for good. Kyle Petty, coming up fast, squeezed by Yarborough for second.

Two down, one to go for the Winston Million. The immediate financial gains were $60,500 for winning the Winston 500 and a guarantee of a $100,000 bonus from RJR for taking two of the Big Four.

Later, Bill Elliott was to say that the most pressurized part of the season was between the Winston 500 and the World 600, leg number three. Everyone wanted a piece of him, the writers, the TV networks, the fans, the promoters, the sponsors, well-wishers and hustlers alike, and he had scarcely a minute to himself.

Unknown two years earlier, Bill Elliott had become a national figure, a celebrity and, for lack of a better description, a corporate prisoner. He was hot property, and Coors wanted him here, Ford there, Melling some other place, and the media were all clamoring for one-on-one interviews. To paraphrase the song, everybody kept talking at him, and it was hard to hear a word they said.

He was torn between the newly defined obligations and his single-minded dedication to the preparation of his car. Between Daytona and Talladega there had been seven races, time to adjust; between Talladega and Charlotte, only one, the Budweiser 500 at the mile Dover track.

Although he slipped to fourth in qualifying, Dover was another successful stepping stone, despite the loss of power steering with another thirty-five laps to go.

He strong-armed the Coors/Melling T-Bird over the finish line twenty-nine seconds ahead of runner-up Gant. Third-place Kyle Petty was a lap down, fourth-place Ricky Rudd two laps and fifth-place Darrell Waltrip three laps. Remember Waltrip? His luck was soon to change.

Dover paid $44,500, and Elliott said he was lucky in a way. "The car held together and several others didn't," he said.

His fourth straight super speedway win tied records held by Bobby Allison and David Pearson, and so far the season had produced five wins in ten races. Tracing back to the shank of the 1984 campaign, Elliott had seven victories in ten super track races.

Ford and Elliott fans loved it, other drivers resented it and NASCAR officials were becoming more frantic by the race. The worst scenario for racing, any kind of racing, is for one car to dominate completely. When that happens, fans grumble, other drivers get heat from their owners and sponsors and, in some cases, teams are shaken up.

NASCAR people had hinted that the Elliotts should slow their man down. Now the weapon, a pencil, came out another time, and the rules were changed again, effective for the Firecracker 400 at Daytona on July 4. Having already raised the Ford and lowered the Chevrolet rooflines, NASCAR vice-president for competition Bill Gazaway announced that the maximum carburetor bore would be $1^7/_{16}$ inches, reducing the opening in the plate base by $^1/_4$ inch.

His reason: "We feel this action will not only improve competition on the track but will also improve durability of engines. Horsepower knowledge has surpassed good parts and pieces. We feel this will reduce speeds in the interest of competition."

In the meantime, the Coors/Melling Ford continued to be inspected and reinspected.

Believing the chase for the million might end in Charlotte, fans from all over the country poured into the state's largest city. For once, Charlotte Motor Speedway president-general manager Humpy Wheeler didn't need to call on his ingenuity to promote the World 600. It was a historic week and event, like Hank Aaron going for his 715th home run, and everyone wanted to say that they were there.

Someone changed the script on them. Instead of seeing a new star's greatest moment, they were to witness the resurrection of an old team, the Junior Johnson and Darrell Waltrip No. 11 Chevrolet.

But you wouldn't have known it from the qualifying.

At 164.703 miles an hour, Elliott's T-Bird was almost two miles an hour faster than runner-up Harry Gant, Geoff Bodine and Waltrip.

Typically, he underplayed his run and was deferential to the old guard, citing cool and favorable weather for his effort and hot and unfavorable conditions for Gant's earlier attempt.

"If it had been reversed, Harry would have won the pole," he said in meeting with the media. "The weather did get better for us, and I hate the way it happened for Harry. But you take what you get, and I'm just glad it's over."

Not quite over. Ahead was a pack of troubles for the Coors/Melling team.

The weekend started with the inaugural, the Winston, with Waltrip and Gant finishing one and two, and Elliott, though on the same lap, seventh. Later he was to describe the Winston as his worst race of the year. Saturday was not his day.

Neither was Sunday.

For a car that had had no ailments all year, the Coors/Melling T-Bird became a basket case. First, the radio lost contact with the pits for some unexplained reason. Then the brakes went. So Bill was in a position where he couldn't talk to anybody, and he couldn't stop, not a very enviable position. He overshot his pit twice and once had to be caught by members of Bobby Allison's crew.

Figuring you don't risk your life for a million dollars, he brought the car behind the pit wall to replace the master cylinder. When he returned, he was twenty-four laps in arrears. Once again, dittoing Saturday's race, Waltrip and Gant finished first and second.

Elliott, like many of the great race drivers, has a bit of fatalism about him, and he accepted the breaks, or brakes, of the game, saying at the time, "We've had our share of good luck this season, and I guess it was about time for something bad to happen. Sometimes it works and sometimes it doesn't. Actually, I'm just glad to be alive.

"It's pretty scary out there when the brakes go. I put my foot down on the pedal and nothing happened. I just kept on getting it down the road when I didn't want to get it anymore.

"It's a long time before the million comes up again, in the Southern 500, and maybe things will work out better. And if they don't, we've had a great year anyway."

The $16,783 purse for eighteenth place was a little less than a million, but Elliott was happy to get out of Charlotte with his health.

At the time the Winston Cup point standings didn't seem too significant. Defending champion Terry Labonte was on top, leading Elliott by twenty-nine, Bodine by thirty-two and Waltrip, who took giant strides after Charlotte, by eighty-two. Later Waltrip would stage a heated battle with Elliott for the title and win out in the last race at Riverside. In looking back, he would pinpoint Charlotte as the turning point.

"Moving into Charlotte I had struggled," he said. "I had some good runs and the car had failed a couple of times, and we were like tenth in the points at one time and Junior was about to pull my hair out and I was about to pull his out.

"Things were not going well at all, and we went to Charlotte on a number of occasions and tested. We spent a lot of test time at Charlotte, and we knew going into the World 600 that had we not had success that weekend I think it would have probably ruined us. I don't think we would have won another race that season because we put so much effort into it.

"So, by virtue of working as hard as we did, and putting as much effort into it as we did, and having the results pay off the way they did, it just turned us around, and, of course, we went on and won the championship that year.

"We were behind two to three hundred points at one time, but that ain't no big deal. If I'm behind, I want to be behind early in the season, not late."

Waltrip and Elliott were on different courses, Darrell going for the points and Bill for the Winston Million and as many races as he could win, but after Labor Day their lanes were to merge on a common destination.

"Our game plan in 1985 was to win races," says George Elliott. "That was our top priority. After that, we'd take what came."

As for Waltrip, he had no choice. He was winless up to the World 600, and the points race was the most logical for him. Having won the World 600, he was still eligible for the Winston Million bonus of $100,000, should he add the Southern 500. If he had done that, then both he and Elliott would have collected a hundred grand each since Bill had swept Daytona and Talladega.

Those who had waited for Elliott to have the basic race driver's slump were wasting their time. With exception of his back-to-back accidents at Richmond and Rockingham, he was never down more than a week or two in a row.

The durability of the Coors/Melling Thunderbird had been a major factor in the season. Disregarding the accidents, the only laps the car lost were on the short tracks, fifteen at Bristol, one at North Wilkesboro and seven at Martinsville. And, of course, twenty-one to repair the brakes at Charlotte. The rivals hadn't seen anything yet. From the Coca-Cola World 600 to the Southern 500, in eight races, there were 1,743 laps run, and No. 9 was present and accounted for 1,742. Elliott was one shy of the five hundred laps run in the Busch 500 at Bristol; otherwise, he was right there at the finish.

Along the way, he won twice at Pocono and Michigan, got a second in the Firecracker 400, a fourth in the Talladega 500, a fifth at

Bristol and a sixth at Riverside. There were four outright poles and two unofficial inside front positions.

At Michigan, where rain canceled qualifying, he was awarded the pole on the owner's car points, and at the Summer 500 at Pocono he was awarded the pole two-and-a-half weeks after the race when it was discovered that the winner had used unapproved fuel.

After Charlotte, the Winston Cup teams made the long trip to Riverside, where Elliott finished sixth. The Budweiser 400 was won by Terry Labonte with Harry Gant (who else?) placing second. The eighth race in the group before Darlington ended up at Bristol, where Bill lost his only lap and ran fifth. Dale Earnhardt won that one.

In between, he was truly "Awesome Bill." The six events went like this:

June 9, Van Scoy 500 at Pocono: The first race at Pocono was almost a replay of the 1984 fall run at Rockingham when Elliott edged Harry Gant by twelve inches. This time Bill started from the pole (152.561 miles an hour), fought off the challenges of Geoff Bodine and Waltrip and beat Gant to the checkers by less than a second. There were only four leaders in the race, and Gant led only four laps before losing the final sprint.

With the win, Elliott completed the cycle of having won on every major super speedway. Average winning speed: 138.974 miles an hour.

June 16, Miller 400 at Michigan: For the second straight race, Waltrip, encouraged by his showing at Charlotte, was hanging on. He'd finished third at Pocono, and now he was right there in second, thirteen seconds behind, as Elliott flashed across the finish line.

The Miller 400 wasn't without problems, though. First, Elliott fell back to ninth and had to catch up; then he had a fuel problem and gambled on a nearly empty gas tank. As Waltrip had said earlier, Elliott was having that kind of year when every decision was right.

Average winning speed: 144.724.

July 4, Pepsi Firecracker 400 at Daytona: The season had now reached its second rules change date, the new carburetor restrictions designed to slow down the Fords and bring parity. Sure enough, his pole-winning qualifying speed was lower than the February effort. At 201.523, some four miles an hour slower. But, then, so were the other cars.

No one expected the Firecracker outcome. Young Greg Sacks, driving an experimental Chevrolet owned by Bill Gardner, the DiGard honcho who prepared Bobby Allison's cars, stunned the racing world by beating Elliott to the start-finish line by 23.5 seconds. As at Michigan, Elliott had fuel system problems, and an unscheduled pit stop with forty-five laps to go enabled Sacks to grab the lead for good.

July 21, Summer 500 at Pocono: The 2.5-mile Pennsylvania track marked the first time that Bill had put together back-to-back wins. Recording his eighth victory of the season, he was five seconds ahead of runner-up Neil Bonnett, with Waltrip third. Unlike the earlier Van Scoy 500, which had only four leaders, this time Pocono saw twelve drivers exchange the baton thirty-six times.

Average speed: 134.008.

July 28, Talladega 500: The return to Talladega clearly illustrates just how close the Coors/Melling team was to having an even greater year than it did. It could easily have won one or two additional races.

With twenty-five laps to go, Elliott held a twenty-three-second lead over Ron Bouchard and had almost a lap on Cale Yarborough. A spinout by Bodine enabled Yarborough to close the gap, and he came out of the last pit stop in position to threaten.

Then, as Yarborough made a move, pole-sitter Elliott's car began to sputter and fade and was passed by a dozen others. Yarborough claimed his first win of the season, and Elliott had to settle for fourth in his wounded charger, the first hint of trouble in six starts. Nonetheless, he finished on the lead lap.

"I thought I could have beaten Cale if not for the problem," he said. "It had come down to the two of us. But we'll have to wait for another time."

Yarborough, who hadn't been shut out of victory lane since 1972, was relieved. "No way we were going to be skunked for the season," he said.

Talladega footnote: A twenty-four-year-old youngster by the name of Davey Allison made his Winston Cup debut in a Chevrolet and finished tenth.

August 11, Champion Spark Plug 500 at Michigan: Having grand slammed at Pocono, Elliott pulled a repeat in the second race at Michigan, and once again, as in the first run over the two-mile asphalt, Waltrip was there trailing him at the finish, four seconds late. The Georgian had won the pole with a record 165.479 run.

Not only did Elliott double his pleasure at MIS, he tripled it by taking his first Run for the Money title, leading at the midway point and banking an extra $10,000. In the first race, Bill had passed Waltrip fifty-one laps from the checkers; this time he whipped past him fifty turns from the finish.

At this stage of the season, Waltrip had moved into second place in the points race, trailing Elliott by 143.

August 24, Busch 500 at Bristol: With the Southern 500 next, this was a week for Elliott to relax, take it easy and get his ducks and priorities in order. For the first time, in a fifth-place finish, he was not in the lead lap, and he lost a few points to Waltrip and the Junior Johnson team, who placed fourth.

With deference to Bristol, Elliott's points performance was caught in the middle of the countdown to Darlington and the last leg of the Winston Million.

The Bill Elliott Show was on.

He'd won at the most festive track, Daytona, and the fastest, Talladega; failed at racing's most famous mile and a half, Charlotte; and now the chips were stacked for the Winston Cup's most historic, Darlington. As untamed and unpredictable as its nickname, "The Lady In Black," this 1.366-mile blacktop, opened in 1950, had been the link between the moonshining dirt trackers and those who genuflect at the altars of speed.

No one epitomized the new breed more than Bill Elliott.

Nineteen races had been run, and he'd won nine of them. What mysterious secret had been discovered in the mountains? George Elliott had said he expected the others to catch up in three or four races. They hadn't in nineteen. There had been charges of illegality, and NASCAR had made two rules changes. Still the Elliott car outran 'em all.

Were the Elliotts legal? Was it plain old hard work?

Prior to Darlington, the enterprising Charlotte Motor Speedway public relations department tried to find out in a survey of a dozen crew chiefs, drivers and other racing experts.

These theories were advanced:

• It's All in the Rear End — The rear axle gear ratio that Elliott uses is numerically lower than that of any of the GM cars, even lower than that of the other Ford Thunderbirds. This allows Elliott a higher top speed, effective on the super speedways but not on short tracks.

• Suspension Is the Key — Elliott has come upon the perfect — and previously thought impossible — combination of left/right weight bias. NASCAR requires that at least 45 percent of the car's weight be placed on the right side. If somehow during the race more weight could be shifted to the car's left side, then back again for the post-race inspection, the driver would have stumbled onto what others thought couldn't be done.

• It's Up Front — Elliott's motor has proven nearly bulletproof, seeming to have more horses pulling for it than anybody else's. His engines are powerful and reliable, a combination which NASCAR racing has not seen before with such consistency. Much talk has centered around the cylinder heads, which may be the hottest thing since the famous Chrysler Hemis were prohibited for being too powerful.

• Down the Tubes — There are people in the sport who say that the lower tubes of Elliott's roll cage may be filled with liquid mercury, a very heavy and dense liquid that would slosh to the car's left side during cornering — counter to centrifugal force — and then level out again when running straight, an illegal practice.

• Blowing in the Wind — Wind-tunnel tests show that the slippery design of the Ford Thunderbird has a lower coefficient of drag than the Chevrolet Monte Carlo, Pontiac Grand Prix, Buick Regal or Oldsmobile Cutlass. Since lower drag becomes more effective at higher speeds, this could help explain why Elliott dominates on the super speedways and falls flat on the short tracks. Subtly changing the T-Bird's bodywork even more, in ways that won't show up during tech inspection, would create a car that no one could beat.

• It's a Family Affair — There are those who think that since the Elliotts are out of the Charlotte mainstream, where most Winston Cup teams are based, and since the main body of the team is family, secrets don't get out as easily as with other teams. Whenever other teams come across a major breakthrough, it doesn't take long for the rest of the racing community to find out about it. Since the Elliott shop is nestled in the hills of Dawsonville, and since the team has not gone through major personnel changes, all of its discoveries and secrets have remained in-house.

• Driving Skill — Bill Elliott may just be the greatest race driver ever. He saves his car, doesn't make silly moves, and he's fast where it counts — at the end. His driving style is consistent; seldom does he make daring moves, such as passing four cars in a turn. His driving is generally smooth, aggressive and fast.

• Star Wars — An aerodynamic engineer was reportedly seen with the Elliotts. This opens the question of whether the team has unlocked the mystery of aerodynamics and handling, better known as ground effects. Ground effects is nothing new in Formula One and Indy car circles, but the term is rarely mentioned in regard to stock car racing. Ground effects involves the forming of a vacuum or negative pressure under the car to pull it down the track.

• The Right Stuff — This is better known as the "Benny Parsons Theory." Simply put, the Elliotts have put the fundamentals together in a near-perfect package much like the "no-magic" of Vince Lombardi and the Green Bay Packers.

• Gambling — The Elliotts are not afraid to take chances — they will try new theories, parts and ideas, rather than stick to the popular setup. Whenever this has been practiced in the past, though, it has usually meant a lot of disappointing finishes for experimenting teams.

• Charlotte Bust — Elliott surprised everyone by failing not only at his first crack at the Winston Million at Charlotte's Coca-Cola World 600 but also in the Winston race the day before, worth a half-million. Was there some mysterious ingredient at Charlotte that kept his magic from working?

There were other theories in the CMS survey.

Hall of Fame mechanic Smokey Yunick said, in his opinion, the secret involved aerodynamics, not a change in the engine. "By shifting a small piece on the body just slightly, you can produce the equivalence of fifty more horsepower," he said.

Former race team owner Ralph Moody pointed to Elliott's skills and his familiarity with the chassis.

"His right foot is worth fifty horsepower," Moody said. "And he has a big advantage in that he gets under the car himself and sets up his own suspension. He also knows where two turns of the suspension jack will work the best. Other drivers are only guessing."

Ray Fox, another Hall of Fame mechanic, saw it in another light. "Their big advantage is they can keep a secret," he said. "Tucked away in the Georgia woods and having the same crew stick with them all the time is their only secret. But when they win the championship, you watch how fast the other teams try to snatch those crew guys up. That's when their domination ends."

There's one flaw in Fox's argument. It is likely that only Bill and Ernie know the secret, and not the other members of the crew.

CMS president Humpy Wheeler said he believed the success was more spiritual than mechanical.

"The Elliotts came at the right time," he said. "They entered racing when the pressure on performance was the greatest. Bill is becoming a fifties-style American hero — no drugs, no complaining and down-home.

"He's a refreshing change to American sports fans who are tired of overpaid, lazy athletes who only think of themselves. What happened at Charlotte? Pressure, pure and simple. After all, they're human. They won't be as bad at Darlington because they're getting used to it."

Wheeler was right.

Bill was more at ease at Darlington. Whereas the World 600 followed the Winston 500 by three weeks, he'd had more than three months to get ready for the Southern 500 and handle the crunch of notoriety. And, with the two bodyguards, he found time to do his thing, tend to his car.

Ironically, the other drivers were beginning to feel the pressure. They were in an awkward situation. The crowd would be there cheering for Elliott, the most popular driver on the tour, and woe be it to the rival who roughed him up. There were a lot of questions. Would the others gang up? Would they move over and let him by? Who knows what's intentional or unintentional? You don't want to hand him a million on a gift plate, and you don't want to be the driver who doesn't give him a fair chance. There's a thin line there.

Tim Richmond voiced the concerns of the other drivers when he said, "If you slip up and knock him out of the race, things could go bad for you for a long time. You don't just pull away and let him by, but if it's a tight squeeze you ease up and let him go. I wouldn't think anyone is looking to take him out on purpose, but stranger things have happened at Darlington."

Richard Petty added that Elliott shouldn't expect anything but the normal racing conditions.

Realizing the squeeze other drivers were in, Bill tried to ease their concerns. "I don't want anybody to just let me have it," he said. "I've worked hard for everything I've got, and I'm not expecting anyone to give me anything now. Whatever happens, happens."

Waltrip, trailing by only 138 points in the drivers' race, didn't exactly stand on the dock and wish Elliott "bon voyage." Instead, he threw in a little sympathetic doubt, saying he wouldn't want to deal with that kind of pressure at Darlington.

For a million dollars, Waltrip would have dealt with Godzilla.

This is just his style. Gamesmanship, word games, the psyche game. As he drew closer in the points standings, he stepped up the tempo of playing with Bill's mind, with such *bons mots* as:

"Experience counts when things get tight."

"Real race drivers don't work on their own cars."

"I can handle the pressure now, but I can remember when it was like a noose around my neck."

Actually, Waltrip and Elliott had had a pretty close relationship prior to 1985. Two years earlier, before the World 600, Bill had consented to drive Darrell's Sportsman car in a preliminary race. Waltrip had spent some time helping Elliott during the week.

"He's really a heckuva nice guy," Bill said at the time. "I know a lot of people dislike him, but once you get to know him, you realize he's a pretty decent fellow. He really knows a lot about what makes a race car go."

A native of Kentucky and a resident of Tennessee, Waltrip was the original villain in NASCAR. When he joined the circuit in the early 1970s, he didn't come with his hat in his hand, as the fans thought he should have, but with a brash and disdainful attitude. He said he wasn't worried about the old favorites, that time was on his side. To fans fanatically loyal to the Pettys, Pearsons, Yarboroughs, Parsons and Allisons, this was shocking blasphemy.

The years mellowed both Waltrip and the fans, and when he joined the team of good ol' boy Junior Johnson in 1981, he began to be accepted by the old guard. They proved a winning combination with forty-three victories, three Winston Cup championships and some $4 million in earnings before they split after the 1986 season.

NASCAR's greatest money winner, with almost $8 million, Waltrip has had reason to mellow. Four of his seventy wins had come in the spring race at Darlington, the TranSouth, but, like Elliott, up to 1985 he'd never won the Southern 500.

Bill himself had finally broken through to the winner's circle in the spring TranSouth, but he had done some of his best early racing at Darlington. With Jake Elder's help, his first pole had come there in 1981, and out of fifteen appearances he'd been out of the top ten only twice. An oil pump failed in 1980, and an accident dropped him to fifteenth in 1984. As early as 1979, when his equipment was inferior, he'd been runner-up to David Pearson in the Southern 500. The way he looked at it, Darlington was a track that rewarded hard driving. It is also a track that doesn't tolerate cavalier driving.

The quest for the million got off to a good start when Elliott blazed to the inside pole position with a run of 156.641 miles an hour. Sitting right there on the outside pole, at 155.986, was David Pearson, Bill's boyhood hero and winner of ten Darlington races. He was an intimidating presence.

"I thought about Pearson beating me more than any other driver," said Elliott.

Benny Parsons lined up third and Joe Ruttman fourth. The other hot Ford, Cale Yarborough's, had some problems and qualified twenty-second, just ahead of Bobby Allison.

Pearson agreed with Elder that Elliott's smooth touch was an advantage on the demanding track.

RJR's president and chief executive officer, Gerald H. Long, was there with the million-dollar check, and the stage was set for the most lucrative race of all time.

A throng of seventy thousand was on its feet cheering when the cars appeared off the fourth turn and the pace car turned into the pits.

Green flag! The million-dollar race was on.

Gunning his Thunderbird, Elliott moved ahead of Pearson and led the first fourteen laps, when he gave way to Dale Earnhardt, who'd come from the fifth starting position. Three laps later, Pearson, the Darlington conqueror, exited the race with a blown engine. He wouldn't beat Elliott today.

Four other drivers — Buddy Baker, Dave Marcis, Geoff Bodine and Bobby Hillin, Jr., — swapped the lead before Elliott accepted the baton again on lap sixty-three. He proceeded to head the parade on fifty-two of the first one hundred turns. Following a caution, he dropped back and didn't lead again until the race was forty-eight laps from conclusion.

During the late stages of the 500, Elliott had to drive fast and react even faster. A spinning Earnhardt almost ended the chase on lap 310, but somehow Bill managed to avoid him. Then he escaped a flying hood that had broken loose from Tim Richmond's car and avoided another crisis when Yarborough's Ford lost its power steering just ahead. The Elliott reflexes were never more evident.

Yarborough, a five-time winner of the Southern 500, had just taken over the lead on lap 323 when his steering went. Reacting with catlike quickness, Elliott moved under him and took the lead. Fighting his car with all the muscle he could muster, Yarborough made it a race but came up two seconds short as Elliott crossed the finish line.

He had survived a battle royal. Harry Gant, the defending champion, Yarborough and Earnhardt all made strong runs, but blown engines and steering problems killed their chances.

Elliott's smooth and conservative style had prevailed. By avoiding trouble, he'd been there at the finish. About his tensest moment, dodging Earnhardt's spinning car, he said, "I don't know how close I came to him because I closed my eyes as I went by."

By the time he crossed the start-finish line, Bill Kiser's Plan A had long been activated. Another chapter had been added to the Winston Cup's most historic track. When Gerald Long presented the million-dollar check to the Elliotts, it was a Horatio Alger story come true. Only five years earlier, George Elliott had decided to pack it in and return to the Ford dealership. Two years ago they hadn't won a race. And now they stood as the number-one team in all of racing. It was heady stuff.

Because of the numerous cautions, the speed was relatively slow, 121.254 miles an hour, but no one cared. As Bill has said often, when it's your day, it's your day. And it was his day.

Proudest of all was George Elliott, who'd always preached hard work and perseverance.

"Back in those struggling days, I could only dream of a million dollars," he said.

It may be strange to say it, but the money was not that big a deal; the chase was more important than the prize. By the time the purse was divided up — taxes, part to the Elliotts and the major portion to car owner Melling, plus members of the crew — the take-home pay was considerably less than a million. Reportedly, Bill got only $100,000 or so. A racing pie has many hands in it. Of course, there are residual benefits such as commercials, endorsements and appearance moneys, not to mention national acclaim. *Sports Illustrated*, which only tolerates stock car racing, put "Million-Dollar Bill" on its cover.

For R. J. Reynolds and Gerald Long, the exposure was well worth the investments. As Long said at the time, "It has been a fabulous year for Bill and his family, and it has been a fabulous year for the

NASCAR Winston Cup Series. The sport has received more national exposure than ever before, and one of the big reasons is Bill Elliott and the quest for the Winston Million. The sport is the big winner." His analysis is correct.

Before 1985, Winston Cup racing had always had some national appeal, but never on the scale that came with the Winston Million and Bill Elliott. Prior to that, it was more of a regional attraction, confined to the Southeast, where it was born and bred, with one exception. Everyone knew Richard Petty even if they didn't know what NASCAR stood for. He was the national symbol of stock car racing. As the Winston Million inaugural season heated up, the national media began to take notice, and such names as Darrell Waltrip, Benny Parsons, Cale Yarborough, Bobby Allison, Dale Earnhardt, Harry Gant, Tim Richmond and Geoff Bodine became more familiar, to the everlasting joy of corporate sponsors.

Following Darlington, that dimension had been eliminated from the Winston Cup season. The million had been won. What was left were the individual races and the points championship. Darlington, where he finished seventeenth, twelve laps off the lead, hadn't been much help to Waltrip. He lost 68 points and now trailed Elliott by 206, Bill's widest lead of the season.

But there was a ray of hope for Johnson's driver. Of the eight races remaining, three were on the short tracks at Richmond, Martinsville and North Wilkesboro where Elliott had never won. Dover, Charlotte, Rockingham and Riverside appeared to be toss-ups, while Elliott was conceded the advantage at Atlanta. It was imperative that Waltrip make big strides early, since three of the first four races left on the schedule measured less than a mile.

First, ol' Darrell had to do something about the Elliott euphoria. That guy was just flat too happy.

"You know," he said for publication, "I've heard tell that being on the cover of *Sports Illustrated* is a jinx. I don't want my picture on the cover of *Sports Illustrated*. Maybe *Rolling Stone*, but not *Sports Illustrated*."

Did you get that, Bill?

Richmond, not *Sports Illustrated*, was more of a jinx for Elliott, and he knocked himself out of contention by slamming into the wall with a brand-new car he'd taken to the Virginia city. With his car heavily damaged, he managed only a twelfth, while Waltrip won his second race of the year and shaved Elliott's lead by 53 points, to 153.

At Dover, where Elliott was expected to have a slight edge and where he'd won in May, there was only more bad luck, or was it the jinx? A broken axle cost him sixty-nine laps in the pits and dropped him to twentieth. Ol' "Hanging-in-There" Waltrip showed up second and picked up sixty-seven more points and cut the deficit to eighty-six.

The Goody's 500 at Martinsville was another disaster.

Up to lap 343, Bill's game plan couldn't have worked better. He was in the lead lap running fifth — he'd run as high as third — when he became the innocent victim of a first-turn pileup. Ricky Rudd got inside of Kyle Petty and nudged him in the rear, knocking Petty into Waltrip, who spun off the apron. Richard Petty, with no place to go up high, slammed Elliott into the wall.

"I just didn't know where to go," said Elliott. "Someone hit me in the rear and that was all she wrote. It's like I said before, who said life's fair? This was one race, and now we'll get ready for another next week. We're not out of it by a long shot."

After the crash, Elliott said he looked across the track, and there was Waltrip, "his car intact and mine torn up." His steering shot, Elliott returned to the track and finished seventeenth.

Late in the race, Waltrip moved up to second and tried to make a move on leader Dale Earnhardt, only to get a dose of metal and be bumped away. That's the way they finished. Elliott's points lead, which was 206 only a month earlier, was now 23 and fading.

Earnhardt, commenting on the points duel, said it should be a tight finish.

"Ernie and Bill are smart racers," he said. "They stayed out of trouble by dodging me and some others and winning at Darlington. I'd say Darrell and Junior have the advantage at North Wilkesboro, which is Junior's home, and Bill and Ernie should have the advantage in Atlanta, where they'll qualify five miles faster than anyone else.

"If Darrell would stop trying to put pressure on Bill mentally, he'll be okay. But if he's not careful, he'll psych himself out. You can go overboard with anything. If he'll keep racing strong and grin real big at Bill, that'd worry him more than anything else."

There were those who thought they saw Darrell grin real big when he saw Bill hanging on the wall at Martinsville.

No one ever sat in a better runner-up position than Waltrip, going into North Wilkesboro, his "home track," only twenty-three points back and having won the Holly Farms 400 four times in a row.

On the Wednesday before the race, track publicist Hank School-field arranged for Elliott to meet the media in Winston-Salem, and many of those present remarked how relaxed and gregarious he was. When you've climbed the highest mountain, the hills don't seem that pressing. Before the Winston Million, he'd been like a man wrestling an octopus and winning. The aftermath can only be relief. He denied it was a letdown, as Waltrip had described it.

"It's not a letdown when you go into Richmond with a new car, fixing to race, and then hit the wall," he said. "Or at Dover when everything is going good and the equipment fails. Or at Martinsville when I'm sitting there on the wall with my car torn up, and Darrell is on the other side of the track with his car intact.

"After Darlington, I knew how quickly everything can change.

"The more you do good, the more you win, the more is expected of you. The Winston Million was pressure time because the expectations were high. I've had days when I didn't want to talk to anybody. But having been under all those conditions and in different situations, I've learned more about coping with it.

"The odds of winning a million are greater than winning the drivers' championship. Winning three of the Big Four races, it's something only two other drivers [David Pearson and LeeRoy Yarborough] have done, and they did it when a million wasn't on the line.

"This [points race] is a different situation. There's as much pressure on them [Waltrip and Johnson] as on us. I'd expect him to say the pressure is on us. But what I've been through this year, there couldn't be any more pressure. The tough time was Talladega going into Charlotte. The hardest thing at this point in time is to get two cars ready for the last five races.

"After Martinsville, we took a few days off. We work so hard and they get tore up so easily, that's the hardest part. As the season nears an end, we've got to start thinking of other things, selling off the old cars and expanding the shop to ten thousand square feet. Ernie's got five thousand square feet now, and I don't know what we need more room for. It's just more headaches. The main thing is that you grow on to other things, but I don't want to lose control of my situation like so many others have."

Beneath his shyness and reserved nature, not always evident even around very close friends, is an Elliott who is a pretty sharp cookie who talks slow but thinks fast. The "country boy" image makes good newspaper copy, but from the way he and Ernie run the racing phase of the team, they're not readily distinguishable from corporate CEOs. George taught them about business years ago.

But you can't do racing business with a broken flywheel, and that's what happened to Bill in the Holly Farms 400 at North Wilkesboro. He had his worst finish, thirtieth, and didn't complete a race for the first time since the Carolina 500 at Rockingham on March 3. Ironically, Waltrip had wire plug problems and could do no better than fourteenth in a race won by another area driver, Harry Gant.

A disappointed Elliott watched most of the race from his perch in the Coors/Melling trailer and declined any post-event comment. His points advantage had completely eroded and Waltrip now led by thirty. Unexpected and unannounced, Waltrip popped up in the press box.

"First time I've ever been here after finishing fourteenth," he said with a smile. "I had problems with a wire plug; otherwise, I think I could have driven a nail in the coffin. As it were, it left the door open a little bit. I would have liked to pick up 75 points, but, on other hand, a month ago I was behind by 206.

"We go back to Charlotte next week, and that's where my season began, really began, in the World 600. I don't see Bill dominating that race like he does on other super speedways. I don't think anyone's going to run off on anyone."

And pray tell, would Waltrip intensify his psyching and perhaps break out a voodoo doll?

He grinned that Waltrip grin.

"You know," he said, "I must have a good script writer. But I think I'll let up for a couple of weeks just to see how things go."

Whether it was voodoo, psyching or just plain bad luck, Elliott's early season magic had turned to stretch-drive miseries. As contrasted to the nine races ending with the Southern 500, when he'd lost only one lap, he'd dropped 287 in just four September events, with finishes of twelfth, twentieth, seventeenth and thirtieth. He had hit the wall, broken an axle, wrecked and broken a flywheel. He was stuck on ten wins.

Indeed, it was Black September.

But now it was October, blessed October, and ahead were three super speedways — Charlotte, Rockingham and Atlanta — and a 2.62-mile road course, Riverside, Elliott's kind of tracks.

At Charlotte, someone forgot to tell Cale Yarborough that Elliott was unbeaten on super speedways when he didn't have a mechanical problem or an accident.

This time " Bullet Bill" went all the way, but the handling was either too loose or too tight, and he lost the dash for the flag by less than a second.

Yarborough, claiming his second victory of the season, was elated. "I'm glad Bill didn't have any problems," he said. "I wanted to beat him fair and square."

Elliott found a lot of consolation in that he was there at the finish. "At least I was watching the race out on the track and not from the truck," he said.

Two days before his thirtieth birthday, Elliott saw another silver lining. He'd gained ten points on Waltrip, who placed fourth, and now the margin was twenty going into Rockingham for the Nationwise 500, which he'd won in 1984.

With things getting tight again, Waltrip figured he'd better go back to talking.

So, prior to the Nationwise 500 he held a press conference to explain how a great season doesn't necessarily mean a Winston Cup championship. Since he wasn't having a great season, he couldn't have been talking about himself. That means . . .

"I'd had a great season in 1979 and that year had a lot of parallels to this one," he said. "I'd won seven races and set a lot of records, and it went right down to the wire. In the last part of the year, we wrecked, blew up a couple of times, did all kinds of things wrong. There was just too much at stake.

"Going into the last race, there was a guy waiting to take my picture for *Sports Illustrated,* and there were two or three major endorsements, and all of it hinged on my winning the championship. Richard Petty didn't beat us, we beat ourselves."

Sports Illustrated? Waltrip was going to let *Sports Illustrated* take his picture? O jinx, where is thy sting?

The 1979 parallel sounded suspiciously like Elliott's 1985 season.

Waltrip talked a good game. Next, he drove a good game, and, for all intents and purposes, the points championship was won at Rockingham. Elliott never had a chance. Early in the race, on a caution lap, he was run over when Richard Petty tried to move in front of Bobby Allison and Allison didn't want him there.

"When you get run over under caution, you know it ain't your day," said Elliott, who finished fourth. "The impact knocked the front end out of line. I never saw anybody or nothing. All of a sudden I was sideways, and I was busy looking out after Bill Elliott. It certainly killed any chance we had of winning."

Waltrip's unexpected win and strong showing at Rockingham increased his points lead to thirty-five and neutralized Elliott's return to form two weeks later in Atlanta.

Starting third behind Harry Gant and Geoff Bodine, Elliott dominated the *Atlanta Journal* 500 from the outset, leading 118 of the first 133 laps and almost lapping Waltrip in the process. But ol' Darrell was living right. At about the moment he was to be put a lap down, a wreck brought out the caution, and he was saved.

Although he won handily, Elliott could not pick up enough points to get an even chance in the last race at Riverside because Waltrip finished third and led on a single solitary lap.

An explanation about Winston Cup points: Beginning with first place, drivers are awarded 175 points with a drop of 5 points for each place through sixth. After that, it drops four points through eleventh, then three through forty-first. Each leader of the race receives a five-point bonus, as does the driver who leads the most laps.

Thus, having gained fifteen points, Elliott trailed by twenty going into Riverside, where a second or a third and a single lap led would have won it for Waltrip.

Elliott, elated over his record-breaking eleventh win, held out hope. "We'll just have to go to Riverside and see what happens," he said. "If Darrell breaks, I win. If I break, he wins. If we both break, it will just come down to whoever finishes worse.

"I won my first Winston Cup race at Riverside in 1983, and the track's been good to me."

But tracks can be fickle. Even Riverside.

It was no horse race.

On the seventh lap of the Winston Western 500, Elliott's T-Bird broke an eight-dollar part, a shift pin in the transmission, knocking out the first and second gears, and was rendered *hors de combat*. Waltrip nursed his Chevrolet home seventh, behind winner Ricky Rudd, and claimed the third Winston Cup title for Junior Johnson.

There was a bizarre twist to the story, as reported by Landmark News Service's respected racing writer, Frank Vehorn. He wrote: "Stranger than fiction, the shift pin had been manufactured in Waltrip's home town of Franklin, Tennessee, by a fellow named Douglas Nash, whose place of business is located about three miles down the road from Waltrip's house.

"Not only that, Butch Stevens, a member of Elliott's crew, charged that Nash knew the part was defective and did not tell anyone. 'They were supposed to be on recall,' Stevens said. 'It looked like the pin we used to replace the one that broke was also defective.'

"Neither Bill nor his crew chief, brother Ernie, commented on the matter.

"'I can't believe someone has the nerve to suggest something like that,' said Darrell Waltrip. 'I'm sure the Elliotts had the best parts they had on the car. They run a Chevrolet gear box, just like mine.'

"Asked from where his team had received its transmission parts, Waltrip shrugged his shoulders. 'From Chevrolet, I guess.'"

The season, which started in controversy over the Fords at Daytona, ended the same way at Riverside. But it did not detract from Elliott's incredible record-breaking eleven super speedway wins and a staggering $2,433,187 in winnings, more than double that of any other race driver in any other season and probably more than any other athlete with the exception of big-name boxers.

The year included:

— Most super speedway wins, eleven, breaking the record of David Pearson (1973 and again in 1976).

— Most consecutive super speedway wins, four (Coca-Cola 500, TranSouth 500, Winston 500 and Budweiser 500), tying records by Bobby Allison (1971); Richard Petty (1971-1972); David Pearson (1973).

— Most consecutive poles on super speedways, seven, breaking record of five by Fireball Roberts (1960-1961).

— Most money won on super speedways, $943,203, breaking record of Bobby Allison, $480,640 (1982).

— Fastest single qualifying lap, 209.398 miles an hour, May 2, at Talladega.

— Fastest 500-mile race, 186.288 miles an hour, May 5, at Talladega.

— Biggest purse, $185,500, at Daytona 500, February 17.

— Most poles in season on super speedways, eleven, tying Pearson (1974).

— Most wins from pole, six, tying Pearson (1976).

— Most popular driver, second year in row.

— Eljer and National Motorsport Press Association Driver of the Year.

— A $175,218 payday for finishing second in the points race; twenty thousand dollars from Eljer, seventy-six thousand dollars from Unocal, thirty thousand dollars for Busch poles, four thousand dollars from STP and thirty-five hundred from Goodyear.

For his Winston Cup title, Waltrip received a check for $350,416 from RJR's Gerald Long, who in turn received the NMPA's Myers Brothers trophy, for contributions to the sport, from the group's president, Harold Pearson of *The Richmond Times-Dispatch*. Right there behind the corporate giant in the Myers Brothers voting was a guy named Bill Elliott, who five years earlier was overjoyed to get five hundred dollars for putting Mell-Gear on his car.

He had run the good race, if not the best, then the most lucrative, but the season had been wearing, demanding and uncomfortable. No one had said it would be easy. Success had left some scars.

1 / Bill, Dan, Ernie & George Elliott with the Coors/Melling Thunderbird

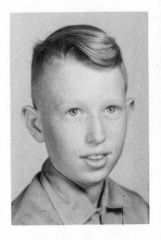

2 / Bill, age 6   3 / Dan, age 10   4 / Ernie, age 12

5 / Mildred & George Elliott, 1945

6 / Bill's high school graduation, 1972

7 / Dan & Bill in the Elliott's lumber yard

8 - 11 / BILL ELLIOTT DAY in Dawsonville
Celebrating the Winston Million, 1985

12 / Bill & his wife Martha in the winner's circle
Darlington TranSouth 500, April 1985

14 / Bill's daughter Starr
Tallagada, May 1985

13 / Bill & friend, Southern 500, 1985

15 / Bill & Starr sharing a victory at the Charlotte Motor Speedway, 1984

1986, Charlotte Motor Speedway; Elliott in the Coors No. 9
16 / followed by Harry Gant (SKOAL No. 33), above
17 / and by Geoff Bodine (LEVI GARRETT No. 5), below

18 / Dan, Bill, Ernie, Mildred & George
at the Coca-Cola 500, March, 1985

19 / Victory Lane, Atlanta International Raceway
1986 Winston Series

24 / Winning the Winston Million at Darlington, 1985

25 / Ninth win for No. 9 in the 1985 season
Michigan International Speedway

26 / The Atlanta Journal 500 win, Nov. 3, 1985

11

Aftermath:
Coping with Success

ADMITTEDLY, THE TOUGHEST TIMES of 1985 for Bill Elliott were the twenty-one days between the Winston 500 and the Coca-Cola World 600, the second and third legs of the Winston Million.

Elliott hysteria was beginning to sweep the country and everyone — media, sponsors, fans, promoters and special interest groups — wanted a piece of the Dawsonville redhead. As he and the Coors/Melling contingent pulled into Charlotte for prerace tests, he felt badgered, pestered besieged from all sides and could work up little enthusiasm for a scheduled press conference.

"I just don't have time," he tried to beg off. "Maybe five minutes."

In recalling the week, Charlotte Motor Speedway president and general manager H. A. (Humpy) Wheeler said, "I understood the situation. Like a lot of drivers, Bill was trying to survive in a hectic time. On the flip side, people were beginning to say he had become difficult to get along with; Huck Finn had become impossible to deal with. I talked with Ed Clark of our staff and told him, 'We're going to change Bill Elliott.'

"We didn't even send out invitations to the press conference. Everyone just knew about it and the Winston Media Center was packed. After Talladega he'd been saying the same old dull things, and they were hoping he'd finally say something.

"He came in late for the press conference, stood there nonchalantly and repeated the same old bland answers like, 'If I win, I win; if I don't, I don't.'

"Very quietly, from behind him, a Wells Fargo truck pulled up, and three uniformed guards grabbed three bags off of the back and came through the door. The press could see this, but Bill couldn't. I interrupted the press conference, took the bags from them and dumped a million dollars on the table in front of him. 'That's it,' I said, 'one million dollars!'

"He was skeptical. 'Aw, that's not a million,' he said. 'It's a few hundreds on top of a bunch of ones.' He was asked to check it, and he thumbed through one hundred-dollar bill after another and his eyes lit up. Heck, I was impressed myself. I'd never seen a million dollars, and the North Carolina National Bank vice-president who let us use the money had never seen a million in person. It was an impressive sight.

"The point is, that light moment changed the press conference. Huck Finn was back, and we had an informative session."

Wheeler had followed the Elliott career closely and CMS had played a major part in Bill's early years. It was there in the Buck Stove Challenge, five years earlier, that he made his first connection with Harry Melling, and it was there in 1982 that he had run second twice.

"First time I noticed Bill was at Darlington," says Wheeler, "where, in timing him, I was surprised to learn he was consistently running a tenth of a second off the leaders' pace.

"In 1982, when he finished second to Neil Bonnett in the Coca-Cola World 600, he was not in shape and simply wore himself out physically; otherwise, he might well have won the race. Bonnett said later that Elliott worried him by staying on the bottom of the track.

"He was beginning to run with the leaders, and that made it a whole new ball game. When he was in the middle of the pack he was good ol' Bill, Huckleberry Finn. It's buddy-buddy until you get with the front-runners and then they turn you every way but loose. You don't go where they're running, take their space. It's the subtle art of intimidation, and it plays with your mind. Also, running with your boyhood heroes, the Pearsons, Pettys, Yarboroughs and Allisons, is intimidating in itself.

"About that time Bill and I made a trip to the monastery at Belmont Abbey [where Wheeler's father, also called Humpy, was a longtime athletic director] and had a little talk. You've got to remember that when Richard Petty won his twenty-seven races in 1967, Bill was just eleven years old, and here he was running with Petty.

"I told him to forget about No. 43, just think of a thirty-seven-hundred-pound car, metal and rubber, and don't worry about the driver. Eventually, he got through that phase and put his time into becoming one with the car."

Ironically, three years later the people along pit row were saying the same thing they were saying during Petty's mastery in 1967 — "Where's the magic?" There was something different about the Petty blue Plymouth Roadrunner just as there was something special about the Elliott red-and-white Thunderbird.

"Where's the magic?" Wheeler mulled over the question. "There were some similarities in what happened in '67 and what happened in '85. One parallel, in each case, was the coming together of back-yard, shade-tree engineering with Detroit, the best of both worlds.

"In 1976 Chrysler engineer Larry Ratchgeb came up with a revolutionary idea, shifting a disportionate weight to the left side of the car. No one had thought of that before. On many tracks the left front does nothing and is, in fact, off the pavement in some cases. The family situation was another similarity. Richard had his brother Maurice as engine builder and his cousin Dale Inman as crew chief.

"People say history doesn't repeat itself, but it always does. Out of Georgia came Bill, the driver/chassis man, and brother Ernie, the absolute perfectionist on engines, a man who drives himself crazy over perfection. Bill became the first driver to have that kind of year since Petty and A. J. Foyt in the 1960s, when Foyt won Indy, LeMans and other majors, and they all had three things in common: (1)He, like Petty and Foyt, became one with the car; (2)he obviously found something in the chassis; and (3)Ernie built a durable and powerful motor."

Additionally, says Wheeler, conditions and timing were just right. As in 1967, NASCAR rules were allowing cars to run on the edge, almost to the point of being out of control. Speeds were reaching two hundred miles an hour at Talladega, 165 at Charlotte and 165-plus at Atlanta, and Ford had come out with a Thunderbird with a different and superior aerodynamic pattern, known as ducktailing. The air came off the fenders, traveled over the car and down behind in sort of a ducktail, making it most difficult to draft off. It created a little pocket for the car, reducing the pull on a lead car. In the past it had taken a speed of two or three more miles an hour to pull out of a draft, but not anymore.

Elliott's style fitted the conditions almost perfectly.

"Bill is not a conflict driver,"says Wheeler. "He doesn't like conflict. At Daytona in the qualifier [1987] Kenny Schrader beat him on the last lap. If there is conflict, he goes for the top five. On a scale of one to ten, in conflict driving, Dale Earnhardt is a 9.9 and Bill is a 3. Say they're under those conditions for ten races. Elliott would have had ten top-five finishes, and Earnhardt would have won five and crashed the other five.

"In that respect, not liking conflict, Bill is a lot like Tim Flock and David Pearson, who depended on strategy and smoothness."

Wheeler has another theory about the 1985 season.

"One of the most interesting books I've read is John Jerome's *Sweet Spot in Time*, which is a study on why athletes produce in one season and hit that highest peak," he says. "Things like Ali beating Foreman, DiMaggio's fifty-six-game hitting streak, Babe Ruth's sixty home runs and Hogan's great golf year. He concludes it's a time when a force within athletes brings their total senses into play for a specific time. It all comes together, and it only happens once.

"According to primitive studies, a race driver, like a fighter pilot, reaches his physical peak at twenty-eight to thirty-two. That could vary a couple of years each way. So, in 1985, Bill was right there."

George Elliott has spoken of Bill's amazing ability to shut everything out and concentrate on the task at hand. Wheeler agrees concentration is the key ingredient in racing success. "For three to four hours, a race driver cannot think of a single thing except what he's doing right now," he says. "Even going into the pits takes total concentration; it's much like landing and taking off in a plane. The only comparable athlete I can liken it to is an NFL quarterback, who must be concentrating and thinking all the time, even when he's on the bench.

"This requirement to concentrate without letup takes its toll on Mondays, when many drivers have the same symptoms as severely depressed persons, light-headedness, lethargy and inability to concentrate. It's a tough business."

Elliott's impact in 1985 involved more than winning races and returning Ford as a challenger. He also changed the demographics of racing crowds and awakened the interest of the TV networks. And Wheeler, along with other super speedway operators, was among the chief beneficiaries.

"I'm sitting here trying to sell the Coca-Cola World 600 against Indianapolis on Memorial Day and that's a tough deal," Wheeler remembers. "The worst thing is that NASCAR is built around seven drivers, and what worries us is that we might have seven drivers from the Piedmont section of North Carolina, and that's tough. We don't have Hispanics to sell to the TV audience in Los Angeles, but we can sell Rusty Wallace and Ken Schrader to St. Louis, Geoff Bodine to upstate New York and Terry Labonte to Texas.

"Atlanta is one of the major TV markets, and Bill made a big difference in that.

"He also made a big difference in the in-house crowds. During the early 1980s we were getting more fans out of Pennsylvania than out of Georgia. From our computer printouts, we can tell exactly where our fans come from, and the ticket sales from Georgia had damn near ceased. Interest in that state had waned when the Flock brothers quit racing.

"Now we're seeing many, many cars with Georgia license plates. He's made a big impact in that respect. And it's happening at other tracks. After Bill failed to win the Winston Million here, I went to Darlington to see how he fared in the Southern 500. Usually, when I go to other races, I must confess that I don't stay to the finish, but I did that day. And I've never seen a grandstand go crazy as it did at Darlington when Bill won.

"It capped a fantastic year."

The one fly in the ointment was Bill's relations with the media. That, he hadn't counted on: the inordinate attention, the full-court press of writers and television sportscasters. He had precious little experience in public relations or holding press conferences, and he admitted he did not react well.

"Having to deal with large groups of people and having to talk with them has been difficult," he told Steve Waid of *Grand National Illustrated*. "I know when I came in I was very shy. I was uncomfortable in front of a camera and even in front of a microphone. It wasn't anything I had done before. I was never used to it. Now, with the way it has grown, I've had to learn to deal with it. But as a person I haven't changed any.

"I've tried to stay the same. I get a little bit more frustrated at times. I have less time to myself that I so cherished years ago. That plays on me every now and then. But I try to take every situation as it comes along and, no matter what, try to make the best of it.

"I've said before I'm a country boy and what's wrong with that? I perceive that everybody says I was a dumb country boy, and country boys are no different than anybody else. They're just a product of their environment. Sure, I'm not brought up to know the ways of the city or what goes on there. But those people aren't brought up in the ways of the country."

Elliott's aversion to interviews and his penchant for disappearing or secluding himself in the team trailer brought complaints from the press. At other times he was curt and uncomfortable, specifically after the fall race at Rockingham. Racing was his game, and he didn't understand why he should stand interrogation on personal matters he wouldn't tell his Dawsonville neighbors about. It didn't help that he lacked the glibness of a Darrell Waltrip, the patient amiability of a Richard Petty or the off-the-wall retorts of a Tim Richmond.

Given his innate reticence, 1985 was a nightmare.

As he told Waid: "There were pressures from so many people, especially after winning Daytona and then coming back and winning Talladega and then going for the Winston Million. It all kind of built up to a deal where it seemed every time I turned around, somebody was pulling at me for some reason or another. It could have been the media, the sponsors, the public. There was so much demand. Thing of it is, if I had been in racing long enough to build up to it a gradual step at a time, it wouldn't have been as hard for me to take. But to have been thrown in there all of a sudden makes a whole different situation. It just took a lot of time to learn how to deal with that.

"It got to the point that it got my mind off racing itself. . . . Once I got to the point where I could say, 'Look, we are going to run and accept what comes along,' then I think that's when I changed my attitude and the way I looked at racing."

Elliott is not the first Winston Cup driver to have a rocky start with the media. Some, like David Pearson and Bobby Isaac, were shy and untutored and had a hard time adjusting to the media. Pearson has said he was not sure of himself, and he dreaded the thought of an interview. Isaac, a grade-school dropout, improved somewhat after he married a schoolteacher. Another old-timer, Jim Paschal, avoided the press whenever he could.

In the main, however, NASCAR has been blessed by drivers who were articulate spokesmen for the sport, among them Richard Petty, Bobby Allison, Cale Yarborough, Darrell Waltrip, Benny Parsons, Neil Bonnett, Buddy Baker and, from the past, Fireball Roberts, Joe Weatherly, Fred Lorenzen, Tim Flock, Donnie Allison, Tiny Lund, Dan Gurney and Marvin Panch.

The late Bob Colvin, president of Darlington International Raceway, used to take Weatherly with him on PR visits to newspapers and television stations. An ebullient, wisecracking, elfish little guy who raced in white saddle shoes, Weatherly was a master at deflating the pompous.

Ned Jarrett was the best example of a self-made communicator. Realizing he needed improvement, he enrolled in a Dale Carnegie course. He is now considered one of the most knowledgeable of track reporters on the Motor Racing Network and CBS.

Traditionally, race drivers have been the most quotable of athletes. But there is, or was, a time and place for everything. Trying to interview Fireball Roberts before a race was not recommended. Moody and preoccupied, he brooked no interference with his mental preparation, and if accosted, he'd either walk away or snap a writer's head off. It was the same with A. J. Foyt at Indianapolis or during his rare appearances in Winston Cup racing.

"The thing about Roberts and Foyt," says Landmark News Service's Frank Vehorn, "is that although they were unapproachable when working on their cars, if you stood back and waited until they finished, they always had time for the press. They were even charming at times."

Perhaps significantly, the all-time public relations king in NASCAR happens to be the all-time winner, Richard Petty, who ruined the public relations game for those who came after him. It is generally agreed that no athlete, in any sport, has ever been more accessible and cooperative with the media than Petty.

And, unselfishly, he shared ink with others, as a veteran racing reporter recalls. "It was years ago and I had gone to Atlanta Raceway to do a column on Petty," he says. "When he finished working on his car, I explained what I wanted and he said, 'I appreciate that, but can I make a suggestion? Everybody writes about me. Why don't you go over there and do a column on Wendell Scott? Nobody writes about him.'"

Scott, the only black in Winston Cup racing, who made a living by running the slow lanes and earning two hundred dollars a week, received unexpected but welcomed attention.

Like everything else, media coverage of Winston Cup racing has undergone a drastic change in recent years. Originally, when Bill France, Sr., founded NASCAR, the sport was reported on primarily as a regional event and usually the low man on the newspaper totem pole got the assignment. Current national coverage of stock car racing is the result of four factors, to wit:

(1) Junior Johnson
(2) Richard Petty
(3) Bill Elliott
(4) The Winston Million.

Johnson was involved in the first national breakthrough when in 1964 *Esquire* magazine dispatched new-breed author Tom Wolfe to Ronda, North Carolina, to profile the old-breed race driver Junior Johnson, the reformed moonshiner from the hills. Not really sure what *Esquire* was, Johnson nonetheless agreed to host the writer for a few days. The article, "The Last American Hero," detailed Johnson's life, his short stay in the Atlanta Federal Penitentiary for failure to pay taxes on mountain booze, his racing success and his almost cult following. It is still considered a definitive piece on stock car racing.

A few days after publication, Johnson visited his old friend Gene White, the Firestone racing tire dealer, in Atlanta, and Gene was anxious to learn what he thought of the article.

"Did you read it, Junior?" he asked.

"Yup."

"Did you like it?"

Johnson shifted his feet.

"Wal . . .

"I'll tell ya, this little guy, he come down from New York, and he's got on a red vest and he wears his hair long like a girl. He follows me everywhere, to the grocery store, to the filling station, even when I go to get a soft drink and a Moon Pie.

"I'll put it this way, if you'd seen the guy what wrote it, you'd have thought it was a good article."

White laughed.

"You know," he said, "in his way, Junior is as eloquent as Tom Wolfe."

Esquire was a giant step forward for stock car racing, which up to that point had been covered by faithful members of the press in the Southeast who had baby-sat a new sport. Eventually, Bill France, Sr., coaxed *The New York Times*, the Associated Press and a few other major outlets to staff the races. The growth from a fairgrounds thrill show to an extravaganza watched by 160 million on TV and 2.4 million in person marked a corresponding proliferation of the media, resulting in facility and space problems.

Like it or not, media relations are a fact of life in Winston Cup racing. It's a whole new ball game. Richard Petty has said that the most revolutionary change he's seen is the absolute requirement that drivers be able to communicate with the media and corporate types. In this regard, Ford has held seminars for its drivers, including Elliott; Kodak sponsored Rick Wilson in a media course, and R. J. Reynolds polished up its 1986 champion Dale Earnhardt and car owner Richard Childress with a refresher course in New York. At these sessions, the same as those held for business execs, drivers are put into difficult interview situations and taught how to react.

"If we spend money and make them a better spokesperson for the sport, help them develop their skills, it's a good investment for us," says Winston Cup Series publicity manager Bob Kelly. "The sport still has the connotations of Southeast, backwoodsy, dirty fingernails and shade-tree mechanics, and it hasn't been that for a long time." Kelly says the sponsors don't want to change anyone, just make them more articulate.

It wasn't that Bill Elliott couldn't express himself — he can — it was simply that he was thrown into unfamiliar surroundings and situations that can intimidate a trained man.

Veteran journalist Chris Economaki, editor of *Speed Sport News* and a fellow who has seen drivers come and go, from Daytona to Indianapolis, says he empathized with Elliott's predicament. "Bill is one of the few drivers who not only drives his car but also works on it and works on it incessantly," he says. "These high-tech cars have to be adjusted all the time and so his time is taken there.

"Then the sponsor Coors has demands on him. They want him to talk to the press and go to dinners, travel here and there and appear in commercials. Ford, which supplies his engines and cars, they want him for public relations work, so there are not enough hours in the day for Bill Elliott.

"Plus the fact that he does not have the congenital appetite for standing up at dinners. Some drivers like it. Darrell Waltrip likes that kind of stuff. He likes to go to dinners and get dressed up. I think Bill Elliott would rather stay home with his family, or be busy under a car, rather than wherever he's being sent by those who pay the bills.

"He's a very sincere, very good fellow, and it's too bad that the first year he achieved so much, people always said, well, it was the car that was winning. It wasn't Bill. That's tough to overcome, but he's shown that he is a first-rate competitor, a very popular guy, and he's learned how to handle the press. Give them a few moments to satisfy them and then go on to other things."

Using other words, George Elliott speaks along the same lines. He says that since he was a junior in high school the only thing Bill wanted to do was race, and, as best as he can, he tunes out all distractions. Unless absolutely necessary, he doesn't want the pit crew talking to him over the car radio. Ordinary humans find it difficult to understand that kind of total absorption, but it's there in a few athletes. Pete Rose was that way as a player, totally immersed in the game of baseball with a one-dimensional sort of dedication. He might not know who the prime minister of England is, but he could quote batting averages of Ty Cobb and Joe DiMaggio and rattle off how many doubles he had in 1977.

Outside of the on-track success, the 1985 season had been traumatic. Rising above the crowd only makes you a better target, as the saying goes, and there were verbal pot shots taken. No one could be that fast; the Elliotts had to be illegal, and being outsiders, away from the mainstream of racing shops in the Carolinas, only made them more suspect.

As Elliott told Waid: "We've been torn down, checked by NASCAR. We just don't work like that. Sure, everybody tries to get by with little things. But to run a big engine or anything like that you are just fooling yourself. I think our cars were probably better than a lot of people's as far as being more equal. You had templates to go by, specifications to go by. I feel like we followed the categories more honestly than a lot of others.

"It was partly jealousy. Any time you've got a guy that is winning or running stout, then there are going to be doubts cast about how he does it — whether by illegal means or using something no one else has got. To me, if I go to a sponsor, I can use that as a scapegoat. I can say, 'We're getting outrun because of . . . ' In this business it's easy to lay the blame on somebody else and that's something we try not to do. If we get outrun, we get outrun, period."

The Elliotts resented the regular breakdown and inspection of their car, but they accepted it as part of the game. Never was anything untoward or illegal found in their Thunderbird. As George Elliott says, "We were probably the most legal car in the garage area."

The most stunning factor, in the eyes of the other teams, was the suddenness of the Elliott explosion. Only twenty-one months earlier Bill Elliott hadn't won his first race on the Winston Cup circuit. He'd spent nine anonymous years in the garage area, and here was a guy nearing his thirtieth birthday. Then in ten months he's transformed into one of the sport's superstars. For him and for them, it was culture shock. Ignored for almost a decade, suddenly he was a frequent visitor to victory lane and to the press box. Expecting a guy to change his private personality in ten months was a little unrealistic.

There was also criticism that the Elliotts, who had been helped by others in the past, now wouldn't give them the time of day. They had found the Holy Grail of speed and weren't sharing, specifically with Ford gurus Leonard Wood and Bud Moore.

Both Wood and Moore say such criticism was overblown.

"First of all," says Wood, "I don't want to take any credit for helping them a great deal in the pre-1985 days. We were always willing to talk to them. They were getting more competitive, and you always seem to talk to people like that. They were up and coming , and they'd come and ask about things and we'd try to provide answers.

"I want to explain some things about racing. About twenty years ago nobody told anybody anything. You didn't discuss any of your secrets and didn't let anybody know what you were doing. You didn't want them to see anything about your car. I think they [the Elliotts] were a little like that in 1985 when they were running so good.

"But nowadays everyone is sharing more than they used to. The other crews are more open and the Elliotts are more open. Like all the rest, they discuss things with different ones now.

"Bear in mind, the sport is so competitive that if you miss one little thing, one item, like in one race, you're just out of it. When you're down, maybe you've got to depend on someone else to give you a helping hand, maybe to get through this one race, and you might have it the next race and they need something. It's more open than it used to be when you didn't tell anybody anything. What it boils down to is that everybody here — in the garage area — is the best friend you have."

While Wood was talking, before the 1987 Talladega 500, Martha Elliott stood by the trailer visiting with Kyle Petty's wife, Pattie, illustrating on the distaff side what takes place between their husbands and the teams. No one has been more successful than the Wood brothers, Glen, the team owner, and Leonard, the crew chief, who in thirty-seven years had eighty-seven poles and seventy-seven wins on the super speedways. It was their driver, David Pearson, and their Ford that had the last Triple Crown — Daytona 500, World 600 and Southern 500 — before Elliott pulled the trick in the Winston Million.

The Woods and the Elliotts have much in common, even to their home environments, the foothills of the Blue Ridge Mountains, one in Stuart, Virginia, the other in Dawsonville.

A devout Christian, Glen Wood never quite adjusted to having to race on Sundays.

It is interesting that Leonard Wood compares Elliott to his old driver, Pearson. He says, "Bill is just that type of driver, you know, he takes a good line through the turns and seems to keep the car freed up and get the most speed out of it. You just watch drivers, and they have certain styles. He seems to have that style similar to Pearson, who, like Bill, always ran smoothly and kept his tires cooler than the others.

"As for the success in '85, I don't think it was any kind of secret or anything like that. It happens once in a while. Sometimes you get everything together — the car's handling well, all your engines are running well and everything falls into place. When those things are happening, there's no stopping you. Then maybe a year or two later it's hard to do even anything. Nothing goes right. Way I've experienced it, these things in racing run in cycles. You can't say it was for this reason or that reason. You just can't explain it."

As Humpy Wheeler said, those years come once in a lifetime. As Bill has said, one of three other drivers — Cale Yarborough, Harry Gant or Dale Earnhardt — should have beaten him in the Southern 500. But two fell out, and Yarborough had late mechanical problems.

"My recollection is I had him beat," says Yarborough, "until my power steering went out late in the race. When that happens, it's pretty much over. But we ran good. It was one of those seasons and he had everything hooked up. He's still running good, but he's not as dominant as he was."

Kyle Petty, who finished second to Elliott in the Winston 500 in the Wood brothers' No. 21, agrees that everything was going Bill's way in 1985. "We run real good in the Winston 500," he says. "Cale led most of the race, and I beat him on the last lap for second, but the way Bill was running, that was the greatest race ever run at Talladega. He was a couple of laps behind and he made them up, and he just went on and went away from us.

"As for his driving style, I'd say he drives more in the style of my father and David Pearson. Laid-back and smooth, he'll lead a race and go away from anybody if he can. He tries to save the car and be there at the end. That's the same style that Daddy and Pearson always had and I guess you go by that because they won more races [305] together than anybody else.

"Racing has gone through some stages. It started with the rough-and-tumble drivers, and then Daddy and Pearson came along and they were real smooth. We had another group come through that were rough-and-tumble, and now you've got another group that is smooth and laid-back. It just comes in cycles.

"I try to take the smooth route, but I don't know, sometimes you do and sometimes you don't. When you first get started and are trying to figure things out, you just keep searching for a style."

When Darrell Waltrip edged Elliott for the points title in 1985, it turned out to be his last hurrah for the Junior Johnson Chevrolet team. His contract ended in 1986, and he left for the Rick Hendrick stable, but not without a parting shot, as only Waltrip can deliver one. "My new car is like a thoroughbred compared to the old nags I used to race," he said. Later, when Johnson's new driver, Terry Labonte, outqualified Waltrip at Daytona, he retorted, "Junior told me I ought to be ashamed for outrunning that thoroughbred with this old nag."

Even mild Junior got into the act, saying, "Last year I had two jackasses, and this year I've got only one mule and I use that mule to plow my garden."

The personable Waltrip can be counted on to stir up things, but when he talks about the 1985 season, now that it's over, he gives Elliott proper credit. "I would have had a great year if it hadn't been for Bill," he says. "He was just having a better year. We ran well at times — I ran second twice at Michigan and a couple of other places — and I was right there, close, each time. But he was just having that kind of year.

"The World 600 in May helped us a lot when we went to Charlotte and won the Winston on Saturday and the 600 on Sunday. That helped us a lot, but, still and all, Bill was having that great season until September.

"In September, he kind of faltered, and because we'd been consistently right there behind him we were able to go on and win the championship. Little things mean a lot in racing. Things happen, little things that go along with racing, and they come along right when you don't want them, when you need them the least.

"Then there's the luck factor, and I'll tell you what it's like. A lot of times you'll win a race and you'll be sitting there in victory circle and you'll have a tire go flat, sitting there as the winner. A lot of times you'll go home after a race after you've won, and they take the engine out of the car and say if we'd run one more lap the engine would have blown. In the 600 we had just enough gas to finish. That's luck.

"It's God-given, God-sent, or whatever, but there is a certain amount you have to have going for you to win a lot of races and to win the championship. I know as well as anybody, and when it's against you, it doesn't matter how hard you work or how well you're prepared, things don't turn out the way you want them. When it's going your way, you just win races and you don't even know why. And you don't even know how."

Elliott had alluded to the intangible, luck or whatever, when he said racing is a sport where one moment you think you have everything under control and it's out of control the next. When an eight-dollar shift pin costs you a shot at more than a quarter-million dollars, that's either bad luck or loss of control.

Wheeler has compared the Elliotts' ascension to the Pettys in that both have close-knit family operations, brothers who build engines and fathers who've been involved on the old dirt tracks. King Richard does not agree totally.

"Well, we'd been there all the time," he says, "and, you know, they kinda hung around and hung around and doing the deal. They just did make some races, and everybody was helping them. Then they got in with Melling, and he brought a lot of expertise and money, and they got their act on the road and were able to do what they needed to do. We did work out of some of the same situations and worked our way to sponsorships and things like that.

"You know, nobody gives you anything, you know what I mean, you gotta pay now or pay later.

"As for Bill's impact, he did have a good impact on racing because it was somebody new, and they come in and did the job, and it was a Ford, as opposed to General Motors, and that helped.

"I look at Bill as a pretty decent driver to run and do what he does. It's a situation where he runs just hard enough to get the job done. He's not hard on a car, not bad about wrecking and things like that. You know he's driving on the safe side of what he can do. Then when he does have to pull it out, he's got a little bit left."

Junior Johnson, whose driver, Waltrip, beat the Elliotts for the points title, scoffs at the idea that Ernie discovered some deep, dark secret. "I don't think there was any secret or anything like that," he says. "They just got a good car and them boys worked hard. The timing was right, and they showed some things as far as the car was concerned. Bill is a good driver, and Ernie is a good engine-builder, but I think their impact has come by Ford having come out with an aerodynamically superior car to the other cars at the time they made their move.

"But don't take anything away from them. As I said, Bill and Ernie are good at what they do. But if you check the statistics, what they did before having a really air-slick car, they did an about-face and moved to another level.

"I think if you put everybody in a Ford right now, they wouldn't be any better than seven or eight other teams. Some think the answer is for NASCAR to approve the Beretta from Chevrolet, but NASCAR says it's smaller than the Ford. Then, of course, the Thunderbird is smaller than the Monte Carlo. That's like comparing apples to eggs."

If anyone should know anything about apples and eggs, Ronda native Johnson should. He's been around them all of his life, as a grower and chicken farmer.

Young Davey Allison, Bobby's son who had driven Winston Cup from time to time and became a regular in 1987, thought there was something there. "Those boys found something, and we'll just have to catch up," he said.

The Elliotts' chassis builder, Edwin (Banjo) Matthews, says their greatest asset was hard work, that and dedication. "I remember when I first associated with them," he says. "They'd just bought the Penske car and they learned a lot of their engine stuff from that. Then we started building cars for them, and we still do. It's just an unwritten thing between us that I build cars and do as good a job as they do. They bought one of those Talladegas that I had.

"I really think the world of those people. They're good, honest, people — absolutely — and they don't ask no extra benefits from anyone. They take what they can take and put back into what they're doing. Just look how the fans respond to them. You know, everybody has his day, and everybody has what others say about them.

"Bill's a winner, and he's a poor loser, which means he's a winner. Junior [Johnson] was that way, Earnhardt's that way and I was that way as a driver. I never wanted to be a loser. I might not have said much about it, but I never liked being a loser. The Elliotts are one of the super teams."

A converted Miamian, who went to school with Bobby Johns and lived a few blocks from Bobby Allison, Matthews now resides in and runs his shop out of the Asheville, North Carolina, mountains. He laughs when asked why mountain boys are so quiet.

"Lord, I don't know," he replies. "When I first went to the mountains, it took me about six years before I figured out how to talk to all those people. Now, I guess, I've turned into one. They've figured out that you can learn more by listening than talking."

Indianapolis ace Mario Andretti, who won the first Eljer Driver of the Year award in 1967 and his last one before Elliott in 1984, says that while he didn't go head-to-head with Bill very often, he was impressed by the Georgian's accomplishment.

"I don't know Elliott as well as I'd like to," he says. "I don't drive and race against him that much. I've got nothing but praise for the man because of what he has on record.

"He seems to be easygoing, real tenacious and intensely professional. Seems like to me he'd be a hell of a nice guy, from what I know. I tell you the man goes for the win, he's a winner, no question, and there's nothing conservative about that."

Being up there on the Eljer honor roll with the Andrettis, Foyts, Pettys, Allisons, Unsers, Rutherfords, Waltrips, Pearsons and Yarboroughs was a humbling experience for Elliott, who said it "sent chills up and down my spine to be in the same category with Andretti and the others. It's hard for me to imagine being in the same league with those drivers."

Upon receiving his second Driver of the Year accolade, the National Motorsport Press Association Award, Elliott confesses that he too was surprised by the extent of his success in 1985. He says, "We had high hopes, but we never imagined all the things that have happened to us. To win the NMPA Driver of the Year is the perfect climax to a sensational year. It is still hard to believe all that happened this year. It certainly was a lot of firsts for us.

"I can't say enough for the job the crew did, especially Ernie and Dan. They were the ones responsible for this award.

"The only regret I have was that we did not win the Winston Cup title. But I guess we used up all of our racing luck during the first two-thirds of the season chasing the Winston Million. We just had too many things go wrong in the last eight races."

While the media and fans hailed him as an instant superstar, Elliott said he knew better. "Recognition is kind of an instantaneous thing," he says. "It's like actors and singers; if you go back, you'll find they've been performing since they were two feet tall.

"Recognition comes when you finally start doing things. People don't hear about you until you're in the media eye. Before that, the tough part is going to a sponsor and saying, 'I can do this job and I need X-number of dollars.'"

The greater the success, the greater the physical and mental costs, and 1985 had left Bill and Ernie Elliott happy but tired, drained and near burnout. They were ready for some R & R.

Much had been said and written about the pressures on Bill the driver. But Ernie was the one who had to keep the engines working, and, being the perfectionist he is, he put intense pressure on himself to maintain a streak of not having had a failed engine since the

Coca-Cola World 600 of 1983. He also has a family predisposition toward hypertension.

For Bill, relaxation didn't mean slowing down. It only meant changing direction. With him, motion and speed are never compromised, even at play.

His favorite methods of relaxing are (1)flying, specifically flying his stunt plane; (2)snow skiing; (3)roller skating; and (4)four-wheeling in the hills. He's not one for curling up with a good book and remaining motionless for long periods of time.

Roller skating was the diversion of his youth. He met Martha at a rink in tiny Suches, Georgia. Snow skiing evolved from his association with Coors and his many trips to Colorado. He's been flying since 1977, the year he became semi-competitive on the Winston Cup trail.

"Flying for me is a great way to relax," he says. "I'd always wanted to, and in '77 I decided I'd do it. After logging forty-three to fifty-four hours in the air, I went over to Gainesville to take my flying test. I almost didn't make the written. Seventy was passing, and that's what I scored, seventy."

He's come a long way from the Cessna that he learned in. There are now two sleek, expensive aircraft parked behind the Coors/Melling compound on Highway 183. One is for business — flying to races, making personal commitments — the other for pleasure. Since one of the planes is almost constantly in use, there is another pilot on the team.

Transportation of the cars and equipment is a separate operation altogether. Unlike the old days when a driver towed his own car to tracks, the modern racer seldom sees his vehicle until he arrives at the race site.

Elliott's funning has also taken a few steps up from clowning on Crown Mountain with Rooster Ingram in a 1963 Fairlane. Now he wings it in his second plane.

Close friend, admirer and business associate Joe Locke, a snow-skiing champion, shares some of those off-duty hours in both flying and skiing, and he marvels at Bill's ability in each. "For Bill, flying is a good way to unwind," he says. "He likes to get in there and do a few stunts, like stalling and spinning just before pulling it out over the trees. The wings come off at five Gs. He takes it up to four-and-a-half."

As on the track, Elliott knows what his limits are, and he stays within that framework. Control, that's the key word. He knows what he has control of.

Not surprisingly, considering their profession, many of the Winston Cup drivers are licensed pilots. In the old days it was quite rare when a Joe Weatherly or a Curtis Turner landed at the rural airport outside Darlington in time for qualifying. Now they come in like a steady stream of corporate executives . . . Elliott, Harry Gant, Tim Richmond, Bobby Allison, Dale Earnhardt, Ricky Rudd, Darrell Waltrip and Cale Yarborough, who, like Elliott, has two planes. In fact, among the well-known drivers, only Richard Petty and Benny Parsons resist the flying urge.

For those accustomed to running two hundred miles an hour on land, driving from track to track can be tedious and nerve-racking. Race drivers are not necessarily patient all on all pavement, as Bobby Allison admitted before the 1987 Winston 500 at Talladega.

"I fly from my home at Hueytown to Talladega, which is a fifteen-minute flight, because I can't stand to ride on the highway at fifty-five miles an hour," he says. "I think I could put up with sixty-five and seventy miles an hour very easily. To someone in my profession who can remember when the speed limits were sixty-five and seventy, fifty-five is aggravating.

"It was a great thing when President Nixon instituted the fifty-five limit. He did a tremendous service to our country, and it's a long and lasting thing, but I think it has outlived its usefulness.

"So I vote for sixty-five. At the same time I think driver education should address interstate highways, entering and exiting and defensive driving."

He added that sometimes kids have to learn the hard way, as his did. "Clifford used up two cars," he says. "Davey used up one. Carrie used up one. Carrie was going on the interstate at night, nice, big Regal, brand-new. All the traffic was stopped and she didn't notice. She was the twenty-first car in one of those majors. I think all of them have learned from their problems."

Proving that the interstate isn't the only risky place, Allison then went out and climbed the first-turn fence, tail end up, in the most spectacular crash of the season, ironically, leading to NASCAR's new ruling lowering speed, not on the interstate but on the roaring roads of Winston Cup. Though shaken, he remained to see son Davey win the Winston 500 before making the safe, fifteen-minute flight back to Hueytown, the most relaxing part of his day.

When Elliott learned to fly, it was more of a desire than a need. He had not yet won a NASCAR race, and he wasn't in great demand for public appearances and sponsor commitments. The challenge and the speed appealed to him. It was something he enjoyed.

The same could be said for snow skiing. He was already into skiing when he met Joe Locke, a Midwesterner who had married and settled at Murphy, North Carolina, through mutual friends, Steve and Curtis Colwell.

Says Locke, "When I first met Bill, I kidded him and told him I knew he was a snow skier, but I didn't know how good he was. I told him I'd like to go out with the team, work with him, try the ski slopes, teach him some new techniques in racing and see how he did.

"I said, 'If you think 212 miles an hour is fast in a race car, wait 'til I take you through a Battleflag Diamond or a Yellow Shoe on the slopes at about seventy to eighty miles an hour. That'll get your attention.'

"He said, yeah, it was fine with him.

"Out in Colorado, before we kicked off, I said, 'We're running underneath a chair lift and you won't be able to make any turns. If it gets too hairy, you yell and I'll slow down.'

"He said, 'Let's have at it.'

"Well, we got up there, we cranked it up, and then we're just flying down the slope. I don't hear a sound and I get a little concerned, but every time I look over my shoulder, he's right behind me, not missing a beat.

"First race I put him in, sponsored by Miller's for Team Members Only, he wins. Later, when Bill, Curtis Colwell and I come back for the next race, sponsored by Hiram Walker and open to everyone, I end up winning and Bill finishing in the top ten in a field of 134 skiers from all over the country.

"I'll tell you, you have to see him ski to believe it. Being a gifted athlete, he doesn't have any fear of the high speeds on the slopes. In the wintertime he does a lot of roller skating, and his leg strength and endurance surpass those of many professional football and basketball players. His eye-hand coordination, leg strength and motor ability are unbelievable."

Contrary to those who question whether a race driver is an athlete, drivers know that theirs is a physically taxing sport that exacts a great toll on the body. The G forces in the corners of super speedways could snap a man's neck if it were not for positioning and harnesses. Upper body and leg strength are vital for survival. More than any other place on the track, that's where the driver and car must become one.

Tim Flock, the last great Georgia driver before Elliott, said the corners were his secret. "I think I had a great advantage in that my father was a tightrope walker," he said. "Let me explain. When the car went into the corners, I had this God-given ability to balance myself. I'm convinced that this balance enabled me to take those corners better than anyone else, get in and get out quicker. I had the perfect feel of the car, every part, every vibration.

"That's important for a race driver. If you don't move with the car, you've got problems. You can't fight gravity."

Thus, in practicality, a race driver's recreation and relaxation outlets serve a twofold purpose, enabling him to get away from it all and sharpening reflexes, conditioning and building strength.

Elliott has his ways; others have theirs.

Tim Richmond plays tennis, races boats, lifts weights and does sit-ups. Bobby Hillin, Jr., a former football player, plays racquetball because, as he puts it, "Racing is like a hard continuous volley in racquetball. You get the adrenalin pumping, and your concentration is the highest possible. There's probably no better exercise for the cardiovascular system and sharpening your coordination. Everything moves so fast."

Weight lifting is not usually associated with race drivers, but a surprisingly large number of them pump iron. Jogging is another popular conditioner.

Physical preparation is one thing, and the proper frame of mind, simply enjoying yourself, is another. Four-wheeling in the hills is an emotional recharger for Elliott. "It's a fun time," says Joe Locke. "The thing about Bill maybe a lot of people don't realize, he's tough. He can take a lot of abuse, and we abuse him. He gets hurt, takes a lot of bad falls and does his share of flips, but he's a good athlete and he bounces back.

"The latest diversion that he's taken up is jet skiing. It's a flotation device that's jet-propelled. You start on your knees, and when it takes off, you come to a standing position. In two days he was literally able to spin it, submerge it and bring it back up.

"We go jet skiing on Lake Knotley in North Georgia and, believe me, Bill could compete professionally on it. You ought to see him ride that thing. He's literally on the edge.

"Anything he tackles, he masters in a short period of time. Frankly, he just amazes me.'

There again, four-wheeling and jet skiing involve movement and speed against a backdrop of tranquil hills and lakes. Even in his quiet moments, Elliott needs a challenge. Others like Dale Earnhardt and Neil Bonnett prefer more sedentary pursuits, such as hunting and fishing. Earnhardt has said he's made some of his most important decisions on a deer stand or in a boat on a lake.

"Thinking is a lot easier in the woods," he says. "There you have no telephone ringing or people around you to bother you."

Clearly, Earnhardt, who describes himself as "One Tough Customer," has two distinct personalities, one for the track and the other for the contemplative life. The outdoors is also a good change of pace for his sometimes partner, Bonnett, who finds escape from the race-a-day world appealing.

"I like to get away from things at times," says Bonnett. "I even get fidgety waiting for a red light."

Running in the fast lane, on asphalt or in life, can have its limits. Even Joe Namath got married.

12

Fred Lorenzen,
The Ford Man
Who Preceded Elliott

AWESOME BILL, meet Fastback Freddie. Before Bill Elliott, there was Fred Lorenzen. There are similarities.

By the end of 1987, Elliott had won twenty-three races, all within a four-year span, and more than $6 million in Winston Cup racing. They didn't call it Winston Cup in the 1960s — it was Grand National — but, nonetheless, on the same tracks, Lorenzen swept to twenty-six wins and $400,000 in six years. That figure might seem like a paltry sum when put alongside Elliott's bank account, but four hundred grand was a lot of bread in the sixties, and, besides, Lorenzen went on to parlay his winnings into millions.

A racer who, like Elliott, worked on his own car, Lorenzen was a NASCAR pioneer, an astute businessman, the forerunner of today's shaven-and-shorn attachecase-carriers in the grease pits.

Despite the years that separate them, Elliott and Lorenzen share a steel bond: Ford.

Of the hundreds of drivers who've turned left since the inception of NASCAR more than forty years ago, only two have been unabashed, unrepentant, unconditional and unflagging Ford men — Elliott and Lorenzen. From divergent backgrounds — Fast Freddie from the suburbs of Chicago and Bashful Bill from the suburbs of Dawsonville — they are brothers under the hood, if not skin.

Ford found a good idea in Lorenzen and a better idea in Elliott.

Now in his fifties, Lorenzen retains his boyish looks and enthusiasm. On a summer evening, he sits in the tastefully furnished living room of his Illinois home and offers advice on his favorite subject.

"Get into stocks," the man says.

"Which stock would you recommend?"

"The biggest. Go with the biggest. You know what that is?"

"IBM?"

"Bigger than that."

"There's something bigger than IBM?"

"You bet there is," says Lorenzen. "Exxon. Go with Exxon. I've got a million in Exxon. It's splitting right now, and you can get it for 47½."

"Should I buy at the split or the full price?"

"Either way is a good buy. I don't think it's splitting until the thirteenth, so at the full price you get two-for-one. Don't forget I told you on August 8 to buy Exxon. After that I'd say go for McDonald's, Waste Management, Ford, GM. How do you think banks pay 6 percent? They take your money and buy Exxon and McDonald's.

"I always follow the advice a friend gave me, 'Go with the best and forget the rest.' You're better off going to the best restaurants, buying the best clothes, picking up the best stocks."

Fred Lorenzen has changed. There was a time, when he was starting out as a race driver in the 1960s, that he didn't buy McDonald's stock; he ate at McDonald's. And he didn't buy Exxon; he bought El Cheapo at the discount station. A blond, handsome, eligible bachelor, he didn't date because it cost money. When Fireball Roberts, Joe Weatherly and Banjo Matthews persuaded a voluptuous blonde to chase him around a pool at a Florence, South Carolina, motel he dashed to his room and locked the door.

For some misguided reason, he thought he'd like to be the subject of a *Playboy* magazine article and asked an Atlanta writer to check it out.

An inquiry was made.

"Tell us something about Lorenzen," the *Playboy* rep said.

"Well, er, er, he's gentlemanly, conservative, thrifty and clean-cut."

"Forget it."

Coming out of Elmhurst, Illinois, as a two-time USAC stock car racing champion, Lorenzen won his twenty-six races and $400,000 before he retired in 1967 due to pressures, nerves and ulcers. He was the first $100,000 regular-season winner. Though others outstripped those figures, Lorenzen remained important in the Winston Cup scheme of things for two reasons:

(1) Among major drivers, he was the godfather of the pure Ford drivers. A host of drivers — Bobby Allison, Richard Petty, Ned Jarrett, Junior Johnson, David Pearson, Fireball Roberts, Cale Yarborough, Buddy Baker, et al. — drove Fords but also competed in other makes.

(2) He pioneered the New Breed before there was a New Breed, being the first businessman-driver to appear at the track with a personal stockbroker.

"Don't mention that broker," said Lorenzen in the comfort of his Oakwood, Illinois, home. "He cost me a million."

Lorenzen, now the father of two, recovered that million and more in real estate and stocks. Outside of the stock market, his favorite small type can be found on the sports pages, under race results.

"Elliott is the hottest thing going," he said. "When Waltrip came up, I said he'd be the next big-timer and I said the same about Elliott. He had all the right things going for him . . . the driver, his brother Ernie, the engine-builder, his brother Dan and the crew and the owner. There's no secret to racing. The way to win is to have the kind of people who'll put the money into it and work all night, if necessary and, from what I understand, the Elliotts are those kind of people.

"Elliott's driving style takes me back twenty years. He drives exactly like I did, smooth and always with something in mind.

"But Bill Elliott can't do it all by himself, just as I couldn't do it alone. A driver is a robot. You've got to have someone in the pits who knows what he's doing. That's where the work is done and big decisions made. Fortunately, he's got his brothers. I had Ralph Moody, a walking computer, one of the smartest racing men who ever came along.

"I remember in the sixties when we went out and started practicing pit stops. The other drivers and crews laughed at us. But they didn't laugh when we were getting in and out of the pits in sixteen seconds. That's where it is, that little edge."

Lorenzen exploded on the NASCAR scene in much the manner that Elliott did, but he had a peculiar disadvantage. He was the first outsider, non-Southerner, to make it big in good ol' boy country and was resented by both the other drivers and the fans. In time, however, their allegiance to Ford overcame regional biases. Elliott had the advantage of being a good ol' boy reincarnated.

The way Lorenzen got from Illinois to Southern racing yards is intriguing.

He says, "As a kid of ten, camping out in a tent in the backyard, I used to listen to the Southern 500 on the radio. I knew all about Curtis Turner, Joe Weatherly and all those guys, and I'd say to myself, 'One of these days I'm going to be in the winner's circle there.' I was always attracted to racing, and I started off in the small stuff and moved up to USAC, where I won a couple of championships.

"Still, I was struggling, building my car behind a pizza parlor in Elmhurst and borrowing four grand from loan sharks at about 100 percent interest to buy engines from Ralph Moody, Ford's man in

Charlotte. Then I got a break. Ford wanted to get back in racing, and Ralph asked if I was interested. Then he went to Ford and said, 'I've got this kid I think can do the job for us.' That's how it started. When I got to North Carolina, Banjo Matthews sort of took me under his wing and helped me until the operation actually cranked up.

"We had all the ingredients that I mentioned, a driver, a mechanical genius, hard work and an outstanding crew, mechanics like Herb Nab. With Ralph Moody, if we finished, we won.

"Most vivid in my memory is the first time I ran at Darlington, the place I had dreamed of. It was the Rebel 300 in 1961, I was on the pole and you can bet I was a little intimidated when I looked out and saw Curtis Turner on the outside. There he was, my hero.

"Before the race, Ralph came up for last-minute instructions and emphasized one point. 'Look,' he said, 'I grew up with Curtis Turner and I want to tell you one thing. Watch out for him.'

"Well, the race started, and I didn't think much more about it. With 150 miles to go, I blew a tire and spent some time in the pits. Once more Ralph told me, 'Watch out for Turner — now go!' I came out a lap down, but I unlapped myself and with seventeen laps to go I caught Turner and made plans to pass him.

"The opportunity came with two laps to go, and I made my move on the outside. He put me into the wall.

"As I came around the pit area, still on Turner's bumper, Ralph held up a big sign that read 'THINK.' He stressed the message by pointing to his head.

"On the last lap I gave Turner a fake to the outside, and when he came up to put me into the wall, I dove to the inside and cleared him, cruising on in to win the race.

"Just as I went past the start-finish line, there he was again, side by side, and what else? He put me into the wall again. My dream had come true, I was in the winner's circle at Darlington, and I had beaten my hero, but, I suspected, I wasn't his hero. Curtis didn't take kindly to losing."

Terrors on the track, Lorenzen and Moody were major contributors off the pavement, specifically in the area of design and equipment.

"As far as I know, Ralph was the first to come up with the rear spoiler," said Lorenzen. "It was either him or Ford, but I'd never seen one until one afternoon when he walked up with a piece of metal and said, 'Let's try this.' It was a half-inch spoiler, though at the time I had no idea what it was. I asked and he said, 'Just get in and drive and tell me what you think.'

"I did, and I couldn't believe what that device did in planting down the rear end. The tail wasn't rising the way it does when the wind plays tricks. 'This is great,' I said, and he handed me a larger spoiler and said, 'Now try this.'

"That was better yet. The spoiler was certainly a revolutionary tool for high-drafting super speedways."

Lorenzen's contribution was equally important, or more so.

Disappointed that his Galaxy wasn't responding as he thought it should, he approached Ford engineers with a complaint and a suggestion. "This car's roof is too square," he said. "The turbulence is holding us back. Can you do something about it?"

Result: The Ford slant back, the most aerodynamic race car of its time. Less than two decades later, Ford's engineers were to deliver an even more wind-resistant Thunderbird to the Elliotts in Dawsonville and set the stage for the most explosive year in stock car racing history.

The slant, or slope, back was to play a prominent role in the future of Lorenzen and Elliott in the purity of the model, but, actually the biggest Ford winner of all time was David Pearson, who posted 52 of his 105 career wins in a Ford or a Mercury. The catch is that Pearson also competed in General Motors and Chrysler products. The same holds true for Bobby Allison, who drove Fords to eighteen first places on the current tracks.

Among Pearson's Ford successes, he had nine at Michigan and eight at Darlington. However, Elliott, with five victory-lane visits through 1987, is closing in on his Michigan record.

There is a lesson to be learned here about the durability of Fords on the long, flat-out tracks as opposed to the dominance of General Motors on the short raceways. Much has been made of Elliott's short-track record, but statistics and facts bear out his contention that Fords simply do not do as well on the stop-and-go raceways.

Through 1987, the results read like this:

At Bristol — General Motors thirty-three wins, Ford twelve, Chrysler six.

At Martinsville — General Motors thirty-three, Chrysler sixteen, Ford fourteen.

At North Wilkesboro — General Motors thirty-three, Chrysler sixteen, Ford fourteen.

At Richmond — General Motors twenty-three, Chrysler seventeen, Ford thirteen.

When Ricky Rudd won the 1986 Sovran Bank 500 at Martinsville, it marked the first winning Ford in twenty-seven races over the .526-mile layout, since Pearson won the same event in 1973.

Based on figures through 1987, the odds are virtually even in the GM-Ford battle at Talladega, Darlington, Atlanta, Charlotte, Dover, Riverside and Rockingham. Ford has the edge at Michigan (19-13) and GM at Pocono (14-4). Factory support, or nonsupport, has always been a major factor. Ford teams headed by Bud Moore and the Wood brothers have persevered over the years, and when the Elliotts came along, they were fortified with an added stablemate at the front. In 1987, the Ranier/Lundy team, with Davey Allison at the wheel, raised the odds on Fords to its highest peak since the Holman and Moody days and Fastback Freddie.

Lorenzen cut quite a swath. He was the first to make a clean sweep of the super speedways in the South, winning four times at Charlotte, three at Atlanta, twice at Darlington and once at Daytona. Talladega, of course, didn't open its gates until 1969, two years after he retired.

When he called it quits, Lorenzen held three major records: most wins in races more than 250 miles, twenty-one; most super speedway wins, twelve; most consecutive wins in major races, five.

His contributions did not go unnoticed.

When he retired on April 25, 1967, at age thirty-one, Holman and Moody also retired his blue-and-white No. 28 Ford and said the number would never again be used. And Jacque H. Passino, then chief of Ford's performance events, said, "No man since Barney Oldfield has contributed more to the performance image of Ford."

Times change and history repeats itself, as Humpy Wheeler said.

Here came Bill Elliott doing for the Ford image what Lorenzen had done, but doing it much faster in the reincarnation of the slant back. And like a phantom out of the past, here came No. 28, not blue-and-white and not retired either, moving to the beat of Davey Allison. Even the Ford driving style remained the same, smooth and unconfrontational. Most of the time.

Elliott has discovered that with the repetition of history comes the return of ghosts. For him, Curtis Turner came back as Dale Earnhardt.

13

1986:
Can a Million-Plus
Be Failure?

BILL ELLIOTT TRIED to tell everyone that 1985 was an exceptional year and not to expect a repeat in 1986, but no one listened.

"Any time you have a good year followed by one that's not as good, there's disappointment," he had said during the closing days of 1985. "Call it ego or whatever. I feel you have to accept what comes along. It wasn't that long ago that I won my first race. Things change, you get older and circumstances differ.

"Look at the Junior Johnson team. Last year [1984] they won seven races. This year they won three, and people say they had a bad year. You've got to accept that, though often it's not necessarily true. If I have any goals, it's to improve our performance on the short tracks. Each year you learn more and more about what you need.

"If I do like everybody else has done, it won't be too good a year. In racing, you have good times and bad times. It seems the guy wins a championship and the next year is bad times. It's been a pattern.

"Truth is, toward the end of last year we weren't that dominant. Those rule changes closed things down."

A "bad year," of course, can be relative. Two wins, both at Michigan, coming off an eleven-win season may be considered bad. But $1,069,142 in purse money and winnings cannot by any measure be judged anything but exceptional. Included in his second straight million-dollar year was a $240,000 payoff for winning the second running of the Winston in Atlanta. That was the single largest purse in the history of NASCAR, and it was also the day he looked most like the Elliott of 1985. There was nothing bad about May 11 in Atlanta.

Earlier, on the first of May, he had retained his title as the world's fastest stock car driver with a qualifying run of 212.229 miles an hour prior to the Winston 500 at Talladega. He also won the poles for the Daytona 500, the Talladega 500 and the *Atlanta Journal* 500, giving him four for the season. At Atlanta, he set a one-lap qualifying record of 172.905 miles an hour.

The real bad luck started during Speed Week in Daytona during February when both Bill and Ernie came down with what they thought was the flu. It turned out that Bill did have the flu, but Ernie had something much more serious — mononucleosis, a debilitating and lingering illness.

It was a major setback. Because of his condition, Ernie could not devote the time needed for engine building and research, and he was absent for many of the prerace practices and qualifying runs, often appearing only on race day. With Ernie questionable, brother Dan stepped into the breach and built the engine that Bill won the Winston with. He also backed up Ernie as crew chief.

Ernie's absence led to some talk of "trouble in River City," perhaps dissension among the brothers, but this was denied by car owner Harry Melling. "We don't have any problems other than that Ernie is sick," he said. "When he was at the Michigan race in August, he was still sick. He stayed in the truck during the race."

Family splits are not unique in NASCAR, as in any other business, and there was a precedent for such rumors. The most glaring of all was the most famous of all racing families, the Pettys. Richard and his engine-building brother, Maurice, went their separate ways after they were fined thirty-five thousand dollars for having an oversized engine and illegal tires. Cousin Dale Inman left Petty Enterprises after a disagreement, then returned later. And son Kyle departed for a better ride.

The patriarch of the clan, Lee Petty, winner of fifty-four Winston Cup races, personally delayed Richard's entry into the winner's circle. In 1958, Richard was accepting congratulations for winning his first race at Lakewood in Atlanta when Lee stormed to the scorer's stand, demanded a recount and was declared the winner.

Then he snarled, "As long as Richard puts his feet under my table, he's going to win fair and square. He didn't win the race, I did. He ain't gonna have it given to him."

Nowadays, Lee Petty seldom attends races, preferring to spend his time on the golf links. The Pettys survive as a family with everyone doing his own thing.

With the Elliotts, there had been a lot of talk in 1985. The engine won it, the car won it and/or Bill's driving won it.

Says George Elliott, "This is an effort where nobody cares who gets the credit. It's the results that count. There's an old saying that human beings can stand anything but prosperity, and I think we've proven them wrong."

Nonetheless, after the champagne in 1985 came the hangover in 1986.

And the head-throbbing started during Speed Week in Daytona.

Prior to the big week, Elliott joined Kyle Petty, Ricky Rudd and Ken Schrader in participating in an IMSA Camel GT event, and they finished fifteenth in the GTO Division. He subsequently took part in four IMSA races and garnered two top-five finishes along with a GTO/GTU most outstanding driver award.

Most of the qualifying day attention was focused on General Motors products, specifically Pontiacs, which had been redesigned to be more aerodynamically efficient. GM had answered the Elliott and Ford challenge by sprinting back to the drawing board. Waltrip went so far as to say that Pontiacs "will be the Thunderbirds of this year."

He missed that prediction.

A Thunderbird, Elliott's, began the season as "the Thunderbird of this year." Little had changed, as Bill turned the track at speed of 205.039 miles an hour, just a bit off his old mark of 205.114. Chevrolet-driver Geoff Bodine won the outside position, and there wasn't a Pontiac in the top ten.

However, with exception of Elliott's and Cale Yarborough's T-Bird (No. 4), the other eight were in GM products. Only Elliott and Bodine, less than a half-mile an hour slower, earned starting positions for the Daytona 500. The rest of the field was filled out by the twin 125-mile qualifying races later in the week.

The Coors/Melling team went through the qualifying process without Ernie Elliott, who was too weak to leave his hotel room. In his absence, brother Dan prepared the engine for the winning effort.

Disappointed that he hadn't broken his own record, Bill said, "I guess I'm glad to be as close as I am after the two rules changes last year."

He went on to win his 125-mile qualifier and finish second to Dale Earnhardt in the twenty-lap Busch Clash. Even at that, he was only two car lengths in arrears. So far he was on schedule to repeat his Grand Slam of the pole, the 125-mile qualifier and the Daytona 500. In 1985 he had become only the third driver to win them all.

He never had a chance. Just past the midway point of the two-hundred-lap race, Elliott, running just behind leaders Bodine and Earnhardt, got entangled in an eleven-car pileup, triggered by a spinning Neil Bonnett, and lost several laps for repairs. Thereafter, he aimed for the highest finish possible.

When Earnhardt gave out of gas eight miles from the finish, Bodine won the race and collected a record $192,715.

Elliott finished thirteenth, perhaps an omen for the season.

In the next eight races, if he hadn't had bad luck, Bill wouldn't have had any luck at all.

They went this way:

Miller 400 at Richmond: Involved in thirteen-car pileup on fifteenth lap, spent forty-one laps for repairs, finished twenty-first.

Goodwrench 500 at Rockingham: Started ninth, lost ground due to gas misjudgment, finished seventh.

Motorcraft 500 at Atlanta: Started fifth and finished fifth, running second when pitted on caution nine laps from finish; problem with lug nut ended chances.

Valleydale 500 at Bristol: Fifth-place finish not bad on short track after running with leaders most of day.

TranSouth 500 at Darlington: Problems on qualifying day relegated him to twenty-first, then forced replacement of ignition coil placed him eighth, five laps off pace.

First Union 400 at North Wilkesboro: Bad news, he finished ninth; good news, he finished on lead lap for second time ever on a short track.

Sovran Bank 500 at Martinsville: For first time in three years, Coors/Melling team suffered engine failure, this time after only forty-two laps, and Elliott had thirty-first finish.

At Talladega, for a change, there was some good news before the bad. No matter what, Elliott always flies with the wind in qualifying at NASCAR's fastest track, and Thursday, May 1, 1986, was no exception.

Driving a spanking-new T-Bird, he sizzled around the 2.66-mile track at 212.229 miles an hour, shattering the world stock car record once more. The standard he had set in previous years was now commonplace as twenty-three drivers ran two hundred or more miles an hour. Three, Waltrip, Tommy Ellis and Pancho Carter, couldn't make the top twenty despite running a little better than 204 miles an hour.

Elliott admitted it was a bit hairy. "My mind was saying back off, but my foot said I'd better not," he sighed in relief. "I didn't think we'd go that fast, but the car was on the ragged edge. Looking back, I don't see how we could have done anything to make it run faster."

Once more the strawberry-haired speed king from Dawsonville had to do it without brother Ernie, who stayed behind at home, and Dan prepared the engine that Ernie had built originally for the Bristol race. Once the race started, the engine ran well as Elliott led

116 of the 188 laps, but it was not totally surprising when it died thirteen laps from the finish.

There was some consolation in the twenty-fourth-place finish. For the first time in weeks he had been in position to win a race, though he didn't quite make it.

Coming up on May 11, the Winston at Atlanta was the focal point of the season for the Coors/Melling team. This was the second running of the Winston, and the R. J. Reynolds Tobacco people weren't quite sure what format to use or where to stage this eighty-three-lap, 126.3-mile added attraction to the regular season. The first one, run at Charlotte as a prelim to the World 600 and won by Waltrip, had been relatively successful, and this led to the belief that it could stand on its own, in concert with an uninspiring invitational race for nonwinners, in Atlanta on Mother's Day.

Wrong.

Fewer than twelve thousand paid customers turned out to see the Winston Cup's all-star show.

In the rules of the Winston at that time, all cars had to pit on the fortieth lap to change two tires.

Elliott saw that pit stop as extremely critical. "With the cars as equal as we expect them, that single pit stop may determine the winner or the losers in this race," he said. "If you don't get the stagger just right, you'd be at a disadvantage."

Returning to Atlanta was a tonic for Bill, who hadn't won a Winston Cup race since the *Atlanta Journal* 500 of October 1985 and had a winless streak of ten races. With Ernie still sick, once more Dan had spent countless hours perfecting the engine for this, the richest run of the year with a $240,000 first-place purse. One thing you learn about the Elliotts, you don't flash the big money in front of them if you don't want them to grab it.

Ernie made an appearance for the Sunday race, but he remained on the catwalk atop the Coors/Melling truck and Dan ran the pits. The pole position was decided by the Winston point standings of the past season, so Waltrip got the inside and Elliott the outside. In less than one lap, Bill was not only inside, he was out front, and that's where he stayed.

Lap after lap, No. 9 led the field around the 1.522-mile oval; in fact, Elliott led eighty-two of the eighty-three laps in a show of complete dominance.

The only crisis came on the pit stop when Earnhardt appeared to have the edge getting out. But as he maneuvered to get back on the track, Elliott came flying under him and cut him off at the head of the pit. It was his slickest move of the day. He averaged 159.123 miles an hour in blowing away the field. Earnhardt was second and Harry Gant third.

"I was hoping this race would turn it around, as it did for Waltrip last year," said Elliott.

Earnhardt, who finished 2.55 seconds behind, was impressed. "The way Bill was running, I got frustrated the first lap and stayed that way all day," he said. "He must have everything back that he had last year. I don't know if he'd put it on the shelf, or if NASCAR had it put on the shelf, but, whatever, he's got it back."

Not quite.

A week later, at Dover in the Budweiser 500, there were more engine problems and a seventh-place finish.

The World 600 at Charlotte was a different story. Everything worked, but there was a human error, a miscalculation. Again running strong, reminiscent of the Winston, Bill had a comfortable lead over Earnhardt for forty-three of the last fifty-nine laps.

It was a test of wills to see which would pit for gas first or if, perchance, both could finish. Elliott ran dry first, and he pitted with only sixteen laps left. Although he returned and remained in the lead lap, the best he could manage was sixth.

Earnhardt, running ninety-six of the six hundred miles on his last tank of gas, beat Tim Richmond to the checkers by almost two seconds for his first victory ever in the World 600. He said that the race was one for his dad, the late Ralph Earnhardt, an outstanding old-time race driver who'd never won the 600.

After an eleventh at Riverside and a fifth at Pocono, the Coors/Melling team pulled into their second home, the Michigan International Speedway, home track of car owner Harry Melling and Elliott's favorite playpen. He had a streak of two wins going at the track, and the extremely wide two-mile oval always seemed to favor the Georgia boy. The track had just been repaved, allowing drivers to use the entire width instead of the one or two grooves of the past, and that was right down Elliott's alley.

Tim Richmond, who was holding the hot hand in 1986, won the pole, breaking a streak of four straight Elliott poles at MIS, and Bill, not quite having his car locked in, qualified eighth for the Miller American 400.

For the fifth time in his career, Elliott found himself in a shootout with Gant for the checkers. He had won three of them, by twelve inches at Rockingham in 1984, by twenty-nine seconds at Dover and by less than a second at Pocono in 1985.

Winding down to the finish, Gant had led laps 174 through 188 of the two-hundred-lap race before Elliott made a move. He nudged ahead, but Gant quickly regained the front spot. Biding his time, Bill stayed on Gant's bumper until lap 195.

He then slingshotted past Gant to take the lead for good.

"I tried a lap earlier but couldn't get a good go at him," said Elliott. "I wanted to get by to take advantage of the lapped cars coming up ahead of us. On that earlier try, I backed off and filed in behind him until I could get a better run."

Gant said Elliott was "definitely too strong to handle, and I guess I was lucky to finish second."

In addition to the $56,900 first-place check, the victory was a blessed relief for Elliott, who'd gone eight months and fourteen races without an official Winston Cup win. No doubt he looked forward to the next race at Michigan, the Champion Spark Plug 400 on August 17.

Meanwhile, in between, there was nothing but trouble.

A pit mistake in the Firecracker 400 cost him a lap, and he had a disappointing sixteenth-place finish. At Pocono, in the Summer 500, he led half the race, but his engine failed at the halfway mark. He was thirty-fifth. At Talladega, where he always wins the pole, he did again with a 209.005, but that was about all as the power plant conked out again. His record-breaking seventh-straight front-row start went for naught, yielding only a twenty-seventh-place finish. In the Budweiser at Glen Watkins, he salvaged a fourth despite a time-trials crash that damaged the car.

When most people lose their way, they retrace their steps to their beginnings. When Bill Elliott loses his way, he pulls out a road map to Brooklyn, Michigan, and the Michigan International Speedway. Whatever ails him, there's a cure at MIS.

Following the pattern of domination or bust, this again was domination for the Georgia redhead. With the T-Bird dialed in, Elliott made the others run his race. He had his way, leading when he felt like it, breathing his car at other times and then, with sixty laps to go, taking total command.

He got some unexpected help and some unexpected opposition.

With fourteen laps to go, Benny Parsons, running second, hit the wall and brought out the caution. That also brought up Richmond, who'd been at the end of the lead lap, and he gave Elliott a chase for the checkered flag. At the finish line, Richmond, riding a streak of either winning or finishing second in eight of the last nine races, was 1.34 seconds off the winning pace, which was 135.45 miles an hour.

It was another good payday, $55,950, for the Coors/Melling team, but more than that, a Winston Cup record for the most consecutive wins on a super speedway, four.

"Anytime you set a record, it's important to you," Elliott noted. "I knew when I went out I had a chance. The car ran so good, it made it look easier. I really made them run my race. That's the first time it's happened here. Last time here, I had to run their race."

Bill, Ernie and Dan would just as soon forget the last ten races of the 1986 season. Other than two third-place finishes, in the Southern 500 and *Atlanta Journal* 500, there wasn't a top-five place to be found. They were nineteenth in the Busch 500 at Bristol, ninth in the Wrangler Jeans Indigo 400 at Richmond, twenty-seventh in the Delaware 500, eleventh in the Goody's 500 at Martinsville, sixteenth in the Holly Farms 400 at North Wilkesboro, seventh in both the Oakwood Homes 500 at Charlotte and the Nationwise 500 at Rockingham and twenty-third in the Winston Western 500 at Riverside. Altogether, the Coors/Melling No. 9 was not around at the finish in six races during this most rare season.

There is a startling contrast in those last ten races and the 1963 season of the last pure Ford driver, Freddie Lorenzen. In that year, Lorenzen became the first $100,000 winner on the NASCAR trail, with $113,570 in moneys from four wins (World 600, Motorcraft 500, Busch 500, Goody's 500), seven second places (Miller, First Union, *Atlanta Journal*, Valleydale and Daytona 500s and Holly Farms and Firecracker 400s), one third (Southern 500), one fourth (Wrangler Jeans Indigo 400) and one fifth (Sovran Bank 500).

Twenty-three years later, in 1986, the Elliotts collected $146,253 for their last ten races, in which they had only two top-five finishes. That provides some kind of measure of how the moneys and prizes have increased in Winston Cup. Theoretically, a modern-day driver can go winless during a season and still earn close to a half-million dollars.

There is another aspect of Winston Cup racing, the hidden money, and no one targets this loot with more zest than the Elliotts. Hidden money is earned by leading the most laps, the right and high-paying laps, pole rewards and bonuses from manufacturers.

In 1986, Dale Earnhardt, on his way to the Winston Cup points title, won five races, had sixteen top-five finishes and won a total of $1,783,880, the first time he and car owner Richard Childress had been over a million. Trailing him were Darrell Waltrip, in his last season for Junior Johnson, with $1,099,735, then Elliott, with only two wins, with $1,069,142. Waltrip and Johnson, like the Elliotts, know where to place their emphasis. Their winnings came on only three wins and twenty-one top-five finishes. After Earnhardt, Waltrip and Elliott finished second and fourth in the points standings.

The season's biggest winner, Tim Richmond, in the Rick Hendrick GM car, earned less than Elliott ($988,221) on seven victories and thirteen top-five places, plus a third in the points. Almost a third of Elliott's seasonal winnings — $352,850 — came from his three wins, the Winston and the two races at Michigan. He also picked up $56,070 in hidden money for finishing thirteenth at Daytona.

Durability was a big factor in 1986. Of 11,447.25 miles run in all twenty-nine races, Winston Cup champion Earnhardt had only 285.25 unfinished miles, while, uncharacteristically, the Coors/ Melling team had 856.95 uncompleted miles. Much of this can be attributed to Ernie Elliott's lingering illness, although brother Dan filled in admirably.

Most amazingly, at the end of the 1986 season, Elliott, whose career began to blossom less than three years earlier, stood fifth on the all-time racing winnings list with total earnings of $5,122,295. Only Waltrip ($7,435,457), Bobby Allison ($6,290,365), Richard Petty ($6,192,102) and Indy ace Al Unser, Sr. ($5,151,834), had won more on the speedways of America. Below Elliott were such names as Cale Yarborough, Mario Andretti, A. J. Foyt, Johnny Rutherford, Rick Mears, Tom Sneva and David Pearson.

The shy kid from the hills of North Georgia, who once had to borrow parts from other drivers, had become a multimillionaire.

And the fans loved him. For the third time in three years, he was voted Most Popular Driver in NASCAR racing. This pleased him. "I'd rather have that award than a lot of them," he said. "It means a lot to me to be liked by a lot of people. Those people out there help you do what you want to do."

What he wanted to do was win more races. Already he had seventeen super speedway victories, tying him for sixth on the all-time rosters, and he wanted more, plus a few scattered short-track successes. Uncomfortable with the "superman" status accorded him and Ernie in 1985, he was now back among the mere mortals, and he had never claimed to be anything else.

Off the track, 1986 was a year of news, primarily the breakup of the Junior Johnson-Darrell Waltrip combination. Waltrip announced he was playing out his option, so to speak, and later disclosed he'd join master engine-builder and crew chief Waddell Wilson under the Rick Hendrick banner. At the same time, Neil Bonnett also left the Johnson team.

To replace Waltrip, Johnson went from one extreme to the other, from a gregarious Waltrip to the quiet and shy Terry Labonte, the Winston Cup champion of 1984. Says Johnson, "Darrell is one of the finest drivers in NASCAR history, but we felt it was time for both parties to move ahead with our professional careers. Terry meets all our standards and he has proven his consistency."

NASCAR also made changes in its rules, going back to a larger carburetor and higher speeds, living on the edge once more as it does periodically. It also approved air dams and rear trunk spoilers to improve handling.

The drivers, Elliott included, awaited 1987.

14

Profit as Bottom Line: Corporations and Stock Car Racing

R ACING IS NOT INEXPENSIVE.
It costs in the neighborhood of $3 million a year to keep a top contender, which would include Coors/Motorcraft team, on the tracks. That breaks down to about $100,000 per racing weekend.

In the case of the Elliotts, the bulk of that expense is borne by the primary sponsor, the Adolph Coors Company, and the associate sponsor, Motorcraft, the parts division of the Ford Motor Company. Car owner Harry Melling had to make a sacrifice to obtain the backing of Motorcraft. He erased the name of the Melling Tool Company from the car and replaced it with Motorcraft, the name of a company with whom he does oil pump business. He considered it good business.

Owner-driver financial arrangements are as varied as the personalities of those involved.

The standard contract calls for a fifty-fifty split of race purses between owners and drivers of the top teams. For some drivers, however, their share can be as low as 25 percent or 35 percent and as high as 60 percent. These terms are seldom disclosed, but garage talk has it that Harry Gant, with the Hal Needham team, has one of the more lucrative driver contracts. Thus, it is little wonder that Gant was upset about finishing only five or six races in 1987.

Personal service and bonus clauses make each contract unique. In addition, a driver benefits from endorsements, commercials and personal appearances.

Some drivers, especially those without a track record, are required to "buy" their own rides. That means that in order to sign on with a team they must bring a sponsor with them.

In view of the various arrangements, big winnings don't always translate into big earnings. For example, in Bill Elliott's twenty-three wins through 1987, the purses totaled $1,489,398. If his contract calls for a 50 percent split, he has cleared $744,699. When he won the Winston Million in 1985, it is said that he banked approximately $100,000 after taxes.

Overall, since he joined the Winston Cup circuit in 1976, through 1987, he had won $6.7 million, including $2,433,187 in 1985, $1,069,142 in 1986 and $1,599,210 in 1987, the first three-year million-dollar hat trick in any form of racing.

His last win in 1987, the *Atlanta Journal* 500 finale, paid $74,200 and was a far cry from his first purse of $640 for finishing thirty-third in the Carolina 500 at Rockingham in 1976.

Suffice to say, he's a millionaire, several times over; he owns two planes, the chassis building in the compound, two homes, one in Dawsonville and the other in Blairsville, and a dozen lakeside lots in the North Georgia mountains. All this before he reached thirty-two years of age.

The name of the racing game is money, and big money begets big pressures.

Jody Ridley, the Elliotts' boyhood hero, understands this. In 1980 he was Winston Cup Rookie of the Year with two top-five and eighteen top-ten finishes and $196,617 in winnings, fourth in all-time rookie earnings. Now in his mid-forties, Ridley is back in Chatsworth, Georgia, running a garage and doing well on the short tracks. Before Elliott came along, Ridley was the last Georgian to win a Winston Cup race, coming from an eleventh starting position to take the Mason-Dixon 500 at Dover in 1981.

Unable to attract a big-money sponsor and tired of the wrangling, Ridley returned to his roots, where he is content. "I'm on the outside looking in," he says. " I'm sure enjoying not having the pressure of politics in racing. The Elliotts have the ideal situation of being a family team and not having to put up with the politics and the finger-pointing.

"Drivers get blamed for almost everything, and most of the time the blame doesn't lie with them. It's usually somebody else's fault, and you end up not having control over your situation."

The Elliotts and Ridley no longer see each other as often as in the old days when he worked on engines with Ernie and took Bill on his first trip away from home. They've gone in different directions.

"We just sort of drifted away," says Ridley.

David Sosebee of Dawsonville, Gober's boy, was another aware of the difficulties in obtaining financial support. He raced from time to time, but lack of funds prevented him from realizing a potential he believed was there. Gober Sosebee said they'd settle for the hundred-dollar patches that the Elliotts used to get started.

In racing, you start with money, but the real key is equipment.

"Look at the winners and in all cases they have good equipment," says Chris Economaki, the veteran journalist. "When Freddie Lorenzen made a big splash in the early 1960s, he had the best equipment that Holman and Moody could provide. And when Pete Hamilton came in and won the Daytona 500 in 1970 he had the benefit of Petty Engineering equipment and expertise.

"Think of what Babe Ruth could have done with a wiffle bat or Ben Hogan with mismatched clubs. In this business if you don't have the equipment you can't win."

A glaring example in 1987 was Davey Allison, a talented rookie who had first-rate equipment and solid backing in Havoline and millionaire sportsmen Harry Ranier and J. T. Lundy, president of Calumet Farms, whose dream is to win the Kentucky Derby and the Coca-Cola World 600 on Memorial Day weekend. With the youngest team on the circuit — both Allison and then-crew chief Joey Knuckles were twenty-six — the No. 28 Thunderbird sat in the winner's circle at Talladega and Dover and just missed at the World 600.

So sudden was winning the Winston 500 at Talladega that young Allison almost forgot standard operating procedure: Forget the race and details; the important part is to give the sponsor full visual and verbal exposure on national television. The guidelines are clear.

First, the winning driver must make himself presentable; then he must don the sponsor's cap, be it beer, detergent, motor oil, an airline or chewing or smokeless tobacco. If he represents a soft drink, he must pop out of the car with a logoed cup.

The first words out of a driver's mouth should include mention of the sponsor. Some things, such as beer and cigarettes, can be plugged with insignias, but not partaken of.

This ritual is reserved for the electronic media — if they want an interview they have to accept the circumstances — and scrapped for print people, who normally ignore the commercial trappings of a race. Except in the case of winners or leaders, print reporters seldom mention even the make of a driver's car.

A Winston Cup race is one gigantic billboard with varying degrees of advertising, from $600,000 for a network spot to one hundred dollars for a car patch. Almost everyone involved wears a cap proclaiming a product, and all roads leading to a track are plastered by signs in Winston red reading, "Welcome Race Fans."

The greatest single benefactor of NASCAR racing is the R. J. Reynolds Tobacco Company, with an estimated $5 million of its advertising budget earmarked for three races (the Winston, Winston 500 and Western Winston 500) and the points race.

This close association began in 1971 when cigarette advertising was banned on television. RJR needed a major outlet, and auto racing met their demographic requirements. They began by sponsoring the season-long points race and gradually added the other areas. Their biggest coup was the Winston Million in 1985, which drew nationwide attention and made Elliott a superstar and a marketable item.

The points race didn't attract a lot of notice until recent years when the winner's payoff reached a half-million dollars. With the huge moneys came a change in strategy for drivers and car owners, who can theoretically go winless the entire season and still capture the Winston Cup and the riches that come with it. In 1985 Elliott won eleven races and lost the driver's championship to Darrell Waltrip, who won three.

In addition to RJR's involvement, some $4 million is made available in sponsorship and manufacturers' contingency prize moneys, featuring such big-time corporate players as Anheuser-Busch, Champion Spark Plugs, Gatorade, Goody's Headache Powders, Goodyear, Holley Carburetors, Ingersoll-Rand Tools, Kodak, Monroe and Bilstein shocks, Moroso Oil Pans, Peak Antifreeze and Coolant, Piedmont Airlines, Procter and Gamble, Sears DieHard, Stewart-Warner Products, STP, True Value Hardware, Unocal Oil and Gasoline, Van Camp's Beans, Timex and Nationwise Auto Parts.

As an example, in 1987 Unocal increased its point fund to $215,000, with $100,000 to go to the highest finisher in the points standing who used Unocal oil and lubricants the entire season and who had won a race since 1982.

True Value's Hard Charger Award contribution of $195,000 goes to lap leaders in each individual race and on the season as a whole. Race winners receive fifteen hundred dollars and the overall leader picks up twenty-five thousand dollars. Stewart-Warner awards twenty-five thousand dollars for the durable driver who completes the most laps in a season, and Gatorade rewards the winners, twenty-five hundred for individual races and twenty thousand for the Winston Cup champion.

Of all the sponsors, Goody's success most closely parallels the success of the Elliotts. Like them, Goody's started small, in a corner drugstore, and like them, with an assist from racing, it grew into a corporate giant.

The Winston-Salem, North Carolina, company, headed by a gracious Southern lady, Ann Lewallen Spencer, and her son, Thad, and run by a former Duke University football star, Tom Chambers, is a classic example of the free-enterprise system. Goody's also has something in common with Coca-Cola and Pepsi Cola. Like those two Southern giants, it had its genesis in a mom-and-pop drugstore.

It is not surprising that Goody's made its appearance in 1932, in the midst of the Great Depression. Everyone had a headache or expected one, and M. C. (Goody) Goodman, a pharmacist, developed a remedy, a mixture of aspirin, acetaminophen and caffeine. His equipment was a measuring spoon, a spatula and prescription scales. Each powder was individually weighed, and women folded glassine paper around it, then placed it in an envelope.

In 1935, A. Thad Lewallen, a customer, purchased the formula and began to expand the business, first into neighboring Wilkes County and later throughout the state and Southeast.

The big break for Goody's came in 1977 when Tom Chambers became president. He had a solid sports background, having been an all-conference player on Wallace Wade's great Duke teams and a senior official in the Atlantic Coast Conference who had once worked the Orange Bowl game.

Given his lifelong orientation, it followed that Goody's would become heavily involved in sports to promote its products. The company aggressively pursued advertising in professional and collegiate sports, fishing tournaments and auto racing.

Lives there a TV or radio soul who hasn't heard Richard Petty drawl, "That was a headache . . . a Goody's headache"? Good ol'boy Petty sold a lot of powders. So did Reba McEntire, a country singer and good ol' girl. They were believable, and no one believes with more fervor than race fans.

From a corner drugstore, Goody's has ballooned into the country's largest producer of headache powders, and in recent years it has added Sayman Skin Care Products, Isodettes Cough/Cold products and Necta Sweet. Its motor-sports program includes the Goody's Headache Award, going to the hard-luck driver of each race; Goody's Pole Day at the World 600 in Charlotte and the Goody's 500, a Winston Cup event at Martinsville. It also sponsors two Busch Late-Model Sportsman events at Daytona.

No one wants to win the Goody's Headache Award, for obvious reasons, but it does provide a five-hundred-dollar consolation on an otherwise dismal day.

Everyone knows that Bill Elliott won eleven races in 1985, but few remember that he clinched the Goody's Headache Award six times that year for problems such as breaking his leg at Rockingham, car failure at Dover, wrecking at Martinsville, finishing thirtieth at North Wilkesboro and falling out of the points race with a broken shift pin at Riverside. All of which proves that when things are going good, you can win three thousand dollars for going bad. No matter what the award, Goody's remains an important part of the racing scene. "We've been pleased with the results of our program in NASCAR," said president Chambers, "both for our company and the welfare of the sport. Our relationship with NASCAR, its people and competitors has been healthy and productive."

Corporate involvement and selling through sponsorship of cars in Winston Cup racing has proliferated in recent years.

George Elliott recalls how it was in the beginning. "STP was the foremost sponsor, and Gatorade stayed in for several years," he says. "Then you had Permatex on the Sportsman circuit. They sponsored it for years and years. In the early 1970s R. J. Reynolds and Anheuser-Busch came on the scene. Sears has been in and out, mainly pushing its Craftsman tools.

"To reap any benefit from advertising in racing, you've got to be a nationwide sponsor. A local sponsor can pick up a small benefit, especially when the race is run in his area, but by and large you need a wider market area."

Sponsors have included deodorant soap, shortening, jeans, coffee, tobacco, beer, auto parts, detergent and, of all things, women's underwear.

Drivers seldom forget where their support comes from. At Daytona in February of 1987 when a young lady approached Darrell Waltrip to pose with her for a picture, he wrapped his arm around her and said, "Honey, you have the sweet scent of Tide."

It's sell, sell, sell, hucksterism at its most intense.

Even the Atlanta South Motorsports Safety Team, which offers paramedic protection and safety at tracks, does its own marketing bit. In a press release, they remind sponsors that their lifesaving vehicle is a good spot to advertise.

"When a crisis happens on the track, we are suddenly the focus of all television and newsprint media as we respond to stabilize the problem at hand," the release reads. "Therefore, your company logo, as a sponsor, placed on our safety vehicles, would generate a public saturation that would exceed that of traditional advertising and increase your overall sales effort."

The exposure potential from racing advertising is vast, an estimated 160 million by television and 2.2 million in person, not counting those along the highways.

Remember the old macho image of racing? Forget it. Racing is now playing to the ladies who make up almost 45 percent of all spectators as compared with 17 percent of a decade ago. Thus, the announcement that Underalls pantyhose would join the sponsorship of the Sterling Marlin team failed to surprise anyone.

"That completes the cycle," says one old-timer. "We started out with good ol' boys in overalls, and now we've got good ol' girls in Underalls."

Despite some grumbling, many view the transformation as natural progression.

Racing is a sport first, but it is also big business. Big, big business, and with big business, profit is the bottom line. If a driver doesn't produce, he's out; if a product doesn't sell, the company is out. Sponsors appeal to women because women do the shopping.

With beer companies, it's different. Federal regulations prohibit active athletes from selling the products. That's why television beer commercials hire retired athletes.

In Bill Elliott's situation, being associated with Coors means he must always be aware of his image. If he didn't project an image compatible with Coors, they'd find someone who did.

Racing has grown by leaps and bounds, gotten more popular with the millions who follow it, but the days of the good ol' beer-drinking boys are gone forever. There is very little sentiment left.

With the big boys who sponsor the races, it's the winning way or the highway.

15

Daytona and the
First Step of 1987

WTBS MOTOR SPORTS REPORTER: "Ernie, after the big
success in 1985, the media said you guys let that get to your
heads and that was the problem last year. Do you buy that?"
  Ernie Elliott: "No, I disagree with that."
  Reporter: "What was the 1986 problem?"
  Ernie Elliott: "I think that mainly it was, you know, sickness, on
the part of myself and the team. You know I had a lot of the crew
members sick. I think that was the biggest problem."
  Reporter: "We're glad to have you back and healthy. Have a great
season."

  Success breeds expectations, and uncommon success breeds unreasonable expectations. As the poet once said, "Blessed is he who
expects nothing, for he shall never be disappointed." Prior to 1985,
nothing had been expected of the Elliotts. Then, coming out of
nowhere, they elevated themselves to another plateau with eleven
wins and $2.4 million in earnings. In racing, as in other sports,
staying there is harder than getting there.
  The expectations and pressures multiplied under critical micro-
scopes. Bill had foreseen such a situation and tried to circumvent it
with the statement that mediocre seasons usually followed great
success. But as the 1987 campaign approached, talk persisted that
there were unrest in the hills, disagreements among the brothers
and distracting outside influences.
  "These things happen," says a veteran racing observer, "even,

maybe especially, among brothers. It happened with Richard and Maurice Petty and with Richard and his father, Lee. Families are not exempt from squabbling. Everyone wants to be the boss, and you can have but one boss."

Being human, the Elliotts never pretended to be in complete harmony. "When they were kids and had fights, it was always two against one and never the same two," George Elliott had said.

Sibling rivalry is a fact of life, and it didn't help that racing experts were divided on the reason the Elliotts did so well in 1985. Some insisted it was Ernie and his engines; others were just as adamant that it was Bill's driving and chassis work. Bill kept saying, "It was a combination of things," which was probably closest to the truth.

In one personality trait, Bill and Ernie are alike. They're driven perfectionists.

As Humpy Wheeler says about Ernie, "He drives himself crazy about engines." He'll work on an engine until he thinks it is just right, and even then he's not completely satisfied. Rooster Ingram spoke of Ernie's rushing home to build a motor from scratch after losing a drag race.

His engine building at Dawsonville with its "Positively No Admittance" warning on the door is protected like a mad scientist's laboratory. A lot of rivals would love to get a peek at what goes on in this top-secret workshop. Ford thinks so much of Ernie's mechanical wizardry that it has put him in charge of its V-6 research and development.

On the flip side, Bill is no less intense and dedicated to his chassis work. As George said, he won't drive the car unless the feel is just right. He doesn't leave anything to chance, checking and double-checking. When he takes the green flag he knows every bolt has been tightened and every part is just as he wants it. In his earlier days he said he didn't sleep well worrying that he had overlooked something. Any distraction, from the media or otherwise, was resented.

Two perfectionists on the same team can be a source of friction, whether they're brothers or total strangers.

The most carefree of the brothers is Dan, who handles the transmissions, rear gears and serves as leader of the over-the-wall gang, or pit crew. He can change a front tire in nothing flat and has been a major factor in Bill's winning most of his pit road races. He is also the most sociable and articulate in interviews with the networks and the media, and excellent buffer for his reserved brothers. He enjoys the notoriety.

On its own merits, two wins and a million dollars in earnings, 1986 would have been a rousing success for the Elliotts of five years ago. Bill was still rewriting pole records at Daytona, Talladega, and elsewhere and leading races and thrilling spectators, but compared to 1985, the year registered as a disappointment, just as anything Babe Ruth did after hitting sixty home runs was a comedown. Like it or not, 1985 had become the standard for future seasons.

The explosive 1985 season also left a lot of shrapnel in the buttocks of some old favorites and regulars in racing who don't cotton to being upstaged. In the sixties, Freddie Lorenzen, not even a Southerner, for goodness' sake, had to pay his dues before he was accepted at the top, and the old guard never appreciated Indy types like A. J. Foyt and Mario Andretti coming in, making one appearance a year and taking their prize moneys. And Darrell Waltrip had a long probationary period because he didn't show the proper respect for rank.

Worst of all, Elliott had come out of the pack. One year he was running with the outhouse gang, then he shows up, without a pedigree check, in the penthouse for a sit-down dinner. That he and Ernie went about their work in mysterious silence only widened the rift.

By the winter of 1986-87, both sides began to settle in, relax, mingle and get accustomed to each other. The Elliotts were still the quickest humans on wheels, strong contenders, but no longer the most dominant team in stock car racing. The hot cars of 1986 belonged to Tim Richmond, with his offbeat charm, the darling of the new breed with seven wins, and Dale Earnhardt, a relic from the Joie Chitwood thrill shows, a driver who thrived on conflict and controversy. He didn't have quite the year that Elliott had in 1985, but his five wins and $1.7 million in earnings beat everything else. The season would have been even greater had he not run out of gas in the Daytona 500, enabling Geoff Bodine to grab his best payday.

Because of Earnhardt and Richmond, the Manufacturers' Championship had been screwed back to its norm of recent years, with General Motors winning twenty-four of the twenty-nine races on the Winston Cup trail. Making up Ford's five triumphs were Elliott and Ricky Rudd, with two apiece, and Kyle Petty with a backdoor sneak at Richmond after Darrell Waltrip and Earnhardt dueled with clashing steel.

Everything is relative. Writers said Elliott had a bad year. He disagreed. "To me, it was defnitely a good year," he said after the 1986 season. "We had two wins, actually four if you count the 125 at Daytona and the Winston. The difference between 1985 and 1986 was finishing.

"We couldn't finish races in '86 like we did in '85, and you can't win if you don't finish. Ernie's absence was part of it, but also racing is a game of odds. You have good luck for a while, and then some bad luck will catch up with you.

"We've worked hard to get ready for the new season. We're all trying to get healthy and stay that way. We've got good cars and good people, and we're in much better shape than at this time last year. The shop is reorganized, and we've been working to have three cars ready for the first three or four races by the time we get to Daytona."

There had been a major change.

For the first time, a top echelon decision-maker had been hired to share authority with the brothers. Hoping to improve their short-track program, they brought in Californian Ivan Baldwin, a former driver often credited with setting up the winning cars of Hershel McGriff, the West Coast's version of Richard Petty.

For years Bill had been saying he wanted to be relieved of the demanding chore of chassis work so he could concentrate on driving, and Baldwin was expected to solve that problem. Yet those who were of the if-it-ain't-broke-don't-fix-it school wondered what this would do to the mystique of the brotherly combination. Or even to Bill's psyche. Adding an outside strong, independent thinker to a family operation may or may not be in the best interests of the group.

But having gone big-time, change was inevitable, and some of the good ol' boys, the Sunday helpers, were replaced by highly trained professionals. When shopping around for experienced help, the Elliotts deliberately stayed out of North Carolina, the hotbed of Winston Cup racing, and there was a reason. They didn't want their business spread around.

As George Elliott says, "Even if they don't chase around and party and fraternize together, there's nothing like alcohol to loosen tongues. There was another thing to think about. By getting people from a wide range, they contribute a different perspective on everything. You get a lot of input.

"As a rule, racing people are very cooperative. When we were starting out, we relied on help from other people. Unlike other sports, racing competitors help each other. Don't misunderstand. They won't tell you everything, but they'll point you in the right direction."

What the Elliotts wanted to avoid was the drifters who go from team to team, carrying inside information and rumors with them. By hiring Baldwin and aerodynamics expert Dave Kriska from Australia, they could feel safe that such leaks were not likely to happen, although the hires did present a communication problem at the Dawsonville Pool Room. Not only did the accents change in Dawsonville, so did the scenery. Where a shade-tree garage once stood, now there was a modern technological and engineering center, a worthy extension of Detroit.

That was the situation when, in November of 1986, the Ford engineers arrived at the Coors/Melling compound to go over the new Thunderbird models with Bill, Ernie and Dan. Already the most aerodynamic car on the roaring roads, the new version was designed to be even more so. The nose had been lowered and pointed and the back deck raised. NASCAR rules had deemed a weight reduction, and the new T-Bird was two hundred pounds lighter at thirty-five hundred pounds.

"We're trying to get used to the 1987 car," said Bill afterwards. "There's not much difference in the handling, and so far I haven't noticed that much difference in the weight reduction, but it should be easier on tires.

"Little things have changed about the body style. There's a difference in the angle of the rear spoiler and the function of the front air dam. It doesn't take much to make a difference, but we're trying to get used to the new body style. To the fans in the stands, it's not that much different, but there are subtle things you have to adjust to."

The shakedown runs were to be made in January at Daytona, when all the major teams tested in preparation for the Speed Weeks of February. As usual, Winston Cup had had its share of musical chairs, the switching of teams and drivers, and there would be a whole new lineup for 1987.

The big item was the Junior Johnson Chevrolet team. Darrell Waltrip, after six years and three driver's titles, had gone with the Rick Hendrick team in a Chevrolet that looked like a huge box of Tide detergent. Johnson replaced Waltrip with converted Texan Terry Labonte, a consistent high finisher who drives and wins as quietly as he talks. In 1984, Labonte had won a quiet Winston Cup championship for another team.

In other major switches, Cale Yarborough had formed his own team after four years with Harry Ranier, and Morgan Shepherd had replaced Joe Ruttman in the Kenny Bernstein Quaker State Buick.

January testing at Daytona was everyone's first chance to evaluate the new rides.

On January 14, Elliott and the other Ford teams arrived on the Florida coast to take their runs. Ricky Rudd, in the Bud Moore T-Bird, had been there two days earlier and registered a 205.011 mile-an-hour lap, comparing favorably with Elliott's track record of 205.114, but short of the new expectations.

The January 14 times were somewhat surprising:

Kyle Petty, 209.059.

Davey Allison, a rookie in the Ranier Ford, 208.547.

Elliott, 208.183.

Kenny Schrader, in the Red Baron Frozen Pizza Ford, 207.134.

Ken Ragan, 202.065.

Alan Kulwicki, '86 Rookie of the Year in the Zerex Ford, 196.421.

The surprise was Allison, beginning a full-time Winston Cup career in the tire marks of father Bobby and uncle Dennis after an apprenticeship in the Grand National division. Having raced the super roads before, for ARCA, he obviously knew his way around.

As the sport has grown, so has the need for testing, though there are some who would limit it because of the expense involved. It is estimated that a testing trip adds fifteen thousand dollars to the average race tab of fifty thousand dollars per team.

Tests may or may not prove a true indication of what a car has. Gamesmanship and intimidation carry over to the practice runs, and there are certain things a driver and a crew chief look for. The way Elliott tests and the way he qualifies are not necessarily the same.

He had already set his goal for Daytona qualifying. He said he wanted to turn the 2.5-mile super speedway in 42.9 seconds, which works out to 209 miles an hour, 4 miles an hour faster than his track record. Kyle Petty had proved it was within reach.

In 1985, when he'd raised the speed ante to 205 at Daytona and 209 at Talladega, Elliott had led the Winston Cup drivers into uncharted waters. It brought questions. Would the drivers and the cars be able to handle the tremendous speeds? Would less than two hundred miles an hour make the starting field at Talladega? And what did the big jump do for strategies and tactics? Answers had to come on the tracks in the heat of competition.

NASCAR history is replete with turning them loose, running on the ragged edge, almost out of control, and then retrenching. When the sanctioning body believes things are getting out of hand, it orders smaller carburetors or others means of reducing speeds. Normally, however, restrictions apply only to the flat-out tracks, where the edges are the sharpest.

Elliott had other goals at Daytona. It was the first step of the Winston Cup point race, first leg of the Winston Million and scene of the Busch Clash. He'd never won either the points title or the Clash, a fifty-mile sprint for pole winners of the previous year.

"If you run well at Daytona, it sets the tone for the entire year," he said at the time. "If not, it's hard to get the momentum up for the next races on the schedule. Doing well at Daytona sets a good, positive attitude for everyone on the team from there on."

Preparation was intense, as it always is in Dawsonville. From the close of the 1986 season in November to February, the Georgia brothers worked sixteen-hour days, attending to every detail.

Says George Elliott, "Actually, though a lot of people don't realize it, this is the busiest time of the entire year. You've got new cars and new personnel, and you're trying to make plans for the entire season. Once the season starts, it's too late to do a lot of these things. Then you're into weekly racing."

Given the time to prepare, the Elliotts are sure to find the short way around any super speedway, and, in the case of the Daytona 500, they'd had all winter to unlock the mysteries. And with six races on the agenda during Speed Weeks, there'd be plenty of time for adjustments.

Bill's schedule called for participation in the Daytona 24 Hours, the Busch Clash, 125-mile qualifier, IROC (International Race of Champions), Goody's 300 Grand National and the Daytona 500, six races in twenty-one days. There was no spare time. When he wasn't racing, he'd be on a plane to somewhere for a sponsor commitment, a public appearance or a commercial venture. And that doesn't include the many, many requests for interviews by the print and electronic media.

Driving, it seems, is the only time when Bill Elliott can be alone, and then he has to be concerned about forty-one other drivers going two hundred miles an hour. The fast lane is no place to relax. Fortunately, he thrives on activity and motion. At first, he had no patience with interviews, but time and experience have brought a mellowing, an acceptance and a more relaxed manner.

He enjoys offshoot races like the Daytona 24 Hours because the pressure to win is less. It's a more pleasant diversion.

In 1986, he had a short race when his car fell out by midnight. But this time, teaming with Lyn St. James and Tom Gloy in a Mustang, he had better luck. They overcame an early flat and a crash to place first in the GTO division.

The next event, the Busch Clash, was high on Elliott's priority list for two reasons. One, he'd never won, having finished third in 1985 and second in 1986. Two, it paid well, fifty thousand dollars for winning and twenty-five thousand in bonuses for leading the tenth and fifteenth laps of the twenty-lap, fifty-mile sprint. That's a seventy-five-thousand-dollar payoff for less than fifteen minutes of driving.

Starting positions were selected by a blind draw, and Bill must have known it was his day when he drew the pole. On the outside was Benny Parsons and just behind them were Cale Yarborough and One Tough Customer, Dale Eanrhardt.

Bill had said the Daytona 500 would set the tone for the season. He was just a bit off. The first lap of the Busch Clash laid down the style for 1987, and it involved the guy in Wrangler jeans. He tangled with Ricky Rudd and Terry Labonte and all fingers pointed at OTC (One Tough . . .).

"Not me," said Earnhardt, whose car was eliminated from contention. "I didn't hit the back of anybody. Somebody hit the front of mine."

The "Who, Me?" season was under way.

When the green flag came out on the second lap, Elliott was on his way, winning effortlessly at a pace of 197.802 miles an hour. Geoff

Bodine, defending champion of the Daytona 500, passed Darrell Waltrip and the Tide machine on the last lap to take second place.

One goal had been attained, but Elliott wasn't gloating. Except for him, Bodine and Waltrip, the other seven drivers in the race had one problem or another, mechanical or otherwise. Parsons, driving the Folger's Coffee Chevrolet as a replacement for pneumonia-sticken Tim Richmond, said he had a faulty start and caused the three-car entanglement behind him.

But for Elliott, who led thirteen of the twenty laps, a win was a win.

He played it low-key. "Just because we did well doesn't mean the Fords are going to dominate," he said after the victory. "This is a new Thunderbird with a new design, but not that much different from what we had last year. The difference, I think, is that we're better organized.

"Winning the Clash might give us some momentum, but we've got a lot of work to do. The pole run is going to be close. I don't see anyone running 210, not even us."

Even at his tender age, Davey Allison had learned to take Elliott's statements with healthy reservations. He said, "It's hard to say how Bill will do. He learned a lot in the last few years, and you never know with him. He'll hold back one time and the next time he'll do something else."

No doubt Allison recalled the day Fords tested in January and he outran Bill. Qualifying day came, and Allison bettered his testing time by almost a mile an hour, registering a 209.084. And, true to Allison's words, Elliott did something different. He did 210.364, exceeding his own track record by more than 5 miles an hour.

Said Allison, "It was kind of a letdown Bill beat us as bad as he did after the way we'd been practicing. His speed didn't surprise me. I had a feeling he'd be fast, but not that much faster than we were."

Elliott said he and Ernie had decided he'd run as fast as he was comfortable with, discounting what others had or would run. And what he was comfortable with was 210.

Qualifying decided only two positions, Bill's and Davey's. The other forty came from finishes in the twin 125s on Thursday prior to the Daytona 500.

Elliott's 125-mile qualifying heat was a different story.

He was right there, inches away from nipping Ken Schrader, in the Junie Donlavey/Red Baron Frozen Pizza Ford, at the finish line, and he didn't make it. Schrader said Bill backed off a little bit, through no one will ever know.

The Ford followers were not unhappy. Schrader, a former sprint car driver, had been making his mark in Winston Cup, advancing each year, and his car owner, the sixty-two-year-old Donlavey, had been a babe in the wilderness, so to speak, an independent fighting the corporates for years. His lone major Winston Cup win came in 1981 with Bill's boyhood hero Jody Ridley driving at Dover.

When forty-six-year-old Benny Parsons won the second heat, the nostalgic day was complete. Donlavey remembered when his car sat there at Daytona in the 1960s, minus a vital part, and Parsons, who had already loaded his ARCA-winning vehicle, jumped on the truck and disassembled the carburetor to provide the missing part and enable Junie's car to run in the 500.

And Parsons, like Donlavey, had come out of retirement and a promising broadcast career to fill in for the ailing Tim Richmond on the Rick Hendrick team. For a few hours, at least, racing had returned to its old-time camaraderie.

Elliott couldn't resent either Donlavey or Parsons, the driver who had helped him the most during his struggling days.

Schrader and Donlavey needed the twenty-two-thousand-dollar first-place check for the 125 more than Bill Elliott did. If it had been the Busch Clash, where the payoff was seventy-five thousand, Bill, who had come up on the outside at the finish, might have taken a calculated risk and gone for it. When the big money is on the line, so is Elliott.

The fifty-lap race had been a good proving ground. At the midway point, on a caution restart, the No. 9 Thunderbird had fallen off the leader board. It took Elliott only fourteen laps to pull up behind Schrader for the shootout.

As the finish wound down, Schrader said he got on the radio and asked what he should do.

"Play it by ear," replied Donlavey.

Added Schrader, "On the backstretch, I lifted and I think Bill played it too cautious."

Said Elliott, "I couldn't make a run on the back side. There was a slower car there. I tried what I thought would work, but it didn't. I'm glad to see Ken win one. He did a good job. The car looked like it ran good."

There is often speculation about whether drivers of different makes stick together, whether a GM driver will help another GM driver or two Fords work as a team.

"From my observation," says a veteran racing man, "the GM drivers are more likely to stick together, which is strange since Fords are greatly outnumbered."

There are instances, of course, of, say, Richard Petty running shotgun in a Pontiac for his Ford-driving son, Kyle, in the the World 600, but that springs more from family loyalty. And Kyle freely admits that Elliott "helped me some" in the 1985 Winston 500, when he finished two seconds behind the Georgia redhead in what many call the greatest race ever run.

But, in general, drivers reject such a theory.

"I haven't seen any evidence of that," says Olds team member Cale Yarborough, a former Ford driver. "Everybody's for theirself, as far as I know. I haven't seen any help from those Chevrolet drivers."

Davey Allison says he doesn't concern himself about ". . . whether I'm teaming up against somebody or somebody's teaming up on me. The way I feel about it, everybody should be out there trying to win for themselves and doing the best job for their teams."

If nothing else, the 125-mile races proved that there was a new and potentially ill wind blowing on the super tracks.

George Elliott, observing from the catwalk atop the Coors/Melling truck, talked about the new development. He observed, "Aerodynamically, these Fords are a lot different from the past, due to design changes. Unless you do it a certain way, with plenty of distance from the lead car, it's most difficult to pass because of the tricky turbulence."

Ernie Elliott, with stopwatch in hand, also kept a close watch on the No. 9 car. Mainly, he observes how Bill gets off the corners. The old racing maxim is if you can't get into the corners, you can't get out. Earlier, in the Busch Clash, Ernie had noticed something he needed to adjust in the engine, and immediately after the 125-miler he was on a flight to Dawsonville.

This was not unusual, according to George. "I'll give you an example. In 1983, Bill had led the 125-mile on Thursday, and Ernie learned something in that race that he wanted to incorporate in the engine. He jumped on a plane and came back home, and from Thursday to Friday night he built a new engine, dyno-tested it, put it on a truck at midnight and made the eight-to-ten-hour trip back to Daytona.

"On Saturday we gave it what we call the 'Billy Dyno Test.' That's Bill taking the car on the track and shaking it out. He has to give his stamp of approval before the engine gets used in a race.

"This year it is the same pattern. We learned something, in the Busch Clash and all, and Ernie and Dan are going back, make some changes and fly it back tomorrow morning. It's a constant learning process, hard work, but if you back off, that's when all those other drivers and cars are going to go zooming by you."

Still to come before the grand finale, the Daytona 500, were two races on Friday, the Komfort Koach 200, a race for subcompact cars; the Budweiser IROC (International Race of Champions); and the Goody's 300 Grand National on Saturday, a day in which the drivers from NASCAR's Triple-A League test their skills against the Winston Cup drivers, or major leaguers.

A chilling accident in the Komfort Koach underlined the old saying that racing is the cruelest sport of all. In football the worst thing you can do is fumble or drop a pass; in baseball, make an error or strike out; in racing, be at the wrong place at the wrong time, and they send you home in a box.

Joe Young, a thirty-eight-year-old journeyman from Richmond, Virginia, had come to Daytona with high hopes for the Komfort Koach, a preliminary race designed to keep the fans occupied. For a day or two, he walked among the Pettys, Elliotts, Waltrips, Earnhardts, Allisons and Yarboroughs, and he felt close to greatness, never mind that his car was parked in the auxiliary garage and few knew him.

On Friday the 13th, Joe Young died at Daytona when his car, No. 5, was hit head-on and set on fire. His wife, Delores, children, Lisa, thirteen, and Jody, ten, and his father, Joseph Calvin Young, Jr., witnessed the horror and tragedy.

Young, a Vietnam veteran, knew the risks. "He knew it could happen to him," said crew member Wayne Hall, "just like it could happen to anyone else."

At Daytona, it has happened to fourteen other race drivers, including such well-known members of the fraternity as Marshall Teague, George Amick, Friday Hassler and two motorcycle racers. Joe Young's name was added to the list. In death, he had gained more notoriety than in life.

"I have become very proficient at writing obituaries," says one veteran writer. "I was at Darlington when Paul McDuffie, a great engine builder, and two others were killed by Bobby John's car, which got on the wall and spun like a top; at Talladega, when Larry Smith hit the wall and died; at Atlanta's Lakewood dirt track when Indianapolis driver Art Bishe became a fatality and at Indy when Swede Savage and a young crew member were killed.

"What bothers me is that no one seems to get upset anymore. It happens, there's momentary sympathy, then it's over. This is the only sport where death is a tolerated part of the outcome."

Of course, drivers can't dwell on the dark side of the sport, just as a football player can't dwell on a crippling injury to a teammate. These things are put in an it-can't-happen-to-me compartment of the mind.

Racing life went on, and at 1:30 P.M., Friday the 13th, twelve of the best drivers in the world lined up for the forty-lap IROC run, with everyone in identically prepared Chevrolet Z-28 Camaros. Having drawn for positions, they appeared in this order: Darrell Waltrip, Wally Dallenbach, Jr., Derek Bell, Elliott, Geoff Bodine, Mario Andretti, Al Unser, Jr., Dale Earnhardt, Scott Pruett, Al Unser, Sr., Michael Andretti and Bobby Rahal. Unser, Jr., was the defending champion of the series, having won two of the four races in the series in 1986.

Appearing in the series for only the second year, Elliott said the experience should help him. "I think I'll make fewer mistakes this time," he said. "I'll know where to be, what to do, and in that type of racing, with all the cars equal, that will make a big difference. I like racing in general, and I liked IROC last year.

"The field should be tougher this year. You don't do anything to set up the car — you just get in and drive what you get, get in and go. Last year at Talladega I had never been in an IROC car before the race. But racing's racing."

Not quite.

Among the four Winston Cup drivers, Elliott was the only non-Chevrolet man. Then go back to what George Elliott has emphasized. Bill has to be completely comfortable in a car, and he's not completely comfortable unless he has checked and double-checked or, preferably, worked on it himself. In this race, as he said, he had to drive what he got, and not what he and Ernie had prepared.

Elliott started strong and held most of the early lead, until he was passed on lap nineteen almost midway, by Bodine, who held off his fellow NASCAR challengers to win in his first IROC race. Earnhardt, who had trouble running low and never led, finished second, just ahead of Waltrip, who passed Elliott a couple of laps from the finish.

With Elliott fourth, Winston Cup had the top four over Indy's and road racing's best. Whether by coincidence or not, the Chevrolet drivers were 1-2-3 and the Ford man fourth.

Bodine's winning speed was 183.673 miles an hour, breaking Cale Yarborough's old standard, set at Talladega. At long last, as Speed Weeks neared an end, Bodine, the 1986 Daytona 500 winner, had scratched. Saturday, and the Goody's 300, was also to have been his day.

By this time, the car business had to be getting confusing to Elliott. He had driven the IROC in a No. 5 powder-blue Chevrolet. One of his old Thunderbirds, sold to Ralph Jones of Upton, Kentucky, and numbered 92, had won the ARCA 200 the previous Sunday. And, now for the Goody's 300, he was in No. 89. That's enough to disorient a one-car man. Only the colors were familiar.

The Grand National jockeys, more accustomed to their cars, led the qualifying, with Tommy Houston and L. D. Ottinger 1-2. Houston's speed was 194.389 miles an hour. Winston Cup's Earnhardt, Bodine, Bobby Allison and Harry Gant started in positions four through seven. In his unfamiliar car, Elliott would do no better than 187.071 miles an hour and the twenty-sixth place in the lineup.

The race developed into a heated duel between Bodine, Waltrip and young Larry Pearson, son of NASCAR great David Pearson. An early domination by the Allisons, Bobby and Donnie, had gone the way of engine and tire problems.

On lap 116, four laps from the finish, the public address announcer excitedly informed the crowd, "Trouble in turns one and two, looks like Elliott, Gant, Hensley, Porter and Standridge!"

Elliott and several others were taken to the field hospital to be checked out. In the meantime, Bodine, with blocking from his brother Brett, beat Waltrip to the checkers and collected $33,147.

Waiting anxiously in the garage area, members of the Coors Ford team were relieved five minutes later when a smiling Elliott walked jauntily through the gate separating the workplace from the medical building and headed promptly for the No. 9 stall, where he chatted with close friend Curtis Colwell. He doesn't usually get himself in a predicament, and on the rare occasions when there's a problem, as in this case, he handles it well.

"This was a case of being with some unfamiliar drivers, not knowing what they were going to do," explained George Elliott. "When Bill doesn't really know a driver, he won't draft with him. Then he'll root him out a hole where he can run by himself. Usually, in Winston Cup racing, that is no problem because most of the drivers are aware of the styles of others."

While George was talking, Bill was already on the track, happy and content in No. 9, for his last practice runs before Sunday's 500. And George, with stopwatch in hand, mounted the team truck to time his youngest son.

Daytona 500 Sunday was the kind of day the Chamber of Commerce likes to advertise, sunny, warm and inviting, the kind of morning perfect for promenading by the rich and famous, not on Park Avenue but on NASCAR's version of Gasoline Alley, where the crews and the cars are as dressed up as the strolling sponsors and corporate giants, with a movie star or an entertainer or two thrown in. Unlike the old days, when crews resembled someone who had popped out of a coal bin, today's racing crowd is more the Ritz than the pits.

Crews break out their neat, pressed, distinctive colors for Sundays, and even mechanics are permed and manicured. Most heroic looking of all, naturally, are the drivers in their tailor-made jump uniforms, not unlike those of astronauts.

A few of the strollers made their way to the stall where racing chaplain Bill Baird had as the subject of his homily: "Be Who You Are."

At the corner of the garage stood big Bill France, Sr., founder of NASCAR and a former mechanic who had made millions. He's still imposing, six-five and ruggedly handsome, the Bear Bryant type, but, nearing eighty, his memory is not what it was.

Thirty-eight years earlier, in 1959, he had launched the Daytona International Raceway, the showpiece of racing, in full-blown controversy. He stood at the start-finish line and called Iowan Johnny Beauchamp, in a Thunderbird, as the winner over Olds-driving Lee Petty.

Three days later, a recount showed Petty had won, and France decided he needed a photo-finish camera.

The scoring system improved, but the controversy remained. That's one of the charms of the sport, its eternal controversy. When he was active, France ran NASCAR as a benevolent dictator. The rules were in his back pocket. He put down several revolts by the sheer force of authority. When Curtis Turner tried to unionize the drivers in the early days, France banned Turner. And, in 1969, when the drivers said it was too dangerous to run at Talladega, he got in a car and turned the track at 175 miles an hour. When they still refused, he ran a race with only one Winston Cup (then Grand National) driver, Bobby Isaac, and a field of unknowns.

Big Bill France also helped shape the politics of Florida. He was George Wallace's campaign manager in a presidential race, and he took on such heavyweights as the state of Florida and the environmental agency in battles over taxes and polluting the atmosphere with automobile fumes.

He owns three tracks — Daytona, Darlington and Talladega — and parts of others.

When family operations are discussed, his is the ultimate. His wife, Anne, whom he met when she was working as a nurse in North Carolina, is NASCAR treasurer, as she always has been. Eldest son, Bill, Jr., is chairman of the board, and Jim France is the new president. Several other family members are in executive positions.

Benevolent dictators are seldom replaced by one man; it's usually a troika or a junta. In that respect, as Bill, Jr., took NASCAR into a new age, the corporate period, he had the advantage of having able, knowledgeable people around him, such experienced racing hands as Jim Foster, vice-president for marketing; Jim Hunter, vice-president for administration; Bill Gazaway, vice-president for competition; Dick Beaty, director of the Winston Cup Series and Les Richter, vice-president for planning and development.

The way corporations are organized these days, Bill France, Sr., may have been the last of the dictators, benevolent or otherwise. What he did single-handedly, as Furman Bisher of *The Atlanta Journal* wrote, was "take cars off the streets and make them a national sport, as national as the National Football League."

By now, France had left, to take his seat in the owner's box; the cars had been inspected by Beaty and his aides, and the drivers were being introduced, individually, to the fans. Some pecked Miss Winston on the cheek, others deferred. That's another thing that's changed. Old-time drivers considered it bad luck to kiss a girl before a race. The late Fireball Roberts used to say that every time he kissed his wife he crashed, prompting impish Joe Weatherly to retort, "Don't kiss her; kiss somebody else."

As expected, Elliott received the loudest cheer from a crowd estimated at 135,000. They love the Georgia boy, his common touch, and, most of all, his flat-out speed. Davey Allison, a second-generation kid making his Winston Cup debut on the outside pole, also got a nice hand, as did Pontiac driver Rusty Wallace, whose team had to scramble to replace twenty-eight thousand dollars in vital parts stolen from the Kodiak team just prior to their trip from North Carolina to Daytona. He had been the fastest-testing GM car in January at 208.237, a mite faster than Elliott, but, following the loss of equipment, he could manage only 204.448 and thirty-second place in the lineup.

In his last press conference, Elliott exuded confidence.

"I'm capable, the car's capable and the team's certainly capable," he said. "You just hope you are not a victim of circumstances early and that you're there at the finish."

He hinted that, if he got the chance, he hoped to move out front where he could run by himself. He said, "I don't like crowds. Group sessions have never been my style."

With everyone worn out from three weeks of one race after another, the main event was off at last, and, true to his strategy, Elliott moved away from the field, leading the first thirty-five laps. After that, he alternated leading and dropping back, breathing his T-Bird.

In between his first time on the point to his ninth, the race had nine other leaders — Buddy Baker, Geoff Bodine, Sterling Marlin, Ken Schrader, Neil Bonnett, Darrell Waltrip, Benny Parsons, Dale Earnhardt and Richard Petty.

In the late stages, pit work became crucial. And Ernie and Dan and the others were operating at peak efficiency, getting Bill out and going like clockwork. They enabled him to beat Earnhardt and Baker out on the last caution stops, and those were the two cars he'd been racing most of the afternoon.

Only forty-three laps remained when they pitted on the caution, and it was certain they'd have to make one more stop, all except Bodine and Bonnett, who were getting exceptional mileage.

By lap 160, Earnhardt had moved out front, ahead of Parsons, Baker, Elliott and Bodine, in that order. By lap 170, Elliott had taken a firm hold on the lead, with Earnhardt beating Baker for second and Bodine fourth.

Now it was a game of chicken. Could the leaders make it, or would one or more have to come in for fuel? Elliott took no chances. Three laps from the finish, he darted into the pits, got his fuel tank topped off and was back in on the track in 6.3 seconds. Earnhardt, Baker and fifth-place Richard Petty pitted two laps later.

Bodine, who gambled and stayed on the track, now had an insurmountable lead, twenty-three seconds, on Elliott, and all appeared lost for the Coors Ford contingent. In the pit stall, Ernie and Dan had resigned themselves to whatever happened.

The roar from the crowd told the story. Bodine was slowing on the backstretch, definitely out of gas.

Ernie Elliott got on the radio and informed Bill.

"Bodine ran out of gas," he said, "You can slow it down."

Parsons gave Elliott a run at the end and lost by only .06 of a second.

Bodine's gamble had failed.

In the Elliott pit, Ernie, Dan and George were smiling and congratulating each other. They don't jump around and hug and celebrate in a boisterous way. They're very businesslike, workmanlike and subdued, as if they never expected to lose.

Later, Bill said he was not surprised Bodine and the Levi Garrett Chevrolet elected to roll the dice. "I knew Geoff was going to do it," he said. "It's typical for the car. Every time I've seen them, they try to go the distance, and I'm glad that last caution wasn't two laps later; then they'd have been able to go all the way.

"We knew we had to stop and get gas and we did it. The crew did a heck of a good job all day long, and I think that showed. The competition would catch up, and then we'd get in and out of the pits and not lose any ground. There at the end we got in, got gas and got out, and that's what won the race for us.

"To beat them the way I did really tickles me, I mean beat them in and out of the pits. That was really a good feeling. For most of the day I was able to make them run my race. And that's a good feeling."

For Bodine, the finish was the height of irony. A year earlier he had won his first Daytona 500 when Earnhardt ignored the fuel problem and gave out two laps from the finish. He said he had no regrets.

"If we didn't think we could [go all the way], we wouldn't have tried it," he said. "It was a calculated risk. I think every team in racing has experienced it at one time or another.

"We're an aggressive team and we'll take chances. Some of them aren't going to pay off. We'll live with this moment.

"When you look back, I made a mistake with the wall, and that should have put me out of the race. My car slid up the track into the wall, and it didn't cause any damage. We were able to overcome that mistake, but not the second one."

After Elliott and Parsons, the top ten of the 1987 Daytona 500 were, in order, Richard Petty, Baker, Earnhardt, Bobby Allison, Schrader, Waltrip, Ricky Rudd, Cale Yarborough and Phil Parsons.

Following the pattern of each new winner setting a record of earnings, Elliott picked up $204,150 to erase Bodine's high of $192,715. Parsons, the substitute driver, didn't do badly himself, with $122,420 for second. The winning speed was 176.263 miles an hour in a race that had only four cautions for fifteen laps.

Daytona marked Elliott's eighteenth Winston Cup victory, all on super speedways, and moved him ahead of Curtis Turner and Marvin Panch on the all-time list of career wins. It was also his first Winston Cup win, outside of Michigan, where he won twice in 1986, since November 3, 1985, when he won the *Atlanta Journal* 500.

In just four short years, he had leaped all the way to sixth among all-time super speedway winners, trailing only Richard Petty (fifty-five), David Pearson (fifty-one), Cale Yarborough and Bobby Allison (both fifty) and Waltrip (thirty). At Daytona, he broke a tie with Buddy Baker.

Elliott had said that Daytona would set the tone, or trend, and the tone was:

— He and Ernie were still the fastest combination around.

— Earnhardt, who had predicted in February of 1986 that he felt that was his year, hadn't slacked off.

— Waltrip and his clean Tide machine were in for rocky days.

— Davey Allison was the most mature and precocious rookie to come along in years.

— The top Ford teams, with Kyle Petty and Ricky Rudd, were on the upswing.

— At forty-six, and even in a subbing role, Benny Parsons could still deal.

— Given top equipment, Ken Schrader and Alan Kulwicki could aim for the top.

— Yarborough was finding it more difficult to run an independent team.

— Rusty Wallace was a future star, and Terry Labonte and Junior Johnson would consistently be near the top.

The only question mark after Daytona concerned Tim Richmond, the object of many rumors. Gossip had him suffering from everything from pneumonia to leprosy. His team said he would make an appearance during the week of the 500, but he never showed. The Rick Hendrick team had already committed with Parsons to run through July 4, with the hopes that Richmond would be sufficiently recovered by then.

Richmond's explanation of his illness was that the hectic 1986 campaign had physically worn him down. "You've heard of running the wheels off," he said. "Well, my wheel fell off."

Daytona marked Elliott's first step toward a repeat in the Winston Million and, in his eyes, success there was vital.

"It doesn't matter whether it's track or basketball or football," he said. "Everybody talks about that explosive 'first step' that gets you the edge. It's the same in the race for the Winston Million. You have to win three of the Big Four, and if you don't win the first one, it's an almost impossible task to win the other three, especially with Winston Cup racing as competitive as it is.

"I'd have to say we have the best chance of anybody right now. That doesn't mean Winston had better start cutting the check. But now we only have to win two of the three remaining races and anyone else has to win all three."

The odds were in his favor.

16

Post-Daytona and the Emergence of Earnhardt

HAVING PROVEN THAT his big-track program was going well, Bill Elliott was anxious to see how the new ideas that Ivan Baldwin brought would fare on the small tracks, and, thanks to the Winston Cup schedule, the transition was immediate.

Richmond, a .542-mile layout, was next after the Daytona 500. But he'd have to wait two more weeks. The Miller High Life 400 weekend was washed out, and the race was rescheduled for March 8, the off-week after the Goodwrench 500 at Rockingham.

The North Carolina Motor Speedway at Rockingham, which measures 1.017 miles, barely qualifies as a super speedway, which, by regulation, must be more than a mile in length. It ranks somewhere between Charlotte and Atlanta and Richmond in degree of difficulty. Historically, Elliott as not done well there. Other than a win in 1984 and a runner-up place in 1983, his highest finish was fourth in the fall of 1985. Of the fourteen times he'd raced there, he'd led only four races.

For a few days, it appeared that rains would delay the Rockingham race. On Thursday, officials managed to get in qualifying, and there was a surprise awaiting everyone. For the second straight race of a two-race season, Davey Allison sat on the front row, this time on the inside, with a record 146.989 miles an hour, breaking Tim Richmond's old standard of 146.948.

More surprising than Allison was his car brand, Ford, the first Ford to start on the pole there since 1979 when Allison's father,

Bobby, did it. Following Allison were Bodine in a Chevy, Schrader in a Ford, Benny Parsons in a Chevy and Ricky Rudd in a Ford. Elliott, with a 145.638, gained the seventh starting position.

"I was trying to be real cautious out there," Elliott said. "It had started to sprinkle, and it was real cold. It's hard to judge what the tires will do here, and you've got so many things going against you. I just decided to go out and get me a good lap and see where I stood. Now I've got to get ready to race."

Allison was elated over his first pole. "To be able to come out and right off the bat sit on the outside at Daytona and then to come to Rockingham the very next race and sit on the pole, I think I'd be crazy to try and fool anybody into believing that we're not all fired up," he said.

"Winning the pole takes a lot of the sting out of what happened in Daytona."

He was referring to a mix-up in which he left the pits too early and lost a wheel.

On Saturday, the rains continued in the North Carolina sandhills, and all events were canceled. There was doubt about whether the race would be run on Sunday. But March proved predictable in its unpredictability, and the sun broke bright and clear. The North Carolina Motor Speedway marked the beginning of the Earnhardt dominance in 1987.

Like Elliott, Earnhardt is not especially enamored of the demanding track, but he had one of those days on which everything, driver, car and crew, come together. He led 320 of the 492 laps and beat Rudd to the wire by 10.5 seconds. So strong was he at the finish, leading 155 of the last 165 laps, that he had a crowd of forty thousand yawning.

His best racing came midway through the event when old hunting buddy Neil Bonnett got door-to-door and challenged him. Bonnett, in a Pontiac, eventually finished third, and Elliott, again uncharacteristically not leading a single lap, was fourth, the final car on the lead lap.

Earnhardt's winning speed of 117.556 earned him $53,900 and gave him great impetus for a shot at two straight points championships.

He also made a prophetic comment. "Last year I led all but three races, and this year I'd like to lead them all and win about half," he said.

Asked why he let friend Bonnett pass at one stage of the race, Earnhardt said, "I didn't just let him by, but I didn't contest him too much either. I didn't pull over, yet I didn't cut him into the infield.

"I ain't changed. Richmond's next week."

Richmond, where Earnhardt and Waltrip had tangled in 1986, enabling Kyle Petty to squeeze through to his first win. Richmond, where the going is tight. Richmond, where Elliott would test his new short-track program under Ivan Baldwin's guidance.

Bill spoke of it: "Today was really one of those days. Nothing went wrong, but, on the other hand, nothing really went right.

"We'll just have to get back together and see what we can do about Richmond. I've been looking forward to that race because I think our short-track program has improved. That's a good yardstick to see how far we've come."

After Rockingham, Earnhardt and Elliott were tied for the points lead with 345. In the Winston Cup scheme of things, Rockingham counts just as much as Daytona.

George Elliott believes there were reasons Bill didn't run as well as anticipated at Rockingham. "We practiced better than we ran," he explains. "I thought we were the strongest car in practice, but because of the rains we didn't get a chance to check the new engine. We had it geared wrong. A couple of poor pit stops didn't help. We lost two seconds in the pits, and two seconds would be five hundred feet."

Also, the team and Baldwin hadn't yet gotten into sync. It takes time for a new man and a team to communicate in the right way, to think alike and to react without holding a committee meeting. The plan at Rockingham was to shoot for the top five, and that's what the Coors Ford team got.

Richmond was to be the first short-track test, a .542-mile exam for the new program. The Elliotts passed, finishing fourth, leading twice for thirteen laps, but Earnhardt trumped the field again by beating Bodine to the finish line by .46 of a second. On Saturday, Earnhardt had crashed and almost totaled his car, but his crew managed to repair it that night.

During the race, Earnhardt, who had to make almost a lap to win, had one of his famous incidents with Harry Gant, up who accused the Wrangler driver of "running all over me." Gant's car was knocked into a spin in the fourth turn and suffered too much damage to contend further.

"I hate it happened, but there was no place to go," Earnhardt said, but Gant replied, "He's blind as a bat. I saw him in my rear-view mirror, and I saw that he wasn't below me so I turned down low. I was in the dirt, and he went down there through the dirt and into me."

The "Earnhardt Problem" was growing.

Other than Earnhardt's winning and Elliott's improvement, the significance of the Richmond race was the performance of Winston Cup sophomore Alan Kulwicki, thought to be a certain superstar of the future, cut from the smooth style of an Elliott or a Petty. He won his first pole, at 95.153 in a T-Bird, and placed sixth in the race.

Those two races, Rockingham and Richmond, offered a preview of Winston Cup's future with the performances of young Allison and Kulwicki, who preceded Davey as Rookie of the Year.

Elliott was looking forward to the next race, the Motorcraft 500, in Atlanta, his backyard. It was a time to get back on track. Also looking forward to Atlanta was Earnhardt, who seemed to take special delight in contending against his chief rival, Elliott.

After Bill broke his own qualifying with a run of 174.247, Earnhardt really got fired up and turned the track in 175.497.

"After Bill got his good lap, I got a little antsy, a little nervous just standing there," said Earnhardt. "I had to go off and do something else to get my mind off it. I went over and watched Rusty Wallace change motors. I knew the car was fast enough if the driver was up to it."

Bill had predicted his time wouldn't hold up. He said, "Earnhardt's going to run a 31.30 or better."

As it turned out, Atlanta International Raceway was not to smile on its home boy or his archrival. Seventy-three laps from the finish, Elliott, who had dueled Earnhardt for the lead all afternoon, went out with engine failure, the first of the mechanical problems that were to dog him for most of the season.

Soon thereafter, a faulty battery switch sent Earnhardt to the pits for repairs. He returned and ran with the leaders, but the time lost had been crucial. He finished sixteenth, to Elliott's twenty-eighth.

For the first time in 1987, Winston Cup had a winner other than Elliott and Earnhardt: Ricky Rudd, driving the Bud Moore Ford. Late in the race Rudd had gambled on a chassis change and hit the right combination. Benny Parsons, driving the Tim Richmond Folger's Chevrolet, gained his second runner-up position of the year, just ahead of Rusty Wallace, Terry Labonte and Davey Allison, who announced his team had picked up Havoline Oil as a sponsor through 1989.

By odd coincidence, Rudd's, Motorcraft Ford had won the Motorcraft 500, just as Earnhardt's Chevrolet had won the Goodwrench 500. It was a big day for Rudd. "Any way you look at it, it was the biggest win of my career," he said. "Before last season, I'd never won a race on a track one mile or longer, except the road course at Riverside. Then last year I won my first super speedway race at Dover. Now I've won at the mile-and-a-half at Atlanta, and to have it come in front of all of our Motorcraft people was really a big boost for everyone."

A defective distributor had stalled the Elliott drive in Atlanta, and now it was on to Darlington for the TranSouth 500 and an extended series of short-track tests, at North Wilkesboro, Bristol and Martinsville.

17

The Cruel Ironies of "The Lady in Black"

"THE LADY IN BLACK," with her undulating curves, teases and then takes away. Everyone, from the Pettys to the Elliotts, has been a victim of her fickle ways.

In 1985, "The Lady," or the 1.366-mile Darlington International blacktop, favored Bill Elliott with two big wins and the Winston Million. There, he's had some of his best races and worst starting positions. He chalked up his first pole at Darlington, but of eighteen races prior to the TranSouth 500 on March 29, 1987, fourteen were begun behind the top ten starters. Yet, he had an incredible sixteen top-ten finishes.

Strategies can change at Darlington. In 1985, when he was on his hot streak, Bill used the frontal approach, winning both poles, his first at the track since 1981, both races and the Winston Million.

But TranSouth pole day, 1987, presented different circumstances and conditions. Early rains had made the track more slippery than usual, and caution was advisable. This time Elliott ran what he was comfortable with, 157.863 miles an hour, and that was good enough for third in the starting order, behind Ken Schrader, seventh different pole winner in the last seven TranSouth races, and Earnhardt.

Bill said he'd take it. "Any time you come back from here with the car in one piece, you're in pretty good shape," he said. "It's in one piece, and I ran a pretty good time, so I'm in pretty good shape.

"The track is still slick. I guess it's because it's a warm day, and there have been a lot of cars practicing on it. The car felt like it wanted to skate around on me.

"I'm not disappointed with our speed. Now we can get down to the business of getting ready for Sunday's race."

There was some flap about letting Davey Allison qualify on the first day with the Winston Cup regulars. Technically, he was a rookie, but he had raced at Darlington the previous year and passed the rookie test. This called for a consultation between Winston Cup director Dick Beaty and the two members of his competition committee, Benny Parsons and Cale Yarborough.

Allison was allowed to qualify for the pole.

Said Beaty, "Dave came here as a rookie last year, attended the rookie meetings, passed the rookie test and ran the race in the Sadler car. He was approved by the rookie committee at that time. I met with the committee, and they agreed that since Davey had passed the rookie test last year and had run the race, we would allow him to qualify."

Allison didn't qualify like a rookie. He had the fifth-fastest time, 157.792 miles an hour, a notch behind the man who made the judgment on him, Parsons.

Spring had just sprung, the season was young and everyone was still optimistic, especially Elliott, then only sixty-one points behind Earnhardt in the points race.

"Everyone is healthy this year, we've got a new chassis man, Ivan Baldwin, who understands the short tracks, and we feel we're ready," he said. "It's way too early to be thinking about the championship, but we're definitely going to be involved in it to the end. Maybe this is our year.

"We had our problems last year. Ernie was sick so much of the year, and that put a lot of pressure on the rest of the team. Despite that, we felt we had a pretty good season. You can't compare it to 1985 because that was an exceptional year for anybody. You don't have seasons like that too often.

"Having Ernie healthy and adding Ivan Baldwin have been pluses for us."

That Earnhardt was the center of attention didn't bother Bill one bit.

"Earnhardt's year has overshadowed everybody," he said. "Just like mine did in '85, and that's made it a holiday for me. The '85 season changed me quite a bit as a person. I got home after the Winston 500, and people were coming from everywhere to see me. It was hard for me to deal with.

"A lot of people wanted to talk who didn't understand racing. That was the hardest thing. They didn't understand I had to work on my race car. I wasn't prepared for everything that happened so quickly."

Nineteen eighty-six had been the buffer year, and in 1987 Elliott enjoyed being one of the drivers instead of *the* driver. He was relaxed. He'd had a good start, a win at Daytona, fourth places at Rockingham and Richmond and a disappointing twenty-eighth at Atlanta, but still it was comparable to 1985, when he was twenty-ninth at Rockingham and twenty-second at Richmond.

It was still a ball game.

The stunning start of rookie Davey Allison had also diverted much of the media attention. Winston Cup veterans weren't accustomed to seeing a newcomer sit on the outside pole at Daytona and set a qualifying record for the inside at Rockingham. The kid was outshining his famous dad.

Recognizing an angle, the racing networks got Davey and Bobby together for an interview in the garage area on the Friday before the race, during a rain lull.

"Here's the scenario," said the racing reporter. "It's the last lap and you're running 1-2. Say one of you is in the trailing car, what would you do?"

Papa Bobby answered first.

"Well," he said, "the outside is the long way around. I'd dive in on the inside."

It was Davey's turn.

He smiled.

"I'd do anything short of crashing to get by. Darlington is a treacherous track, but I like it. It's a challenge."

Unbeknownst to anyone at the time, the scenario suggested by that reporter was to be alarmingly real on race day.

By Sunday morning, the rains had subsided, and the South Carolina sun broke from the eastern beaches, a good day for racing Darlington-style. At 8 A.M., Bobby and Davey Allison, devout Catholics, were in St. Anthony's Church in Florence for Mass and Communion, spiritual fortification.

Schrader, the pole winner, found his stay at the front fleeting, as Earnhardt let out the throttle and passed soon after the green flag. From then and until lap 214, he swapped the lead with Dave Marcis, Ricky Rudd, Darrell Waltrip, Bobby Allison, Schrader and Buddy Baker.

On 214, with Baker leading, a chilling accident occurred.

The No. 28 Ford, driven by Davey Allison, either had a flat or broke an axle on the backstretch, and he went out of control in the three-four turn, only to be smacked into the wall by his father, who found himself trapped by his careening son and Cale Yarborough.

No dreamed-up scenario could have been more horrifying.

As the twisted metal of the Havoline Star erupted in flames and black smoke, members of his crew left the pit *en masse* and headed for the scene of the wreck, one carrying a heavy jack with him. Davey's wife, Deborah, was advised that she was wanted at the medical center. No one knew it at the time, but Davey was already out of the car. With the aid of the safety crew, he had extricated himself even before his father hurtled out of his car and rushed to the No. 28 window.

Davey said it took him all of ten seconds to get out of the car. It would have been sooner if the safety crew hadn't been pulling him by the arm before he got his neck harness off. But he praised the rescue people for their prompt and efficient action.

Those who gathered around young Allison in the garage area, next to his totaled car, were impressed by his calm and professional demeanor.

"I kept thinking, 'be calm, be calm,'" he said. "Flames were everywhere inside the car, but it's no big deal if you keep your head. I just want to thank the Good Lord that no one was hurt."

He then walked over by a transport truck and talked with his father, who was also calm and collected. When you're around race drivers long enough, you learn that they must possess a certain temperament. These things happen. You just go on from there.

The Allisons would go to Mass again the next Sunday. Then they'd go out and run two hundred miles an hour again. There will be more crises, and one in the Winston 500 was to scare Davey Allison more than the fire and smoke at Darlington.

In this, his rookie season, "The Lady in Black" had thrown a guttest at him, and he had passed.

"She" had also taken out Terry Labonte with a broken collarbone. You don't fool with "The Lady."

After the caution was lifted, Baker regained the lead but soon gave way to Schrader. Until then, Elliott had been conspicuous by his absence from the point. Mechanical failure in the last race at Atlanta had made him more cautious than usual.

However, with race moving to the serious stage, he made a move and whipped past Schrader on lap 258 of the 367-lap race. He then diced with Schrader, Earnhardt and Neil Bonnett until the turns had run down to the last ten.

It was now or never, and the No. 9 Ford thundered to the front.

There was a problem for almost all the drivers, a fuel problem. Ernie Elliott had calculated the Coors Ford could go 71.8 laps per tankful of gas. When Bill made his last stop, under caution, seventy-three laps remained in the race.

"There was nothing to do but gamble on last lap and a half," he said.

In an effort to conserve fuel, Elliott had earlier fallen behind Schrader and drafted off him. But, to make his move on Earnhardt, he had to let out the throttle, and this depleted his fuel supply. In hindsight, if he had drafted Schrader for two or three more laps, it might have made a difference.

Both he and Earnhardt gambled.

The Wrangler driver dashed into the pits with eleven laps left, giving up his twelve-second lead, got his tank topped off and returned in third place behind Elliott and Schrader. Five laps later he passed Schrader and trailed Elliott by 2.5 seconds. In his exhuberance to catch the Coors Ford, Earnhardt smacked the wall and dropped back to a four-second deficit.

With the laps becoming history, Earnhardt's chances appeared small and nil. Then, with a single lap remaining, the Darlington crowd jumped to its feet.

The first indication of the race outcome came when Elliott, on the backstretch, steered off the next turn's banking and down to the apron of the track — a standard maneuver in trying to slosh the remaining gasoline into the fuel line. For Bill Elliott, it had to be the most helpless feeling in the world. He was almost there, a few hundred yards, with nothing to propel his Coors Thunderbird.

Earnhardt cruised by easily and won his third Winston Cup race of the five that had been run. Elliott managed to coast in second, with fifty-year-old Richard Petty third, Sterling Marlin fourth and Schrader fifth.

Bill lost the way he had won at Daytona.

"I still can't believe I won this dadburned race," said Earnhardt. But as Waltrip had said, "When everything goes your way, you win and you won't even know why. And you don't know how." That applied to the way Earnhardt's season was going. He couldn't lose for winning.

In all fairness to logic, however, Earnhardt's had been the strongest car on the track all afternoon. He had led 239 of the 367 laps.

"We did the only thing we could," said Elliott. "Gambling to go all the way was the only way we could have beaten Earnhardt. He was playing with us."

"It was a gamble that we lost," said Ernie Elliott. "But that was the only call we could make."

True, the Elliotts gambled for first place. But it was a smart move in another way. If Elliott had come in for gas, his highest finish would have been third or fourth. As it was, he collected $31,485 as the runner-up. Not a bad payoff for leading only forty-one laps.

In his press interview, Earnhardt said the 1986 Daytona 500 was on his mind when he came in for gas.

"When the fuel gauge bobbled, I said, 'Guys, I'm coming to the pits . . . I'm not doing Daytona again.' Then when I came back out and Elliott got caught behind traffic, I said, 'I've got him now.' But with all my anxiousness catching Bill, I lost it and knocked the hell out of the wall.

"I started talking to myself down the backstretch, but the sun came out again when Bill ran out of gas."

It was not one of the better pit work days for the Elliott crew. Once he came out a second behind Earnhardt and later in the thick of a chain of slower cars.

The dominance of Earnhardt was beginning to worry the other teams. Just as in 1985, when Elliott was winning everything in sight, there was talk of something illegal or favoritism from Chevrolet on parts or breaks from NASCAR.

Following the TranSouth 500, Earnhardt held a comfortable seventy-one-point lead over Elliott in the Winston Cup points race.

He had a total of 840 to Elliott's 769. Trailing were Neil Bonnett, 700; Waltrip, 690, despite a struggling year, and Richard Petty, 678.

18

Tackling the
Short Tracks

THE SHORT-TRACK swing is usually a relaxed time on the
Winston Cup circuit, but in 1987 the "Earnhardt Problem" was
beginning to get to some of the drivers and the crews.

Gant had complained at Atlanta, Kulwicki had gotten the "treatment" at Richmond and intimidation had become a buzzword. But
few were speaking openly until the usual informational press conference held in conjunction with the First Union 400 at North
Wilkesboro. Track publicist Hank Schoolfield always manages to get
a leading driver in relaxed circumstances and, as a result, everyone
learns a lot. In 1985 Bill Elliott gave his best interviews there.

This time the driver was genial Benny Parsons, who had come out
of semiretirement to sub for Tim Richmond.

Schoolfield's meeting coincided with a press conference at the
Charlotte Motor Speedway announcing Richmond's plans for the
season.

In answer to a question, Parsons said his deal was to race through
the Firecracker 400 at Daytona. After that, he didn't know. But just
as he finished speaking, Don Wilson, Schoolfield's able assistant,
said the news out of Charlotte was that Parsons would continue for
the full season, and Richmond would return for the Winston on May
17 and then play it by ear, depending on how his health was.

Parsons was delighted to hear he'd get the full shot.

Until this stage of the season, there had been a lot of grumbling
about Earnhardt's style but no public statements. Veteran racing

writer Benny Phillips of the High Point, North Carolina, *Enterprise* brought it out in the open by asking Parsons about the fine art of track intimidation.

"It's there, sure," replied Parsons. "You can intimidate in a lot of ways, on the track in races, practice runs and qualifying and off the track in the garage area in how you handle things.

"Earnhardt, he's a race driver; Richard Childress, you've got to give him credit for the car. And the intimidation factor is always there. You handle it in different ways. Personally, if it's me and I look in my mirror and see Earnhardt coming up, and it's early in the race, I might let him by. If it's late in the race and you've got a shot at the checkers, the situation is entirely different."

Since the First Union 400 was only the sixth race of the season, many of the drivers were still in the shakedown stage, trying to solve one problem or another. Elliott, with Ivan Baldwin in tow, was looking for improvement on the small tracks. Waltrip and Waddell Wilson were still trying to work the kinks out of the No. 17 Tide machine. And Terry Labonte, with a broken collarbone, planned to start the Junior Johnson No. 11 Chevy and then turn it over to Brett Bodine.

Young Brett was to qualify the car.

Saturday, April 4, was a milestone day for Elliott. His 116.003 record speed was good enough for his first pole ever on a short track. The next nine cars behind him were all GM products, with Parsons, Earnhardt, Bobby Allison and Terry Labonte (Brett Bodine) making up the top five. Brett was two positions ahead of his brother Geoff, who good-naturedly complained, "It's kind of embarrassing to have your little brother beat you; maybe we ought to have a nepotism rule."

Elliott considered the pole a big step forward in his team's program. "I thought it was a pretty doggone good lap," he enthused. "I don't care what anybody thinks. It sure did feel good, let me tell you. The car's running super good. Whether I'm on the pole or not, I'll take this lap for sure. I'm pretty happy, let's go race.

"Without a doubt, it's the best short-track car I've ever had. Give a lot of credit to Ivan. He's the short-track expert. He had a lot to do with building and getting this car ready. That's what we brought him on board for was to shore up our short-track program.

"We know now, too, that we've got to be consistent during the races on short tracks. You've got to stay up front consistently in order to win and survive. We know that, and I think we're improving on that aspect."

The Coors Ford at North Wilkesboro was a totally new car, built specifically for the First Union 400. In its first shot, it had beaten the North Wilkesboro track record. Now Elliott had to improve on his record of having finished only twice on the lead lap in short-track racing.

Weather must always be considered during the early part of the Winston Cup season. Rain had postponed the Richmond race and delayed events at Rockingham and Darlington. At North Wilkesboro it had snowed on the Friday preceding the race.

But all was clear for the race on Sunday.

Everyone knew the driver to beat — Dale Earnhardt. Coming into North Wilkesboro, the North Carolinian had had an incredible season, leading almost half of the miles in the races up to that point. In winning three of five races, he had been at the front for 1,065.5 miles, more than tripling the miles led by the runner-up, Elliott, who had been in front for 394.3 miles. Durability was another plus. Of the 2,216.89 miles run, Earnhardt had failed to finish only 9.95.

If those facts weren't enough to discourage the others, Earnhardt was also the defending champion of the First Union 400 and hadn't finished out of the top ten in the past six races.

When Elliott is out front at the start, you can bet the farm that he'll lead, and he did at North Wilkesboro, for ten laps. Then he fell back. The race setup wasn't running as well as the qualifying setup, and he continued to lose ground, little by little.

As everyone had feared, Earnhardt dominated the race after taking over from Elliott on lap eleven. In all, he led 314 of the 400 laps, including the last 84.

Elliott finished tenth, two laps down.

"Something ain't kosher," said George Elliott after the race. "Earnhardt's car certainly didn't run like a light car. What I wish they'd do is make a public display of the car weights, put them on the scoreboard like they do everything else.

"But give NASCAR the benefit of the doubt. In 1985 when we were winning we had the same things said about us, and we were the most legal car running.

"There is still some adjusting to be made in the chassis department. Ivan is regarded as a good chassis man, but you've still got to make the car fit Bill. Once they get to communicating, they won't have to communicate, if you know what I mean. He'll know what to do without communicating.

"I remember when Fred Lorenzen and Ralph Moody were at Daytona testing for Goodyear.

"Lorenzen came into the pits and Moody asked, 'How does it feel?' Lorenzen said, 'Perfect.'

"'Not perfect,' said Moody. 'You were a little bit loose in turns one and two.'

"That's what I mean about it not being necessary to communicate."

Despite the race problems, something had been achieved at North Wilkesboro. The Coors Ford's first short-track pole was a start. And Bill had come out of the First Union 400 only twenty-seven points behind Earnhardt in the Winston Cup race.

Bristol would be the second test. It would also be the place where the complaints about Earnhardt would heat up.

At the .533-mile Bristol track, not as wide and inviting as North Wilkesboro, the Coors Ford team reversed the pattern of the previous race. Bill started eleventh and finished fourth after leading the most laps, 147, a performance considered his best effort to date on the short tracks.

Late problems with tire stagger prevented a real shot at winning. "We did all we could do," he said. "The track changed on us, and we could never get it back. We were able to lead some laps, and I think that our short-track program is coming around."

Elliott managed to avoid all the crashes and fender-bending that occurred. Everyone was complaining about Earnhardt, winner of his fifth race of the seven run. He tapped Elliott on the very first lap, and on lap 252 of the 500-lap race, with ominous rain clouds threatening to shorten the afternoon, he got into leader Sterling Marlin, who spun, damaged his car and was eliminated from contention.

This caused a lot of flap after the race.

Marlin's father, Coo Coo, an old-time driver who seldom won a race, leveled a blast through the Associated Press. "I'd like to take him [Earnhardt] out behind the barn and beat the hell out of him," said the senior Marlin. "He's bullying his way through racing. Earnhardt has set Winston Cup racing back twenty years. . . . Somebody who drove back then like Earnhardt is driving now wouldn't have lasted many races. Something would have happened to him. We raced hard and there was a lot of contact, but we didn't deliberately wreck each other.

". . . I blame NASCAR more than I blame Earnhardt. Earnhardt's getting away with what NASCAR lets him get away with. NASCAR's about to sit around and let this thing really get out of hand."

Some were of the opinion that Coo Coo Marlin picked the wrong incident to protest. While Earnhardt appeared to have been clearly guilty on other occasions, the Bristol incident was not that clear-cut. TV replays show that Earnhardt had wedged inside and Marlin might have drifted down a smidgen.

"Earnhardt's not doing anything everybody else in racing hasn't done," says Junior Johnson. "It's a little rough for some of those drivers out there, but there's nothing wrong with that. From where I was standing in the Bristol deal, it could have gone either way.

"Earnhardt just pushes that. It goes on in racing. If they don't like it, they should get behind him and do it to him.

"His style is just like his daddy's [Ralph Earnhardt]."

Former racer Ned Jarrett, now a radio and TV analyst, agrees with Johnson. "Dale drives like his dad did," he says. "It's a thin line, a style that causes controversy. There was not as much attention to racing, as much notoriety, then, but it can certainly cause some controversy now."

It's been said that Jarrett himself was no powder puff on the tracks. Mention of that fact brings a knowing grin.

"I was aggressive, yes," he says, "and certainly Junior [Johnson] and Curtis Turner were aggressive."

Even Richard Petty, nearing fifty, was spotted banging around the Bristol track as he finished second, his highest place since a third at North Wilkesboro in 1986.

"I've heard a lot about how the King is getting old and all that," said one of the younger drivers after the race, "but did you see that body block he threw on Bodine?"

"That's the way Bristol is," said Petty. "If you ain't hitting somebody, they're hitting you."

Elliott, the quiet one, let all the others fight it out at Bristol. He jumped into his van and made the long trip back to Dawsonville to prepare for the Sovran Bank 500 and test number three on the short tracks at Martinsville.

Once again, as the Winston Cup caravan pulled into the Virginia city, all the attention centered on Earnhardt, who'd won three straight and five out of seven. His triple was the first by a Winston Cup driver since Bobby Allison turned the trick in 1983 on the way to his first Winston Cup championship. The last to win four in a row was Darrell Waltrip in 1981 during his first championship year, and the last to take five consecutively had been Richard Petty ten years earlier.

The all-time high, of course, was Petty's ten straight in 1967.

At Martinsville, Elliott had two objectives. The first, another exam for the short-track program. At the same time he had to be thinking of the next race, the Winston 500 at Talladega, the second leg on the Winston Million. You don't want to get so out of shape at Martinsville that you're not ready for Talladega.

Qualifying day found the Coors Ford with its hood up and Ernie Elliott and his aides working through the whole run for the pole. Ernie reported that it took the crew much longer than normal to replace a faulty engine because the old engine required some configuration work to enable it to fit into the new Ford.

Despite the delay, Bill was in a jocular mood. "Me? I'm here psyching everyone out," he said. "I want to start twenty-first and then come on. That would psych 'em out — if I loaded up and went home."

He had planned on qualifying the next day, a Saturday.

For a change, a new name and car were on the pole, Morgan Shepherd and the Quaker State Buick. His speed of 92.355 miles an hour was a record. Earnhardt had qualified fourth, behind Terry Labonte, now healthy, and Harry Gant.

With Saturday came another chapter of the 1987 monsoon season. There was no qualifying and Elliott drew the thirty-first and last position in the field. Back there, he was more amused than angry, saying, "It really ought to be fun starting last. The way I look at it, it's more impressive going from the back to the front than from the front to the back. I'd rather be up front here, but I don't want to be in the middle, so I might as well start in the back."

Elliott wasn't the only one having problems. Short-track expert Waltrip, who'd had ten top-five finishes in the last fifteen Martinsville races, was starting in the eleventh position and the Tide machine was more clean than mean.

Once the race started, Elliott put on one of the most exciting shows of the season. While Shepherd, Gant, Earnhardt and Waltrip took turns at the lead, he was passing cars in wholesale numbers. From his caboose position, he'd whipped past nine by the fourth lap.

And by lap 126 of the 500-lap race, Bill Elliott was in first place. He had passed the entire field, thanks to heady driving and alert pit work by Ernie and the crew.

He then fell back, relinquishing the point to Earnhardt, who in turn gave it up to Rusty Wallace. A fast pit stop on lap 204, when Ernie changed two tires while others were taking on a set, enabled Bill to grab the baton again.

"The tires were not wearing," said Ernie. "We thought we'd take a chance."

After trading the front with Earnhardt once more, the Coors Ford ran into an old Martinsville bugaboo, brake trouble. When Bodine jumped to the front, passing Wallace on lap 368, and appeared certain to break his long winless streak, Elliott was out of brakes and just holding his position and turning laps.

It was a piece of cake for Bodine, or so everyone thought. Then, with only seventeen laps to go, he brushed Kyle Petty's Ford in the first turn and spun, allowing Earnhardt, who was a full four seconds behind, to catch up and slip by for his sixth win in eight races. Bodine finished third, behind Rusty Wallace. Phil Parsons was fourth, Labonte fifth and Elliott sixth, two laps back.

The Coors team had made a strong bid and possibly didn't get enough credit for its last-to-front effort before the brakes went.

Bill was not discouraged. "On the short track it's more the car and how it's set up than anything you can do," he said. "You're still turning the wheels and telling it what to do, but you've got to have something telling you what to do. In the past I'd find something and end up tearing the car up, but I've got the cars and we keep taking them back to the race tracks. We keep making them better and better."

Bodine was having the opposite kind of year from Earnhardt. He had lost two races, Daytona and Martinsville, that he thought he had won. Nothing was going his way. It was hard to rationalize, but he tried.

"Everything was in good hands and then I spin in the corner," he said, trying to find the words. "My family was here and my wife, and they keep telling me it's all right and I try to tell myself it's all right, but inside it's hurting. My crew chief, Gary Nelson, tells me eventually we're going to win and don't worry about this.

"My whole crew feels that way. It's hard to get mad or yell or scream when people feel that way around you. But this has got to stop. It can't continue. You know we have a strong team. We'll go back to the shop like we did last week and the week before and work hard. Like we won . . . almost."

Earnhardt, knowing he'd gotten a king-sized break, was subdued in the post-race press conference. To have an extraordinary season, a driver needs the kind of break he was handed on a platter at Martinsville.

"Lady Luck can smile on you or bite you," he said. "She smiled on me today. I was giving it all I had, but I don't think I could have beaten Geoff. After he spun, I just concentrated on not making a mistake."

The oddity was that Dale Earnhardt won a race and no one accused him of using dirty tactics.

On the short road at Martinsville, Elliott played on the home court of others. The good part about Martinsville is that it leads to the long road at Talladega, where Bill Elliott is the fastest man alive.

19

The Winston 500 and the Failed Engine: Problem or Providence?

IF YOU PLAYED a word association game and mentioned "Talladega," the most likely reply would be "Bill Elliott." The Alabama International Motor Speedway, fastest racing road in the world, belongs to Elliott, fastest driver in the world of stocks.

It was at AIMS that he elevated street car racing to a higher, riskier dimension, beginning in 1985 when he won his first pole in the Winston 500 with a blazing 209.398 miles an hour. The next year, he raised that a notch to 212.229. By running that fast, he forced the others in the field to come up to his standard. And the 1985 Winston 500 will always be regarded as a legendary race because of the phenomenal way Elliott made up almost two laps under green to win at a world record of 186-plus miles an hour over five hundred miles.

No other driver is identified with a particular race to the degree that Elliott is with the Winston 500. It is not so much that he always wins at Talladega — he doesn't; he's won more at Michigan — as it is that his style is the one most suited to the 2.66-mile, high-banked runway. Despite this relationship between man and asphalt, he is not one to show a lack of respect for the strip of land built on ancient burial grounds of the Creek Indians, who reportedly placed a curse on all who followed.

"So many things can happen fast here," Elliott said prior to the 1987 Winston 500. "The best thing about this race is leaving on Sunday night."

Winston 500 week is not a casual time for Elliott. He is expected to win the pole, and he is expected to lead and perhaps win the race despite a record that shows that prior to 1987 he'd won only one. All of these expectations add to the pressures of the second leg of the Winston Million. Having already won at Daytona, Elliott stood to gain at least $100,000 in the 1987 Winston 500. That's the consolation prize for winning two of the Big Four.

There were other pressures building up. More and more, the Earnhardt Problem was surfacing. Slowly but surely, a confrontation was building between Elliott's finesse style and the North Carolinian's root-and-move ways. It was a showdown waiting for a place to happen.

Talladega, in the spring, wasn't the place.

Instead, as the events unfolded, it was to be the scene where Winston Cup racing gave birth to a young man with superstardom written all over him, twenty-six-year-old Davey Allison, a rookie who'd more than paid his dues in all types of lower-classification racing.

He was a rookie who thought and spoke like a veteran.

In a meeting with several reporters during the week, Allison, participating in only his fourteenth Winston Cup race, had displayed track savvy far beyond his years. He pointed out that a change in car designs had resulted in a drastic change in the laws of aerodynamics on such high-speed tracks as AIMS. He had figured out something that many of the other drivers, including veterans, had only suspected.

"It's a strange thing," he said, "but now the second-place car can control the race leader. Everyone assumes the leader sets the pace. The second-place car these days has a lot of control over how fast you go.

"Let's say cars are running nose-to-tail, and the leader of the pack is running wide open. The guy behind him is running at three-quarters throttle and staying there, content to ride at that pace, and he looks in his mirror and sees somebody gaining on him. He says, 'Well, I can use a little bit of my power and push this guy a little faster.' He can gain as much as three-quarters of a second.

"A lot of things can happen. You can slip on the outside and steal his air, dive in on the inside and upset him, get him out of control. Or you could sit behind him and catch that air coming around his car before it can funnel out.

"Believe me, it's no fun. I've been there. I drove Neil Bonnett's car here last year and whoever was behind me, whichever way their car went, I was hanging on for dear life. Sometimes I'd ask myself, 'Why don't they just drive straight?' Then the guy behind might be thinking, 'Why am I driving all over the place, why can't I be still?'"

His father Bobby had won the Winston 500 in 1986, and Davey said even then the tricky winds had caused big problems.

"Dale [Earnhardt] and Dad almost got into it," he said. "Dale drove up to Dad going into the third turn. They came close to touching, and the only reason they didn't was that Dale's car caught coming off the fourth turn. He was far enough out of shape where he had to lift and give Dad room. Dale had no control over what he was doing and coming off the fourth turn you couldn't have slipped a piece of paper between the two cars."

"Yeah," said Charlotte racing writer Bob Myers, "and I'll bet everyone in the stands said, 'There goes that danged Earnhardt again.'"

A smile creased Allison's youthful face. "I don't think anyone was thinking along those terms last year," he said.

Many had expected Elliott to qualify for the 1987 Winston 500 at better than 214 miles an hour. In a January test, he'd run 214.600 and had the racing world buzzing. But he said he wasn't disappointed with 212.809.

"Under the conditions, we ran as fast as we could run," he said. "You've got to take under consideration that the air makes a lot of difference. You've got to do it on the day you do it. Everybody's been asking me since last weekend what we could run, but you don't know until you run."

With Bobby Allison's LeSabre on the outside pole at 211.797 miles an hour, it was the same front row as in the 1986 Winston 500. In third place was Davey Allison's Thunderbird, at 210.610, almost 2 miles an hour slower. The Allisons had done well at their home track. Bobby had won four times and brother Donnie, now semiretired, twice.

Elliott, of course, had been the dominant driver on the treacherous Talladega track for two years. In 1985, the Winston Million year, he had made up two laps under green to win at the all-time high speed of 186-plus. And in 1986 he was leading the field when engine problems sidelined him with fourteen laps to go.

But Bobby Allison thought the margin was narrowing.

"He was far ahead then," said Allison. "He was running 212, and we were only running 200. Now he's still running 212, and we've caught up a bit."

Davey agreed that Elliott would be the one to beat. "The thing about Bill," he said, "is sometimes you hang on for dear life, and sometimes you run off and leave him, depending on where you're at and what kind of day he's having."

In a week, Elliott had gone from the last starting position to the first. Engine problems delayed his qualifying at Martinsville, and he and Ernie never did get the car on the track, having to settle for thirty-first position.

"From thirty-first to first ain't bad," he said. "It may be getting boring to you writers [to have him win the pole], but I enjoyed the heck out of it. First time I don't win it, y'all gonna ask, 'What happened?' I'd rather keep on winning and not have to answer that question."

As they went into Talladega, Earnhardt had won six of eight races amid charges of rough tactics, and the other drivers were depending on Elliott to take the initiative away from the North Carolina villain.

"I know some say it's me versus him," said Elliott, "but I don't see it as a last stand. I still have to run my race. I don't see it as a two-car race. I look for Waltrip, Baker and Dave Allison to be among the leaders."

For young Allison, it was to be the most traumatic and exhilarating day of his career, a day in which he was to experience heart-stopping horror and the thrill of his first victory.

Just twenty-one laps into the race, Bobby Allison's Buick cut a right rear tire, got airborne upside down and rode the first turn grandstand fence, ripping out fifty feet of wire and coming to rest on all four wheels in a totaled car. Debris from the flying car injured several spectators, one suffering a serious eye injury.

Davey Allison, who'd been dicing for the lead with Elliott during the early stages of the race, saw the accident and said "That was the scaredest I've ever been in my life. My heart sank. I asked the Good Lord to let him stay on this earth with us a while longer."

His prayer was answered. As he came around on the caution, he sighed with great relief as he saw his father climb out of the twisted metal.

Flagman Harold Kinder, on the stand about fifteen feet in front of where Bobby Allison hit, remained at his post and waved the yellow flag to warn the other drivers. Fortunately, the hurtling steel did not reach the stand.

"Thank the Good Lord no one was seriously hurt," said a shaken Bobby Allison during a delay of two-and-one-half hours for repair of the fence.

Upon the restart, Davey Allison and Elliott resumed their duel at the front. On this day, Allison was a bit stronger than "Awesome Bill," and Elliott had a little power on the rest of the field. But, alas and alack, twenty-eight laps from the finish Elliott's engine quit, and his day had ended.

When he had gotten out of the car, Elliott said, "You've got to live with things like this. I thought the car was driving pretty good, but I couldn't get a chance to stay with Davey. I'd get in that traffic and drive as hard as I could to get caught back up. Davey's car was running good, and he had the car I was trying to run with, but who'll ever know if I could have caught him?"

In retrospect, that might have been the luckiest day of Bill Elliott's life. When the Coors/Melling Thunderbird was examined, crew members found that a lug nut on the left rear wheel had been left off in the excitement of a pit stop.

"Can you imagine what could have happened if that wheel had come off at two hundred miles an hour?" asked George Elliott. "It could be engine failure was a blessing in disguise."

With Elliott out, Davey Allison went on to edge Terry Labonte for the checkers in a race shortened ten laps by another accident, this one involving Ken Ragan. Kyle Petty was third and Earnhardt fourth, ending his four-race winning streak.

With victory in only his fourteenth race, Davey Allison became one of the earliest winners in the history of Winston Cup racing. Ron Bouchard won the Talladega 500 in only his eleventh race, but through 1987, it was his only win.

As a matter of comparison, Dave Marcis also posted his first success in the Talladega 500, but it was his 250th start. Earnhardt and Morgan Shepherd won on their fifteenth starts. Elliott's first win didn't come until his 116th race. Tim Richmond won on his forty-fourth. Kyle Petty went 170 races before he won.

By winning at Talladega, Allison joined Elliott in the side race for the Winston Million. But to win, one or the other had to sweep the remaining Big Four races at Charlotte and Darlington, a tall order for anyone.

20

The Disneyland of Auto Racing

CHARLOTTE HAD TO HAPPEN. It was the OK Corral, a place to settle things between two racing philosophies. Like Greta Garbo, Bill Elliott adhered to the "I vant to be alone" school of thought; and, like Ma Bell, or Ma Barker, Dale Earnhardt was happiest when he could reach out and touch someone.

All signs pointed to an eventual showdown or shootout. Elliott believed Earnhardt had done more than touch him at Watkins Glen in 1986, and there had been several incidents during the 1986 season. Labeling himself "One Tough Customer" in Wrangler jeans, Earnhardt had become the Great Intimidator on the Winston Cup circuit. When he was on your exhaust, he was a physical threat or a mental hazard, and neither one was conducive to total concentration. Waiting for the other shoe to drop could be unnerving.

Until Charlotte and the third running of the Winston, there had been only words.

Both had strong things to say in the April 26 edition of *The Atlanta Journal-Constitution.*

Earnhardt: "I scared hell out of ol' Bill at Daytona. That little boy will never forget that deal. I didn't hit him. I just got up there and got the air off his spoiler and got his ol' car loose.

". . . As dominant as Bill has been on super highways, that's the only way to lead a lap on him. Move him. Scare him. Mess with his head."

Elliott: "He wants to intimidate me, but that can turn both ways. I ain't taking anything off him anymore. I've got my style and I win races. He's got his style and he wins races. I'm not out to wreck anyone or hurt anybody. I just want to race.

". . . Last year at Watkins Glen, after what he did, if I could have gotten back on the track I'd have driven right over him."

The stage was set for a classic confrontation in the Winston, racing's version of the hundred-yard dash. In boxing it would have been the slugger against the boxer, in hockey the checker against the skater. In racing it was Ford against Chevrolet, the points leader against the runner-up: Elliott against Earnhardt.

Based on his super speedway credentials and his performance in the second Winston in Atlanta, in which he led eighty-two of the eighty-three laps, Elliott was a prohibitive favorite. He was a chassis man, and the two ten-minute breaks in the 135-lap race were a chassis man's dream. The new Winston format called for a seventy-five-lap segment, a ten-minute break, a fifty-lap middle segment, another ten-minute interval, then a ten-lap shootout for $200,000. By leading all three parts and the most laps, a driver stood to collect $300,000, the largest single-race prize in NASCAR history.

Racing men agreed with the odds.

"Bill's 100 percent ahead of everyone else," said chassis builder Banjo Matthews. "He's super at strategic planning, and he's already won the Winston once."

Charlotte Motor Speedway general manager and president H. A. (Humpy) Wheeler saw it from a different perspective. He said, "Bill's chances of winning are high because he's combined the characteristics of the best drivers. He races with the aggressiveness of Curtis Turner, the finesse of Tim Flock, the daring of Fireball Roberts and the intelligence of Fred Lorenzen."

Wow!

The Winston, the tenth event of the season, marked the return of Tim Richmond, who felt sufficiently recovered from his bout with pneumonia to try a 135-lap sprint. The biggest winner of 1986, with seven victories and just under a million dollars, Richmond saw the less taxing Winston as the perfect spot to test his stamina.

"I've run a lot of races in my life, but the toughest was battling pneumonia," said Richmond. "I'm not coming back to run second."

As expected, Elliott was the fastest in qualifying with a run of 170.827 miles an hour. He bumped Richmond who, in turn, had bumped Geoff Bodine.

Several questions remained. Would Elliott run off and leave everyone? Would Earnhardt be a good little boy, or would he brand a few other cars with Wrangler blue? Finally, can *anyone* be good when $200,000 is at stake?

Veteran driver Neil Bonnett didn't think so. "Whoever wins the last ten-lap segment will not be a gentleman, and he'll get more bad press than you can imagine," he warned. "Shoot, you run ten laps for $200,000, the guys are going to take off the gloves and go at it. That's what this sport is all about."

The Elliotts pronounced themselves ready. Early on race morning, the twenty cars, covered with formfitting canvas and lined up, resembled iron thoroughbreds in a paddock. They were the elite of the mechanical world, the top twenty powertrains to be ridden by the top twenty drivers.

"Hopefully, I can lead the first lap," said Bill Elliott. "That's the advantage of starting first. I'd rather be there than anywhere else."

He did lead the first lap. Except when he was in the pits under green, he led every lap of the first two segments. Never had Ernie Elliott prepared an engine more beautifully than he had No. 9 for the Winston. It was complete dominance. During the break before the ten-lap shootout, Bill told the media that nothing was changed. You don't change perfection.

There was only one flaw during the first 125 laps. So excruciatingly boring were they that many fans left the premises before Elliott, Geoff Bodine, Kyle Petty and Earnhardt lined up for the $200,000 shootout. The spectators who left had overlooked a couple of salient facts. Number one, Earnhardt was sitting right up there where he preferred to be, right where he is most effective, behind the leaders. Number two, Bodine, winless and struggling in the Levi Garrett Chevrolet, was having one of his better runs, and he was hungry.

The gloves were about to come off. Just ahead were the most controversial ten laps in NASCAR history, twenty-five thousand dollars in fines, intentional attempts to ram, pit crewmen squaring off and shaking fists, a near-fight by two drivers in the garage and utter chaos. The man who had predicted the finish, Neil Bonnett, wasn't around to see it. He was on his way to the hospital because of elbow and knee injuries suffered in a midrace wreck.

The strategy was no mystery. Because of his style, Elliott needed to get the jump on the start. He knew it. So did Earnhardt and Bodine. Their mission: somehow, perhaps anyhow, prevent him from getting to the front.

They got some unexpected help. Elliott had to back momentarily off the throttle when the pace car was slow in leaving the track. This gave Bodine an opening, and he filled it. However, in the first turn they somehow tangled and Bodine spun. Elliott got into the right side of his car, and Earnhardt into the No. 9's rear. Niftily, Earnhardt cut to the apron and took the lead. Bodine managed to control his car and continue.

All combatants had time to stew during a brief caution.

On the fourth turn of the restart, Elliott and Earnhardt tangled, knocking the No. 3 Wrangler yellow-and-blue Chevrolet to the grass, where Dangerous Dale recovered and, with a daring maneuver, shot back in front of the Coors/Melling Thunderbird.

Now it was war.

When Elliott tried the outside on the backside, he was pushed up high near the wall by Earnhardt. The brush with Earnhardt bent a fender on No. 9, resulting in a cut tire and the end of chances to repeat in the Winston. He finished an angry fourteenth.

Slowing on the last lap, Elliott waited until the race was over and then turned No. 9 into No. 3. He also took another swipe at Earnhardt in the pit area, as did Bodine.

Earnhardt's victory was lost in the pandemonium of the finish.

His crew and Elliott's crew stalked each other and shook fists, and Papa Richard Petty had to break up a heated argument between his son, Kyle, and Pontiac driver Rusty Wallace, who edged young Petty for fifth.

The accusations flew.

Elliott said Earnhardt deliberately pushed him up to the wall.

"When a man pulls over on the backstretch and then runs you into the wall, I'd say that was pretty deliberate," he fumed. "I was a sucker for going, but, yes, he hit me several times and everyone saw it."

Replied Earnhardt, "I just wanted him to know I was upset for knocking me through the grass."

Elliott did not deny that his postrace jostling of Earnhardt was intentional. "Very much so," he said. "He liked to wreck me and several other people. When a man's got to run over you to beat you, it's time to stop. I'm tired of it. This is Saturday night racing, Saturday night wrestling."

Bodine, who denied he and Earnhardt were teaming up on Elliott, offered his version of the incident.

"It was a combination of three drivers, just driving very hard, going for the win," he said. "I got a good jump on the start, had a good move there, and got into the corner about three-fourths of a car' length ahead of Bill Elliott. I was on the outside and tried to keep him low on the racetrack, to give him just enough racetrack to get through and hopefully he'd let up on the gas.

"Before that, Dale Earnhardt was behind me, and before we entered the corner he bumped Bill Elliott. Well, I guess to Bill that looked like we were teaming up on him. I was ahead of him and Dale was bumping him.

"So Bill, instead of going into the corner and letting up, he went in there and stayed in the throttle. When I squeezed him down in the bottom he came up and tapped me in the quarter panel. So that was really a reaction to me trying to keep him low and Dale running into him and maybe getting him a little hot and he went in there and ran into me, and I spun around in front of everybody.

"There wasn't any teaming up. I was just trying to get out front, and he [Dale] was trying to intimidate Bill maybe. I have no hard feeling about any of that. I thought it was kind of what everybody expected would happen for that kind of money and that kind of race."

After the restart, Bodine managed to come from last to finish fourth behind Labonte and Richmond. Only Kyle Petty's Ford prevented a GM sweep of the top ten despite the fact that for 90 percent of the race the Chevys needed binoculars to see Elliott. Sheer numbers had done him in.

More than anything else, the 1987 Winston underlined the contradiction in stock car racing.

Neil Bonnett explained it well. "The thing I don't understand is that all the press here in Charlotte is bad-mouthin' all the beatin' and bangin' that was going on. I guess that's both the selling point and the problem in our sport.

"The press thinks it's awful that guys race the way we do, but if nobody bumped fenders, it would have been the most boring race in the world."

Drivers must live that contradiction. There are NASCAR rules, and then there is the code of the drivers, unwritten and seldom mentioned, but very real. It boils down to this: Don't get mad, get even. When something is done to you intentionally, you retaliate and at the earliest moment. Otherwise, you've been intimidated. The intention is not to endanger the other guy, only to get his attention.

Publicly, racing officials, promoters, media types and fans moaned about how horrible the finish was. Privately, they couldn't have been more pleased with the outcome. Until the last ten laps, the Winston was a competitive flop. For the press, a no-story turned into a real sizzler. Fans had renewed vigor in choosing up sides, Earnhardt versus Elliott, Chevrolet versus Ford. They'll be talking about the 1987 Winston for years.

Of course, with NASCAR, it can't end there. There had been violations out there in the open; therefore, judgments had to be made. Racing people wiped the smiles off their faces and solemnly announced activation of a high tribunal to try the offenders. Sitting in judgment were Bill France, Jr., NASCAR president; Jim Hunter, vice-president of administration, and Dick Beaty, Winston Cup director. Those to be judged were Earnhardt, Elliott, Bodine, Petty and Wallace.

Since garage squabbling is commonplace, Petty and Wallace were quickly dismissed.

Earnhardt and Elliott were each fined twenty-five hundred dollars and required to post seventy-five hundred in bonds against future behavior. Because he tried but couldn't hit Earnhardt's car in the garage area, Bodine got off relatively light, a one-thousand-dollar fine and a four-thousand-dollar bond.

"We have to preserve our integrity," intoned Beaty.

It was a tough week on Bill Elliott. Retaliating on the track and speaking out in anger were against his quiet and reserved nature. He keeps his opinions on other drivers to himself. Publicly, he says only nice things about them; you have to be really close to Elliott to know what he really thinks. Earnhardt's car owner, Richard Childress, said he was not upset with Elliott. He thought Bill acted "out of frustration." But it was more than that.

Elliott feels that sometime, somewhere, somehow, a person has to take a stand. In 1985, when the media and sponsor crush got to him, he secluded himself in the trailer, away from it all. This time he had met the challenge head-on. As painful as it was personally, he had gotten Earnhardt's attention. And, unlike other occasions, he had made himself immediately accessible after the race to charge that the event had deteriorated into "Saturday night wrestling."

He had not planned on returning to Dawsonville between the Winston and the Coca-Cola 600, but, given his state of mind, he decided he needed the solace and peace of the hills. He spent Monday at home.

"He's some kind of ill right now," his father said at the time.

Returning to Charlotte the next day to prepare for Wednesday's 600 qualifying, Bill ran only five or six laps and requested that the crew park No. 9 and adjourn early. At the same time he and Earnhardt patched things up.

"I did something wrong, and I'm willing to pay for it,"he said. "I do think the fine was a little stiff, especially since it's my first incident. This is something that has been building up for a long period of time, and something needed to be done to put a stop to it. I apologized to Earnhardt, their crew, everyone.

"These are people you have to deal with and race with every week. Now, let's hope it's all over and done with, and let's just get on with the racing."

Having made his peace, Elliott was ready to concentrate on the run for the pole. He had been cheered by a letter from Georgia governor, Joe Frank Harris, citing his contributions to the state and offering, along with friends, to pay his fine.

Earnhardt also spoke his piece. He said, "I'm not Black Bart, but I'm a tough racer. Bad and tough are two different things. I am tough on the racetrack, but I ain't got a bad bone in me. I don't want to see people get hurt."

The week of controversy and name-calling had its desired effect on the turnstiles for qualifying, which drew an unusually large crowd to see if anyone could beat Tim Richmond's track record of 167.078 miles per hour. In the field of fifty-six trying for the top twenty starting positions, Earnhardt was thirty-sixth in line and Elliott fiftieth.

Harry Gant held the top speed of 168.562 when Earnhardt scratched off to an almost equal mixture of boos and cheers. He bettered Gant's speed by more than a mile an hour, 169.733.

Many expected this to hold up until Elliott came up for his four laps, but, surprisingly, Bobby Allison, forty-eighth off the grid, pushed his Buick to 170.160 and broke up the anticipated showdown. Bodine was next. He spun out and was forced to wait another day.

Less than three minutes after Allison's record, Elliott was on the track to thunderous applause, foot-stomping and whistling. The crowd never sat down as he circled the track.

First lap: 171.712.

Second lap: 171.636.

Third lap: 170.713.

Fourth lap: 169.561.

Four-lap speed: 170.901, new record.

"Big time!" Elliott exclaimed as he wheeled into the garage area, his twenty-fifth career pole secure, in third place among active drivers behind Darrell Waltrip (forty-six) and Cale Yarborough (thirty-five).

He added, "You kind of judge your run by the crowd, and I just kept going and going. There was a lot of pressure, but everyone knew I was running good."

Elliott was right where he wanted to be, in the catbird's seat, for the third leg of the Winston Million. On the flip side, his only challenger, young Davey Allison, had had an atrocious qualifying run (167.456) and a disappointing sixteenth starting position.

"I don't understand it," Allison said. "Yesterday we practiced consistently at 171."

Ironically, the guy with the best chance to win it turned out to be Allison.

Earnhardt had woes from the first lap when a tire went flat. Between that faulty start and a mysterious pinhole in the cylinder, he became a non-factor early.

That left Elliott in a commanding position, and he had, by far, the strongest car, leading seven times for 181 laps before his engine locked up just past midpoint of the race. Ernie Elliott and the No. 9 crew brought him behind the pit wall, jacked up the car and quickly determined whether it could continue. A few feet away, behind the next pit, Earnhardt and No. 3 were on jacks. There wouldn't be any more showdowns on this day.

In order to lose as few points as possible from his Winston Cup lead, Earnhardt returned to finish twentieth in the race, three spots ahead of Elliott.

The attention turned to Davey Allison, now, by process of elimination, the strongest entry on the track. For him, at least, the Winston Million was still a viable target. His luck didn't last. His engine failed forty-nine laps from the finish, and he parked the Havoline Ford.

By now, the baton had been turned over to the equally young Kyle Petty in his Woods brothers Ford and, with Papa Richard riding shotgun, he cruised to an easy win and a ninety-thousand-dollar payday, his largest.

What started as a week of wrangling, acrimony and finger-pointing ended in an uneventful Coca-Cola 600.

All was peace and harmony, or was it?

Two days later NASCAR announced that Geoff Bodine was fined fifteen thousand dollars for getting into Earnhardt during the previous Saturday's Winn-Dixie 300 Grand National race. A radio station in Greensboro, North Carolina, led a campaign to raise the money for the fine, but the penalty was quickly rescinded by an appeals commission.

In all, during the week, NASCAR had levied forty thousand dollars in fines, six thousand of which was collectible.

The biggest laugh of all came in a press release from the CMS that read: "Dick Beaty, Winston Cup director, today cautioned the drivers about *wreckless* driving, telling them it would result in a back flag and cars being brought to the garage area and parked."

A Freudian slip, no doubt.

Lost in the week of controversy was the recognition of Elliott's amazing ability of not only winning races on the super speedways but also winning money even when he doesn't win races. At Charlotte he didn't win anything except the Goody's pole, yet he came away with $225,000, again displaying a mastery of hidden earnings.

For example, in the Winston he finished fourteenth and won $110,150 for leading the first two segments and the most laps. And it defies logic that he parlayed a twenty-third finish in the Coca-Cola 600 into a payoff of eighty-two thousand dollars when the winner, Kyle Petty, collected only ninety thousand. But Elliott led the most laps and the right laps, the big-money laps.

When the money was on the line, so was Bill Elliott.

Actually, CMS hadn't been that kind to him in the past.

As a youngster in a modified, he had always failed to qualify. In his pre-Harry Melling days, his highest finish was sixth, and in 1980 he wrecked on the sixth lap and was the first car in the garage.

The biggest disappointment had to be the Coca-Cola 600 of 1985, the year of the Winston Million. Having wrapped up Daytona and Talladega, he needed only the 600 for the million. He appeared a cinch after winning the pole at almost 165 miles an hour. The race, however, turned out to be a nightmare. First the radio went out, then a tire and eventually the brakes. He drove the wounded Thunderbird to an eighteenth-place finish.

On the positive side, he won the Miller High Life 500 in 1984, his third Winston Cup win and second on an oval track, and he had two second places in 1982 and another in the fall race of 1985. And Charlotte had helped during his struggling days. It was there that he made his connection with Melling.

"We've had mixed luck here," Elliott reflected in 1987. "We've won here, and we've broken here."

In retrospect, Charlotte, with its atmosphere and personality, was the logical place for the showdown between the two faces of racing, an infant sport, not yet forty years old, trying to find an identity and still ironing out wrinkles.

Is stock car racing deadly serious, or should it be lightly entertaining? Is it physical or finesse, or a little of each? Should it sell those who run up front or help the back pack and try for more parity? What can it do to meet changing demographics?

Charlotte provides the laboratory for all these questions.

Its atmosphere, its personality and its modus operandi contrast sharply with the other four traditional Southern tracks. The atmosphere at Daytona is speed and resort country; at Talladega, unleashed speed and backwoodsy, the Salt Flats of stock car racing; at Darlington, history and tradition; and at Atlanta, compactness and track visibility. The buzzwords at Charlotte are showmanship and luxury.

Three of the tracks — Daytona, Talladega and Darlington — are NASCAR owned and operated. The other two are independent. There's little doubt that Charlotte is the Cadillac of racetracks. With its balloons, clowns, stage and stunt shows, boxing and wrestling matches, skydivers, VIP boxes, condos and private club, it is the Disneyland of auto racing.

CEO and founder Bruton Smith and president-general manager H. A. (Humpy) Wheeler do things their way. When they see fit, they offer advice and a helping hand to make pack drivers more competitive. In the early 1970s, then-president Richard Howard brought Junior Johnson and Chevrolet back into the sport by sponsoring a car. Johnson had retired when the factories withdrew support in

1969. Howard also provided Wendell Scott, the sport's first black driver, with better equipment.

And, in those struggling days, Wheeler helped Bill Elliott with the acquisition of sponsor support. It was at Charlotte that Elliott was first introduced to Melling.

While acknowledging some of this, the self-appointed purists of racing delight in ridiculing what they consider the prostitution of The Race by CMS. It's a thinly veiled philosophic stance on which came first, Barney Oldfield or P. T. Barnum. Raised eyebrows are directed at Smith and Wheeler, a couple of soulmates of baseball's Bill Veeck and Charles O. Finley and unrepentant twitters of tradition.

Sometimes even the locals look askance and forget CMS's potential.

In the spring of 1987, when Charlotte landed a National Basketball Association franchise, it was described as "the first major league sport" between Washington and Atlanta. Admittedly, the NBA was a step up from the defunct World Football League, but, nonetheless, Smith and Wheeler did not take kindly to the slight.

There are only two major leagues in racing, Winston Cup and Indianapolis. And the biggies in Winston Cup are Daytona, Talladega, Atlanta, Darlington *and* Charlotte. Evidently, the purists, in knocking Charlotte and CMS's promotional strategies, overlooked the obvious promotional trends in professional basketball, baseball and football. And the not-so-obvious selling of college sports by administrators.

The NBA is choreographed for limited defense, high scores, pretty cheerleaders who don't cheer, slam-dunk contests and box office. Anyone who can deify a playground gimmick like the slam dunk can surely sell a lackluster eighty-two-game regular season in which players rest for the playoffs.

Long before racing's Smith and Bruton, baseball's Veeck and Finley shocked the establishment by playing midgets, outfitting teams in short pants and hokey softball uniforms, using clowns and mascots, laying the groundwork for such now-standard promotions as Bat Day, Glove Day, Pantyhose Day, Groupie-in-the-Third-Row Day, Little League Day, Fireworks Day and Old-Timers' Day. Baseball's biggest draw is not Darryl Strawberry, but a guy who dresses up like a chicken and clucks.

Until recent years, professional football was above admitting The Game needed promotional boosting. You can be that way when you've got the only Sunday war going and such military analysts as Howard, Dandy Don and Giff shooting it to fans, so to speak, foxhole by foxhole. As it turned out, the only war was in the TV booth. The network broke up their first team, and viewers were left with post pattern and draw plays.

Troubled in the ratings and at the gate, the NFL is discovering The Game is not enough anymore. Even Sunday wars get old.

Humpy Wheeler, the promotional wizard, picked up on that important sports trend long ago. There was method in his madcapness.

By incorporating entertainment and something for everyone into the racing experience, he broadened the base of spectators, for the first time appealing to the upper-middle class, women, children and even people not especially attached to racing. Then he went about cleaning out the ruffians and brawlers from the infield to make the surroundings more palatable. A major problem in the past had been that undesirables regarded admission as an open invitation to behave boorishly.

Unlike Daytona, Talladega and Darlington, Charlotte had seen more than its share of hard times. The track was practically born in Chapter 11 bankruptcy. It didn't help that Bruton Smith's original partner was Curtis Turner, a great race driver but a lousy businessman. Always described in news accounts as " a millionaire lumberman from Roanoke," Turner was more like a broke bloke who lived like a millionaire.

Like almost everyone else in racing, Richard Howard has a Turner story. He says, "I was standing in my front yard when this sleek, black limousine pulls up and parks. There's a chauffeur in the driver's seat and Curtis and this gorgeous blonde in the back.

"He gets out of the car, all slickered up, grabs me by the arm and leads me out of hearing range and says, 'Richard, I'm a little embarrassed. I'm going out to dinner and I went off and left my wallet at home. Could you let me hold fifty dollars until Saturday?'"

That is vintage Curtis Turner. Later, when he was in semiretirement and promoting a race at the Lakewood mile dirt track in Atlanta, he participated in one of the most amazing race results ever.

The crowd was small, the field irregular and organization nonexistent. Not intending to drive, Turner changed his mind, donned a helmet over his street clothes and borrowed a car.

He drove the race of his life, sliding deep into the corners, nudging others out of the way and intimidating everyone but the flagman.

He won easily.

When complimented on his victory, he pulled out a handkerchief, wiped the perspiration from his brow and replied, "Hell, I had to win. I didn't have the money to pay the purse."

Flamboyant and likable, he was a disaster for Smith and CMS. The track went under, and Smith with it. Later, Smith returned and acquired majority control, and, in 1976, the year Bill Elliott moved up to the Winston Cup tour, Smith made his wisest decision. He hired Humpy Wheeler.

So CMS has been through the hard times and the good times. Under Wheeler, it went from the old ways of doing things to the modern, making it an appropriate setting for the major confrontation, old versus new, that dominated the week from the Winston to the Coca-Cola 600, May 17-24, 1987.

Despite the sheet-metal rhubarb between Elliott and Earnhardt, the questions about aggressive driving weren't completely resolved and probably won't be. What distinguishes stock car racing from Indianapolis racing is contact. With their roll bars, fuel cell tanks and other protective parts, stocks are much safer than Indy cars and can stand some battering.

The question remains: What is hard racing, and what is unnecessary roughness? The half-mile Martinsville track is one gigantic traffic jam, some say a demolition derby.

Like boxing, which has never solved the boxer-versus-the-slugger riddle, it is doubtful if racing will ever resolve the age-old adversarial relationship between the rough-and-tumble and the smooth.

21

In Pursuit of the Points Championship

FOR JUNE AND MOST OF JULY, the Coors Ford team was up and down, erratic, and something seemed to be missing.

Following the Coca-Cola 600, Bill registered a couple of runner-up places, in the Budweiser 500 at Dover and the Miller 500 at Pocono, and a fifth at Riverside. There were more valve problems at Michigan, his patsy track, and he parked No. 9 after only 126 laps.

Everything, it seems, was going wrong. In the Firecracker 400, Bill was sitting in good position, despite the loss of power steering, with five laps to go and a caution about to end. Just as the green flag went down, he had a flat and was forced to follow the pace car to the pits. He finished twelfth, which enabled him to maintain his second place in the points standings and collect the hundred-thousand-dollar first-half award. Leader Earnhardt pocketed $150,000.

There was a smidgen of encouragement between the Firecracker and the Summer 500 at Pocono. Traveling to the West Coast short-track circuit, which was Ivan Baldwin home country, the Coors Ford beat the field in the Washington 500, but it was a race that doesn't count toward the Winston Cup.

At Pocono, overheating limited Bill to seventy-two laps and a thirty-second-place finish. And for the first time during the season, he fell lower than second in the points standings. As the Winston Cup trail led south, to the Talladega 500, Elliott was third, with Neil Bonnett having moved into the runner-up position.

That midsummer stretch after Charlotte belonged to Tim Richmond, who finally got into full-time action and won successive races at Pocono and Riverside; Earnhardt, who won at Michigan and in the second race at Pocono; and the Allisons, father and son. Davey set a Winston Cup rookie record by winning his second race at Dover, and Papa Bobby, nearing fifty, broke his season-long winless streak by slipping through the confusing finish of the Firecracker 400.

The Charlotte debacle was on everybody's mind as drivers moved into Delaware to begin their midsummer northern and western swing. Elliott said he did not expect to see the banging and bumping that started at Bristol and carried over to the Winston. The stiff fines levied at Charlotte tended to discourage such misbehavior.

If nothing else came from the 1987 campaign, Elliott once more proved that when it comes to qualifying he has no peer. He shattered the Budweiser 500 mark with a qualifying run of 145.056 miles an hour, breaking Ricky Rudd's old record by almost 5 miles an hour. It was his fifth pole of the season, and no other driver had more than one.

Elliott suspected the heat would be a factor in the race. "It's going to be tough like Charlotte last week," he said. "The heat is going to take a lot of cars out of the race. The main thing I want to do is finish the race. This is always a tough track to finish on."

After all the problems during the first half of the season, the Coors/Melling team had changed its game plan. If the wins came, fine, but now the strategy was to place high, chip away at Earnhardt's point lead and concentrate on the points championship. As Bill said, his main objective was to finish the race.

Two Thunderbirds flashed across the finish line ahead of the field. Elliott's was the second one. The first belonged to Davey Allison, setting a new rookie record with his second win. Davey led 149 of the last 152 laps and beat Elliott by almost seven seconds. Together, he and his father led 359 of the 500 laps. They were running one and two when Bobby's Buick went sour on the 349th lap.

It was becoming evident that Davey Allison, who'd spent a lot of time on the Winston Cup tracks in another racing division, wasn't an ordinary rookie.

Nor did he speak like a rookie. "They say your first victory is the hardest to get," he said. "It took me fourteen races to get it. And, after that, it took only two races for my second win. I hope that is sign of even better things to come."

At least one part of Elliott's plan was working. With Earnhardt finishing fourth, he picked up a few points and trailed by 209 after the Budweiser 500, still within striking distance. He said that on this day Davey and Bobby "were just too strong."

Enter the most emotional part of the Winston Cup season, the Miller 500 at Pocono. Significantly, Tim Richmond had decided to return for his first official Winston Cup race at the scene of two of his seven 1986 wins. He had taken part in the Winston, a sprint event, but this was to be his first real test of stamina following his serious illness.

In appreciation for his stand-in role, the Rick Hendrick team had prepared another Chevy for Benny Parsons, who in "retirement" was approaching a half-million dollars in earnings.

The pole went to Terry Labonte, and Parsons showed the "old man" could still do it by qualifying second, ahead of Richmond and Elliott. In a script worthy of Hollywood, Richmond, the sentimental favorite, beat Elliott to the checkers by seven car lengths to record a victory in his first race of 1987.

The usually flip Richmond, the circuit's swinging bachelor, was all choked up after the race. "I thought I could dry the tears on the cool-down lap," he said. "But as other drivers passed me and offered their congratulations, it just made me cry harder. I couldn't see the pit road for the tears so I decided to take another lap, but that didn't do any good either. I was still full of emotion in victory lane."

At first, Richmond tried to talk to TV analyst Ned Jarrett but couldn't. Jarrett told him to take it easy, and they'd do the interview later.

It was the most dramatic and emotional moment of the season.

The Coors team's decision to go for the points was a negative factor in the Pocono race. The tall gear set up to aid in durability was a handicap in the late five-lap shootout with Richmond. A lower gear would have given Bill the impetus to challenge.

Nonetheless, he gained 15 points on Earnhardt, who finished fifth, and was inching closer, trailing now by 194. The Elliotts had calculated that if they gained 15 points a race, they would have picked up 224 by the end of the season and be right on the verge of victory.

Moving to Riverside, a 2.66-mile road course with nine turns, the odds favored one of the younger drivers. Elliott, Richmond and Rudd had won their first Winston Cup races there. Road courses had never appealed to Earnhardt, so it was logical to assume Bill would gain more points in California.

Bobby Allison explained the young driver's advantage, saying, "Young drivers don't have twenty years of bad habits to break. That's why they do better on road courses." Rudd added, "The new tire compounds favor aggressive drivers, those who throw their cars around."

That description seemed to fit Richmond. At least, Earnhardt thought so. He said, "You've got to be cautious around Richmond. He's a little wild. With all the stuff that's gone on recently, who can afford to get in trouble? We can't; he can."

Earnhardt was upset. "Richmond knocked me down the straight-away and cut me off twice in the corners at Pocono," he told racing writer Ray Cooper of *The Greensboro* [North Carolina] *Daily News*. "I can't afford to get in trouble. I've got to mash the brakes, but it's sort of like driving with your hands tied.

"The way we're having to race now, we're going to start losing fans because it won't be as exciting."

If Richmond was aware of Earnhardt's complaints, it didn't bother him. He pulled off a second straight miracle at Riverside, where he finished ahead of Rudd, Bonnett, Labonte and Elliott, in that order. Earnhardt was seventh and lost nine more points to the Coors driver. The deficit was now 185.

This time the irrepressible Richmond was more composed in his interview with Jarrett.

"How about that, Ned?" he said. "I want to dedicate this race to my dad, for Father's Day. I don't think I'm a father, so I'm going to dedicate this to him, and all the dads out there. If it wasn't for the dads . . . I guess you'd have to include the moms to go along with them . . . . "

Obviously, Richmond was in a grateful mood.

In the past, when things were not going right, Elliott could always bank on finding the cure at Michigan, where he'd won four straight and five of the last six races. But the Miller American 400 on June 28 was an exception.

He qualified third behind pole-sitter Rusty Wallace and Derrike Cope, and things went downhill from there. For the fourth time during the season, there was a serious malfunction in the valve or the valve spring, and he was forced to the garage after completing only 126 of the 200 laps, his worst finish of the year, thirty-fourth, dealing a serious blow to his chances at the driver's title.

Ironically, the man who broke his Michigan streak was Earnhardt, who'd never won there before.

By edging Davey Allison at the finish, Earnhardt assured himself of another million-dollar year. All he had to do was start the remaining races on the Winston Cup schedule. He also gained 129 points over Elliott and stretched his lead to 314, making it extremely difficult for the Coors team to make up that deficit in the fifteen remaining races.

It was a crucial reversal for the Elliotts. The one consolation was their money winnings. With $698,550, they were well on their way to their third straight million-dollar year.

For Elliott, things were really going bad if he didn't win a pole at Daytona, and that's what happened in early July when he returned for the Firecracker 400. He didn't sit on the pole at Daytona for the first time in four races. That honor went to Davey Allison who, under the new carburetor restrictions for Daytona and Talladega, qualified at 198.085 miles an hour. Elliott was a tad off at 198.050, and Ken Schrader, who did so well during Daytona 500 week, gave Thunderbirds the top three positions.

What the new rule did, in effect, was bring Elliott down to the rest of the field. It assured cars running in clusters, which is not Elliott's style.

Elliott had a dual purpose in the Firecracker.

First, of course, he wanted to win the race. That would have been ideal. But there was a more lucrative prize at stake. Following the Firecracker, the points leader at the midway stage of the season would receive $150,000 and the second-place driver $100,000.

Elliott was second by a mere twenty-five points over Neil Bonnett. So he had to make sure he finished ahead of Bonnett or high enough not to lose more than twenty or so points. He calculated that Bonnett usually ran fourth or fifth, so Elliott's work was cut out for him.

In store for the holiday crowd was one of the most confusing finishes in the history of Daytona, dating back to 1959 when Bill France, Sr., stood at the finish line and called the wrong winner. During the winding-down stages of the race, it appeared that veteran Dave Marcis, known more for his appetite than his familiarity with the winner's circle, would win his first race since a Richmond triumph in 1982. He was running strong at the front until Rick Wilson lost it and wrecked with nine laps to go, bringing out the yellow flag.

Most of the drivers pitted for fresh tires, and Bobby Allison, running at the tail of the lead lap, took on four. When they came around for the restart, Elliott was right there, near the front, ready for the shootout with Marcis, Schrader, Buddy Baker, Waltrip and six others.

But, suddenly, as the pace car rolled off the field, Elliott followed it to the pits. He had detected a tire going down. It must be noted that at the time, Bonnett, his rival for a hundred grand, was two laps down.

When the green went down, Marcis and Schrader jumped out front again. No one noticed Bobby Allison coming up through traffic.

As they barreled around the fourth turn on the last lap, a three-car accident involving Marcis, Gant and Schrader, who flipped several times and slid on his top, left the finish in chaos. Allison crossed the finish line ahead of Baker, but everyone, including the radio network guys and scoreboard keepers, thought he was a lap down. They called Baker the winner. Marcis was knocked across the start-finish line.

Who won?

NASCAR said Allison had taken the lead two laps earlier and was the winner, followed by Baker, Marcis, Waltrip, Morgan Shepherd,

Earnhardt and Schrader. Hard-luck Gant was ninth, behind Rusty Wallace. Elliott's Ford was the twelfth car in the lead lap, two laps ahead of Bonnett.

In retrospect, Elliott's priority was to beat Bonnett and win the $100,000, considerably more than the race payoff of $57,375. By ducking into the pits for a fresh tire, he nailed down the points money, giving him $116,900 for the day. If he had lost the points duel to Bonnett and won the race, he would have been $59,525 poorer.

Again, Elliott proved that no one figures the "hidden money" better than the country boy from Dawsonville. Through the Firecracker, he'd banked $815,450 on only one win; Earnhardt, on the other hand, had won $782,890 on seven victories.

There was a touch of irony in Bobby Allison's Daytona victory, for it was he and his airborne crash in the Winston 500 that prompted the speed restrictions at the two tracks. Nonetheless, it was a victory he needed for bragging rights around the dinner table with son Davey.

While Daytona had its consolation, the Summer 500 at Pocono two weeks later was frustrating for Elliott and the Coors team. After only seventy-five laps, twenty-six of which he led, he parked the T-Bird because of overheating and had to be content with thirty-second.

Since Earnhardt, rooting out young Alan Kulwicki at the finish, swept his eighth win in seventeen races, Elliott's dream of winning the points race ended for all practical purposes. He fell to third behind Bonnett.

"It just broke," said a disappointed Elliott. "The car was handling super, and it was hooked up. When we were there, we were there, but if you can't finish, you sure can't win. When you start running into motor problems, it seems like it takes forever to overcome them.

"It's out of my hands. I just drive the car."

A perplexed Ernie Elliott surmised that a rock might have been responsible for the front-end damage.

22

Reverend Bill, Burial Grounds, And a Return to Victory Lane

B IG, BURLY, WITH STOOPED SHOULDERS, Bill Baird jab-
bed at the air with his right hand as he spoke. He was talking
about how Solomon was the wisest of men. Yet he had sinned against
God. All of us are weak, and none of us are exempt, he said.

There is no one else quite like Bill Baird. He preaches, yet he is not
a preacher. He is a Southern Baptist psychology major. He played
football at little Guilford College in North Carolina, and he had a
cup of coffee with the Minnesota Vikings of the NFL. He doesn't
claim to be a saint; in fact, he says he's "marginal," but he consented
to serve as chaplain to the Winston Cup drivers and try to seek the
paths of righteousness with them. His sermons, he says, are just like
everyone else's — average.

Richard Petty, Cale Yarborough and Benny Parsons, impressed by
his counseling with the Fellowship of Christian Athletes, ten years
ago convinced him to hit not the sawdust but the grease-pit trail. He
operates on a year-to-year contract paid by a private fund supported
by drivers, sponsors and collections.

There are no glass cathedrals. On race day, when cars are rolled
out and the stalls cleared, he chooses a place in the garage and sets
up his church: a battered and chipped speaker's stand, a cardboard
box for offerings and a huge banner reading:
Let's Talk About Jesus
Worship Service, 10:30 A.M.
Jesus said, "I am the Way, the Truth and the Life."

On this day, July 26, 1987, prior to the Talladega 500, his congregation included drivers, mechanics, pit crewmen, wives, children and those connected with racing, about a hundred in all. Among the worshippers were Petty, Parsons, Yarborough, Lake Speed, Ernie and Dan Elliott and Bill's wife, Martha. Others follow their own dictates. Bobby and Davey Allison always attend Mass and receive Communion on the morning of a race. When Bobby crashed on the same track in the Winston 500, Davey said, "I'm just thankful the Lord let him stay with us."

Baird led the group in prayer and meditation, which won't put horsepower in a reluctant engine but won't hurt if you crash at two hundred miles an hour. You wonder if anyone prayed the previous day prior to the ARCA Permatex 500 when twenty-six-year-old Tracy Read of Charlotte crashed and died. His last words, reported in a press release, were, "You're going slower, you're a little more comfortable." But not necessarily safer. Primarily a pit worker for Yarborough, Read, like most young men at the track, had a racing career in mind.

To survive in racing, a driver must have a strong feeling of indestructibility carefully diluted by a healthy dose of fatalism. Perhaps old-time Indy winner Bob Sweikert said it best.

"I know so many people who hate to get up in the morning because they detest their jobs and their lives," he said. "I've loved every minute of racing, every aspect of my life, and if I die tomorrow, it won't change anything. I would have made the right choice."

Soon thereafter Sweikert was killed in a track crash.

Life goes on.

Baird didn't mention the Read tragedy. That is sort of an unwritten rule around racetracks. Instead, he talked about Solomon and sinning and human frailty. Though he preaches on Sundays, Baird spends the bulk of his time counseling.

"Drivers have the same problems as everyone else," he said. "They talk about money, families and children. There's a lot of stress in this business. I don't put myself up as any example. I tell them, 'Don't look at me,' and I point them toward God."

Baird knows the Elliotts well.

"They're fine people," he says. "Dan and Ernie are always there at the services, and Ernie is on our board of directors. When their families are here, they always attend. George and Mildred I consider the salt of the earth. The sport needs more people like the Elliotts.

"They invited me down to the First Baptist Church in Dawsonville for a revival, and I went there and preached a week. Ernie and Dan and Sheila and all, I stayed at their home and, really, it was an enjoyable visit."

As with much of his life, Bill Elliott keeps his religious orientation to himself. His prerace time is spent checking and rechecking his car and going over his game plan in the seclusion of the transport trailer. Before the Talladega 500, he made a personnel change and was back in charge of his own suspension system.

No one knew exactly what the situation was with Ivan Baldwin, the Californian who'd been hired to relieve Bill of the chassis work. There was talk that there was conflict between him and Ernie Elliott. Another report had it that the duties had been split and Baldwin would handle preparations for short tracks, his specialty, and Ernie for the super speedways. Then it was said that Bill and Ivan had rented one of George Elliott's properties in Dahlonega, an old skating rink, and were planning to build cars for other drivers.

For Bill, the whole chassis situation had been a dilemma. He needed someone to provide relief from a time-consuming chore, yet, at the same time, he was most comfortable when he was handling his own setting up, a practice some considered one of the "Elliott secrets."

Says George Elliott, "I've always said if you listen, the car talks to you. No one tells better what it wants than the driver. If the driver can translate that into the chassis set-up, that's a big advantage. There are lots of symptoms to different ailments. It's a fine line. In the past, Bill wouldn't carry the TV camera simply because it upset the delicate balance of the car weight.

"The trick is in narrowing the symptoms to two. Then you've got a fifty-fifty chance of finding the solution instead of a ten-ninety chance. Next you fix or adjust the easiest of the two that can be handled in a race. It's a game of odds, and no two race cars are the same."

Whatever the combination, Bill had it for the Talladega 500 qualifying. Sitting on the pole for a record sixth straight time at the track, his speed of 203.827 miles an hour, due to new carburetor restrictions, seemed a snail's pace compared to his track record of 212.809 set in the May Winston 500.

The surprise was that Dale Earnhardt and not Davey Allison, winner of the Winston 500, was on his outside. Qualifying earlier and under cooler conditions, Earnhardt had a 203.459 clocking.

The Elliotts were pleased to be on the pole, but not with the speed.

"NASCAR is trying to see how slow the cars can run," George Elliott speculated. "If they get any slower, I'm going to grab a helmet and start driving myself."

Still, it was a welcome change from Martinsville, where Elliott had started thirty-first and last, his first provisional start.

"I went from last last week to first this week, " he said. "Last week some of our crew members thought we were beat before we started.

At least this week we won't have that problem. On the other hand, qualifying is one lap and the race is 188. Our success depends on how well we get the car set up.

"If Earnhardt gets his car working good and is running out front toward the end, he'll be one of the cars to beat."

On July 26, 1987, by 10:45 A.M., Bill Baird had removed his banner, packed up his podium and dismantled his portable church. The ninety-five degree Alabama heat was oppressive, and many of the drivers gathered in an air-conditioned infield building to cool off before donning their cool suits.

The atmosphere had changed since the Winston 500. There wasn't much talk about the Earnhardt menace. Rivals felt that NASCAR, because of the uproar at Charlotte, was scrutinizing Earnhardt, and, besides, his huge point margin didn't make winning critical for him. Having been eliminated from Winston Million consideration, both Elliott and Davey Allison were now taking it one race at a time, hoping for the best possible finish.

Elliott knew he could run at the front. What was beginning to become doubtful was whether he could be running at the finish.

Sixteen races had been run and Earnhardt had won eight, Davey Allison and Richmond two apiece, Elliott, Bobby Allison, Kyle Petty and Ricky Rudd one each — eleven General Motors cars, five Thunderbirds. Ford, which won only five races in 1986 after sweeping fourteen in the previous year, was hanging in there, thanks to the emergence of Allison.

Once the Winston 500 began, Elliott and Allison quickly jumped to the front. Elliott led the first six laps. Then they swapped the front position for thirty-three laps, at which point Dave Marcis and Earnhardt assumed the lead until Allison retook it on lap number forty-one. Elliott, concentrating on finishing, dropped back and ran with the lead pack until the 110th turn of the track, when he shot to the front again. After ten laps, he dropped back to bide his time until he encountered a problem some sixty laps from the finish.

He thought he had a broken axle. Ironically, so did Earnhardt, and they both pitted under a caution. From the descriptions given over the radios, both crews were convinced that they had serious troubles.

"It felt just like I had a broken axle," Elliott said. "The rear of the car started jumping up and down and only one tire was spinning. But the problem just disappeared after they took the axles out and looked at them."

Earnhardt was just as baffled. "The car felt like it had a broken axle, but it must have been something else," he said. "It was just fine at the end."

Due to the time spent in the pits, Elliott fell out of the top ten and began to work his way through the field again. Finally, with only thirty-seven laps remaining in the race, he made it. An outstanding pit stop under caution, in which Ernie changed only two tires while others were taking on four, was a major factor.

That efficiency made up for an earlier pit stop, when there was some confusion and lost time.

But Elliott himself had called the shot on tire wear. At the slower speed, he was getting more mileage out of tires, and he felt changing only two was not that big a gamble. Ernie had used that tactic at Martinsville to enable the No. 9 Thunderbird to go from thirty-first to fifth during the Sovran Bank 500.

Once back on the track, however, Elliott had to fend off Davey Allison and was fortunate Allison had to struggle to get back in line with a tight leading pack to be in position to challenge. Keeping his eye on the rearview mirror, Elliott did a superb job of working the traffic behind him, holding his position by moving back and forth. Allison said he had wanted to get to second earlier, but no one would work with him in the draft and he had to do it on his own.

He said, "It's the hardest I've ever worked for a position. There were just too many cars in the lead draft."

That's the way it finished, with Elliott and Allison one and two. For his second major win of the season, recorded at 171.292 miles an hour, the Georgia redhead banked $70,920.

The Talladega 500 had several Winston Cup ramifications. For one, it put Earnhardt, who finished third, over the million-dollar mark earlier in the season than anyone in history. Elliott, who hiked his earnings to $897,445, now had only to run out the season to hit the million plateau for the third year in a row. There was also a change in the point standings.

Neil Bonnett, who wrecked and finished thirty-second, fell to fourth, and Elliott regained his runner-up place, 430 points behind Earnhardt. Terry Labonte, with a sixth place at Talladega, moved into third.

Both Earnhardt and Elliott continued to add to their vast earnings. By winning $35,050 at Talladega, Earnhardt hiked his lifetime winnings to $6,004,331 to trail only Waltrip, Bobby Allison and Richard Petty in racing moneys. And Elliott, close behind at $5,940,565, stood in position to equal or surpass Earnhardt by the end of the season.

When Elliott reached his million, it marked the seventh time a Winston Cup driver has won that much in a single season. No other motor-racing single-sanctioning series has recorded a driver's winning as much as a million dollars during a single campaign.

There is always relief when the two obligatory visits are made to Talladega, the world's fastest stock car racing track, said to be built on the ancient burial grounds of the Upper Creek, or "Red Sticks,"

Indians. Legend has it that there is a curse on those who would defile their happy hunting grounds. Tracy Read was the last of three drivers to die there in the last twelve years. North Carolinian Larry Smith was killed at Talladega in 1973 when the G-forces snapped his neck; big, amiable Tiny Lund, who once saved Marvin Panch from a flaming wreck at Daytona, crashed and died two years later.

Weird things happen at Talladega.

In that same 1973 race, Bobby Isaac, who had set a world closed-course speed record with 201.104 miles an hour during a special event at Talladega, was running fourth in the Winston 500 when he inexplicably pulled into the pits, exited the car and departed the premises.

Later he said, "Something inside me kept telling me to come in. When that happens, it's time to hang 'em up."

That was August 14, 1973. Four years later, to the day, Isaac, winner of thirty-seven NASCAR races, collapsed and died of an apparent heart attack during a Sportsman race at Hickory, North Carolina.

For Elliott in 1987, the Talladega was a moment for revitalization, but the problems and inconsistency returned in the next race at the Watkins Glen road course, where he started ninth and finished twenty-eighth due to rear-end problems.

The Budweiser on the Glen, a ninety-lap race, was won by Rusty Wallace, in a Pontiac, his first success of the season, and he earned it the hard way, by making a pit stop for fuel at the start of the last lap. Fortunately for Wallace, he had a twenty-two-second lead on Terry Labonte when his red warning light came on.

He gave out of gas just as he rolled to his pit, and there were some anxious moments when his engine almost didn't refire.

But, as Elliott has always said, "When it's your day, it's your day," and the Watkins Glen race, run on a Monday because of a rain postponement, was Wallace's day.

23

Michigan International Speedway: Elliott's Home Away from Home

IN MODERN STOCK CAR RACING, the Golden Rule is slightly revised. The track's guideline goes: Do unto others and yourself what you'd like, or before they do unto you, but *never, never* embarrass your owner or sponsor. The name of the game is making the money men look good, preferably in the winner's circle, but certainly among the front-runners. If you can make them look good before their friends and neighbors and business associates, all the better.

No one does a better job of making a sponsor look good close to home than Bill Elliott, who has virtually monopolized the Michigan International Speedway, located just twenty miles from car owner Harry Melling's home and industrial empire, not to mention its being the home track of the Detroit automakers. Time and again, Elliott has provided Melling with bragging rights and given Ford a showcase for its Thunderbird line.

Needless to say, because of Melling's business interests, the lanky redhead is extremely popular in the Brooklyn, Michigan, area, where fans have adopted him, drawl and all, as one of their own, prompting him to call MIS his second home. He is to Brooklyn, Michigan, what the Dodgers were to the other Brooklyn.

From 1982, when Melling bought the team, through the 1987 season, Elliott won six of the twelve Michigan races run. Amazingly, those six came in the last eight races of that period, and it would have been seven if he hadn't given out of gas within sight of the checkers in 1984. Additionally, he had five inside poles, two outside starts and three from the second row. That's as close as a driver can come to complete domination.

The spring of 1987 was not one of those joyous visits to Michigan. Nothing, it seems, went right. Elliott qualified third, but in the race itself a broken valve spring relegated him to a thirty-fourth-place finish and snapped a string of four straight wins at MIS.

When the Winston Cup drivers returned for the Champion Spark Plug 500 on August 16 and qualifying on the day before, fans were treated to a preview of stock car racing's future. Young Davey Allison, already winner of two races and a rookie who took things in stride like a veteran, won the pole with a run of 170.705 miles an hour, and Alan Kulwicki, the 1986 Rookie of the Year, beat out Elliott for the outside. It was Allison's third start on the point.

At 169.932, Elliott was almost a mile an hour off the pace, and for first time in a few years, he found himself the underdog at Michigan. Allison, who had qualified in racing setup, looked extremely strong.

The 1987 Champion 400 was one of those should-have and could-have races.

Richard Petty, who hadn't won since the Firecracker of 1984, could have won but didn't when he pitted for tires with eleven laps to go and then wrecked on the final go-around. He finished eleventh.

Rusty Wallace, coming off his win at Watkins Glen, could have won but didn't. He took the lead after Petty made his pit stop, but with five laps remaining he hit the wall on the fourth turn, giving up the lead to Earnhardt, winner of the spring race.

"This is a big disappointment to me," said Wallace. "I felt I had a good chance to win the race."

Meanwhile, in his own words, Elliott kept digging and digging. It had not been one of his dominating afternoons. In fact, he had led only once, from laps 138 to 150 of the 200-lap race.

"With thirty laps to go, I was thinking we were pretty much in a no-win situation," he said. "It just shows that if you get a little luck and keep driving, driving, you can find yourself in a position to win."

With thirty laps to go, Elliott was in eighth place, 1.2 seconds behind leader Petty. Then all the leaders started falling out, and the Georgia redhead found himself running behind Earnhardt. It was a dream position for him. He was second on his favorite track, a layout wide enough for passing without interference, and he felt he could outgun Earnhardt.

With two laps to go, just before Elliott made his move, Earnhardt dropped down to the apron of the track, a maneuver used to conserve fuel. Later he indicated that he also had a tire going down.

"When he took the low groove, I stayed on the throttle," said Elliott. "His car was a little looser than mine at the end. I don't think I needed a mistake to beat him, though. If it's like they say that

Earnhardt had a flat tire on the last lap, then it never hurts to be good here at MIS. And sometimes I'd rather be lucky than good."

Whatever, good or lucky, Earnhardt problems or not, Elliott swept by to win over the Wrangler Chevrolet driver by .76 of a second, at a winning speed of 138.648, and collect a first-place purse of $52,875. It was his third Winston Cup win of the season, matching the record of 1984, his best year other than the million-dollar 1985 season.

Earnhardt's explanation: "I couldn't hold off Elliott because I was running out of gas. That's why I was running the low line. The car was running good all day."

Finishing behind Earnhardt, in order, were Morgan Shepherd, Wallace and pole-sitter Davey Allison. The first ten finishers were all on the lead lap.

For Elliott, the race proved one thing. Sometimes you don't have to overwhelm everyone to win a race. He was just stroking it, racing to finish, going for the points, when his perseverance was rewarded.

"The way this race went, it just blew me away," he said. "I just kept digging, kept working my way to the front and hanging in there. I ain't believing this victory."

The win marked Elliott's twentieth Winston Cup victory and, significantly enough, six, or almost a third, had come at the Michigan International Speedway, where Harry Melling had bragging rights.

At that point in his career, in addition to the Michigan success, his wins had come as follows: Daytona, Atlanta, Darlington, Talladega and Pocono, two each; Riverside, Charlotte, Rockingham and Dover, one each. It's true his Winston Cup career was in its twelfth year, but, for all intents and purposes, it had begun in 1984, when he became competitive.

After Michigan, the Winston Series moved on to the .533-mile track at Bristol for the Busch 500. In the spring, Elliott had had his best finish at Bristol, a fourth in the Valleydale 500, but historically the compact layout had never been kind to him.

His main objective at Bristol was to keep Earnhardt within range in the points race. Dogged by tire problems, Bill qualified fifteenth and ran ninth in the race. He was not a factor as Earnhardt, on a short-track roll, swept to his fifth straight victory on raceways of less than a mile.

When the points had been awarded, Earnhardt led Elliott by 545.

More than battling Earnhardt, Elliott was trying to hold off Terry Labonte, Rusty Wallace and Neil Bonnett for the runner-up position, which pays handsomely at the end of the season.

24

The September Jinx And Circling the Wagons

B Y LABOR DAY and the Southern 500, the Winston Million had become a pipe dream.

The first three of the Big Four had been won by three different drivers — Bill Elliott, Davey Allison and Kyle Petty — and RJR safely tucked away its million for another year. What remained was the $100,000 consolation bonus for a driver who could win two of the four races. That added some suspense to the 1987 Southern 500.

Of the three Ford drivers, Elliott had to be the favorite. He had won twice at Darlington, both in 1985, while Allison and Petty, both twenty-six, had never scratched on the "Track Too Tough to Tame." But, then, Darlington races seldom follow expected patterns.

In the spring TranSouth 500, Elliott had had the race in his back pocket but gave out of gas two hundred yards from the finish line, allowing Dale Earnhardt to snake through to his third win of the season. Going into the TranSouth, Bill trailed Earnhardt by only sixty-one points in the points race, and a success there would have made all the difference to his overall strategy, but it was not to be. Now, as they returned to Darlington, he trailed by 545 points and, for all intents and purposes, was out of contention. The spread was the largest since Richard Petty led Dave Marcis by 573 points after twenty races in 1975.

Although having what, for him, was considered a down year, Elliott was virtually even with Earnhardt on the super speedways. He had three wins there (Daytona, Talladega and Michigan) to

Earnhardt's four (Rockingham, Darlington, Michigan and Pocono). The difference was on the short tracks, where Elliott had improved, but the Wrangler driver was five-for-five.

"You can't win the Winston Cup without strong showings on the short tracks," Elliott said. "We put a lot of effort into improving our short-track program this year. The results show it. And if Earnhardt weren't having such a phenomenal year, that improvement in our program would have us neck-and-neck with him for the title."

Up to the Southern 500, the twentieth event on the schedule, it had been virtually a three-car season, Earnhardt's Chevy and Elliott's and Davey Allison's Fords. Wrangler had nine wins, Coors/ Melling three and Havoline two. At midseason, there was a brief interruption when Tim Richmond, 1986's leading winner, returned from his serious illness to win back-to-back races at Pocono and Riverside, but Richmond soon had a relapse and faded, being forced to withdraw at Darlington. The single-race winners, to that point, were Petty, Rusty Wallace, Ricky Rudd and Bobby Allison.

Otherwise, it was a most uncommon year on the Winston Cup trail. Missing from victory lane were such familiar names as Darrell Waltrip, Geoff Bodine, Cale Yarborough and Neil Bonnett, all having atrocious seasons in comparison to their past records. In terms of points and money, Junior Johnson's new driver, Terry Labonte, was having a commendable year, but, surprisingly, he hadn't caught a checkered flag. And if Skoal Bandit driver Harry Gant didn't have bad luck, he had no luck at all.

Labor Day weekend is an important race date on the Winston Cup calendar, but it is more than that. It is the juncture of the year when race teams begin to assess and reevaluate their personnel and equipment, and sponsors get very concerned if they're not doing well. The corporations want their logos in victory lane and on national TV, and prolonged absences don't make their hearts grow fonder.

One change had already been announced. After four years, Rudd decided that he would leave the Bud Moore/Motorcraft team and shop for a more competitive option. The Rick Hendrick team disclosed that Richmond would be out indefinitely and that Ken Schrader would replace him in 1988. It was also hinted that Benny Parsons would not return to the Hendrick group.

The Coors/Melling team was in a state of flux. There were whispers that the Ivan Baldwin experiment — the fractured setup whereby Baldwin handled the short tracks and Ernie Elliott the long — wasn't working out. By strange arrangement, Ernie stayed away from the short tracks and Baldwin from the super speedways. And yet, in name, Ernie Elliott was the crew chief. The Elliotts' greatest success had come as a brother act, and some said that was now being threatened by outside voices.

For the Southern 500, at least, it would be like old times. Ernie was fine-tuning the engine, and Bill was doing what he had preferred to do in the past, setting up his own car.

Based on the record, six poles to that point of the season and twenty-five in the last three years, no one prepares for qualifying better than the Elliott brothers, Bill, Ernie and Dan. They work at it; they take it seriously.

"Bill's good at his own chassis," says Glen Wood, senior member of the Wood brothers. "He's one of the few that gets out and does that himself. When he changes the spring, he knows what he did. When he changes that screwjack on that spring during a race, he would know more about what that does than a lot of the drivers. A lot of the drivers are very, very uneducated about what all that does."

On Thursday, September 4, the Elliott stall in the garage was a beehive of activity before the 3 P.M. qualifying sessions.

The prequalifying action went something like this:

12:45 P.M. — Bill takes the No. 9 Thunderbird onto the track, runs a few laps and comes back in.

1:05 — Most of the front-running cars return to the track and test against each other. Before Bill goes out, he and Ernie tighten rear lug nuts on wheels.

1:08 — Dale Earnhardt strolls out of transport truck, munching a sandwich, slips through window of Wrangler No. 3 and takes a spin on the track.

1:09 — Bill returns from track, car goes up on jacks and he and Ernie check things on right side of engine, with hood up.

1:11 — Elliott tries out changes on track for two laps, then returns.

1:15 — Back out for another run.

1:17 — Returns to garage. Hood raised, setup changed, Bill stays in car while crew changes all four tires, right side first, then left side.

1:24 — New tires tested on track.

1:28 — Back in garage, hood raised, Bill once more doesn't leave driver's seat, Ernie works on engine, car jacked up again and tires changed.

1:40 — Back for another test on track.

1:44 — Back in garage, Ernie goes over to window and has a conference with Bill, still in car. Hood raised and engine checked.

1:52 — Last trial run on track, Bill gets out of car, now satisfied for qualifying, about an hour away. A stall away, Earnhardt also seems satisfied and gets out of car, returning to truck.

If it isn't done by now, it's too late.

As has been the case all season, most of the prerace attention is on Earnhardt and Elliott.

Buck Baker, one of the early pioneers in NASCAR racing and father of current driver Buddy Baker, talked about that situation as he visited in the garage area.

"You take Bill Elliott and Dale Earnhardt out of racing right now," he said, "and you'd cut the field and the grandstand in half. They are the two drivers who maintain the interest in the sport.

"Bill has made more of an impact because of his style and his character than because of the Ford he drives. His upbringing has a lot to do with it. It's kind of like writing a book on the history of NASCAR. The guy is nice and presents himself well, drives real hard, and he's a good, hard worker and down-to-earth, and I think people like to see that. That's what made NASCAR. And him being from Georgia and the Carolinas, that's where it originally started.

"Earnhardt has done as well with a different philosophy. He's a little more aggressive, but, on the other hand, that's the same environment he was brought up in. His dad raced, and Earnhardt learned a lot of his tactics from him on the short track around Concord.

"I don't see that much wrong, really, with Earnhardt's style of driving. Whenever you drive as hard as he does, you just get yourself in a tight spot once in a while. It's kinda like dancing. If you dance too fast, you kinda get out of step once in a while. I don't think Earnhardt does anything intentionally; he just enjoys a good tight, hard race."

Thought he's been retired for years, Buck Baker remains close to racing. He runs a drivers' school at Rockingham, teaching young drivers the rudiments of racing.

"They come from all over the world to learn to race," he said. "We're turning people away. At first, I had the school at the Atlanta International Raceway, and on the second day those guys would be running 160 miles an hour. That was too fast. So I switched to Rockingham, a mile track, so they couldn't run that fast.

"I've got ten cars in the school that I could put on the Winston Cup circuit right now."

Shortly before three o'clock, the cars were lined up for qualifying over the 1.366-mile track, and, as usual at Darlington, officials were hopeful of beating the low-hanging rain clouds.

Crowd reaction to the drivers was predictable. Darrell Waltrip got a modified Bronx cheer, a reminder that fans still recalled his earlier, cocky years, though the hooting is now more habit than genuine feeling. Earnhardt's arrival brought a mixture of cheers and catcalls, a reminder that Elliott fans hadn't forgiven him for Charlotte. Davey Allison got a good hand and the reception for Elliott was thunderous applause, whistling and cheering.

Fast times during practice had been turned in by Davey Allison, Elliott and Labonte, and it figured that one of them would sit on the pole, which, in the spring, had surprisingly gone to Kenny Schrader.

Labonte, first off the grid among the leaders, held true to form. His 156.313 miles an hour run in the Johnson Chevrolet led the field until Elliott scratched off. The Georgia boy ran just a little faster, 156.487, and appeared to have the pole clinched as one by one, the others failed to match the speed. "Bad Boy" Dale Earnhardt said he was not unhappy with his 154.953.

"That's race pace," he said. "I can run five hundred miles at that speed."

After making his run, Elliott adjourned to the back of the Coors/ Melling transport where he sweated out the field. His challenger for the Winston Hundred Thousand, Kyle Petty, had his problems.

Glen Wood explained, "Kyle's been pushing ever since he's been down here and they did something to his car, and whatever they did made it a little too loose. Here they've got only one lap for qualifying, and you've got to make the best of that one lap."

The other challenger for the Winston bonus, Davey Allison, was the last driver to qualify, and the screaming of the public address announcer told the crowd that he had won the pole. His 157.232 run was well below Tim Richmond's record of 158.489 but almost a mile an hour better than Elliott's time. He replaced Bill on the inside and bumped Labonte from the front row.

"I thought Bill's speed would hold up," said a surprised Allison. "I didn't even think I could beat Terry's time."

However, Elliott had suspected his time might not hold up.

"Frankly, it [the car] ran a little quicker than I thought it would," he said. "The lap was about what we practiced."

Lake Speed and Earnhardt rounded out the top five.

Following the Darlington 500 qualifying, Ernie and Dan Elliott packed up and returned to their motel, but Bill and the drivers stuck around to qualify their Grand National cars for Saturday's Gatorade 200. For Elliott, that event marked a significant change. For the first time since he had driven some else's Chevrolet in 1979, he would be in a GM car, a V-6 Buick prepared and owned by Butch Stevens, a member of his crew.

It was a most uncommon sight, Elliott in a GM product, and a most uncommon speed for him, 152.097, for a most uncommon starting position, twelfth.

Grand National qualifying just beat the monsoon season at Darlington. Persistent rains on Friday and Saturday scrapped the rest of qualifying, practice and the Gatorade 200. And up to noon on Sunday, there was some doubt that the Southern 500 would be completed on schedule.

As usual, Elliott approached Darlington with a healthy dose of respect. "A lot of people tell me Darlington owes me a victory because of the last two races and the way I lost them," he said. "I'm not sure I agree with those people, but if this old track is honoring IOUs, I'll be happy to cash one in during the Southern 500.

"But, I might not have any IOUs from this old place. I might have used up what I would have gotten when I was lucky enough to win the Southern 500 in 1985 and cash that check for the Winston Million at the same time.

"That victory remains one of the brightest lights in my career. To win the Southern 500 is a goal of every driver. But to win it and also win the Winston Million at the same time was very, very special.

"A lot of people ask me if I remember much about that race. The answer is yes, I do. I remember that we didn't have the best car that day and didn't dominate the race.

"Instead, it was like we were supposed to win it. We were about a fourth- or a fifth-place car, but when it came down to the end, we won the race. And most of all, I remember the victory ride around the track with Ned Jarrett and the cheers of that huge crowd.

"It made chill bumps stand up on my arms and neck at the time, and when I think about it, it still does.

"What a difference a year made. Last year, when the Southern 500 came around, I didn't figure in the money at all. I hadn't won any of the Big Four races that counted toward the bonuses.

"All I could do was try to win the Southern for a second straight time and be the first driver to do that since David Pearson in 1976-77. And I had it in hand — and then let it go.

"I led that race after the rain delay with just seven laps to go — and then hit the wall in turn two and threw away my chances. It was my fault. I guess what they say about this old track reaching out to grab you when you least expect it is true.

"Then here in the TranSouth 500 this year, I had a chance to win. When it came down to the end, it was going to be either Dale [Earnhardt] or myself.

"Gas was a problem. We knew it was going to be real, real close, but if we stopped for fuel, we lost.

"We had to chance it, and on the backstretch on the final lap, my Coors/Melling Thunderbird came up empty. Earnhardt passed me in the last turn to win the race while I coasted home.

"I'll do my best to win the Southern 500 here this year. We need to win as much as we can if we have any chance at all of catching Earnhardt in the Winston Cup points chase.

"If we can win the Southern, we'll also win the Winston $100,000 bonus. That will be whipped cream on the peach cobbler. I sure love peach cobbler with whipped cream!"

On Sunday there was a break in the clouds, a glimmer of the sun, and the race was started under caution forty-five minutes late. When Elliott, running up front with Allison, radioed that he thought the track was dry enough to race, flagman Harold Kinder dropped the green. NASCAR officials hoped to get in at least half the race, or 184 laps, before threatening clouds erupted again. That would make it an official race and not disrupt the holiday plans of the fans. Because of a 70 percent chance of rain, it was a race against time.

The event was run under caution for the first twenty-four laps before Kinder gave the green. Shortly after the start, Earnhardt whipped past Lake Speed and moved into fourth place. On the forty-sixth lap, he nudged ahead of Labonte and fell in behind Elliott, who had held his runner-up position behind leader Davey Allison. Two laps later, he wedged inside Elliott on the homestretch and made the pass.

Allison, however, did not give up the lead as quietly as the others had. Earnhardt kept testing him, and young Davey kept pulling ahead on the turns.

Obviously, Elliott was biding his time, content to run with the leaders, let time take its toll and make a late move. Usually he ran second, third or fourth. Of the three Ford contenders for bonus money, Allison seemed to be the strongest. Kyle Petty, who'd started twenty-first, was moving up, but slowly.

Then, for Allison, disaster. On the 164th lap of the 367-lap race, he fishtailed against the fourth-turn wall, spun and sustained a great deal of sheet-metal damage. It was almost the identical spot where in the spring he had crashed and caught fire when he was hit by his father's No. 22.

Limping to the garage, Allison explained that he'd cut a tire a lap earlier and failed to heed a radio call to bring the Havoline Ford in for a quick change. He thought he could make one more lap.

"That was a mistake on my part," he said. "Next time I'll bring it in to the pits."

Actually, even though this accident wasn't as scary as the Tran-South inferno, young Allison seemed a little more shaken. He kept telling reporters to move back and "give me some air."

Shortly thereafter, Elliott, pitting under caution, and brother Ernie decided to correct a handling problem by slipping a support under the front right spring. Time spent making that repair dropped him from the leaders. Once back on the track, he found his radio had gone out and, consequently, he missed his next pit stop and was forced to go around one more time before the crew was ready.

Making the repairs was a miscalculation because of the weather conditions. The race was almost certain to be stopped by rain.

As the dark clouds grew ominous, drivers jockeyed for the lead. Earnhardt led on laps 166 to 188, at which point the race was over the halfway hump and official. Then Richard Petty came out of the pack to pass Earnhardt on the front straight, and the crowd went wild. It was the first lap after the last caution and Petty made his move on the third turn.

"Richard was going a little faster than I wanted to go on that first lap on new tires," said Earnhardt. "Sometimes you don't know how those tires are going to work out."

Since it was sprinkling at the time, Petty no doubt hoped for a red flag and the stopping of the race at that moment, but it wasn't to be.

Earnhardt, who seemed to be toying with the King, let him lead for two laps and then passed him on lap 191. Seven laps later the caution came out for rain, and on lap 202 the red flag stopped the race. After an hour and a half of waiting, it was declared over, with Earnhardt the winner for the tenth time during the season.

Finishing behind Earnhardt, in order, were Rusty Wallace, Richard Petty, Sterling Marlin, Labonte, Bobby Hillin, Jr., Ricky Rudd and Elliott. The race was 224 miles short of 500 miles, the shortest Southern 500 on record.

It was the kind of year Dale Earnhardt could do no wrong. He'd won in the spring at Darlington when Elliott gave out of gas; he'd won at Martinsville when Geoff Bodine spun out with a thirty-second lead. He'd been a leader in nineteen of twenty-one races and led the most laps in eleven of them. As Darrell Waltrip had said, "Sometimes you win and you don't know why."

That was the way it was for Earnhardt in 1987. Everything was coming up roses.

After the Southern 500, he had collected $1,186,970 in prize moneys and held a 583-point lead over Elliott in the Winston Cup Series. He was well on his way to a $2 million year without benefit of the Winston Million, a rare feat indeed. As for Elliott, his financial rewards were nothing to sneeze at; he was just fifteen thousand dollars short of a million, nearing that magic mark for the third year in a row. He would become the seventh NASCAR driver to reach the million level.

He'd had his great season in 1985. Two years later, Earnhardt was having that kind of year. It was the kind of year in which speed was paying off but not paying up. Two nights before the Southern 500, a highway patrolman stopped Earnhardt for speeding, then let him off with a warning. That was the kind of year it was.

Three of the four races after Darlington marked a return to the short tracks for Elliott and the Winston Cup gang. The exception was the Monster Mile at Dover sandwiched between the Wrangler 400 at Richmond and the Goody's 500 at Martinsville.

The short tracks had been neither an Elliott strength nor a Ford playground, as Elliott reminded everyone. Of the 222 races held over the years at Richmond, North Wilkesboro, Martinsville and Bristol, Ford had been in the winner's circle only fifty times, and Fred Lorenzen, David Pearson and Junior Johnson had twenty-three, or almost half, of those.

Lorenzen was the all-time Ford winner on less-than-a-mile tracks with nine, followed by Pearson's eight and Johnson's six. Next came Bobby Allison with four and, after him, Ricky Rudd, Ned Jarrett, Richard Petty, Fireball Roberts, Marvin Panch and Dick Hutcherson, all with two. Outside of recent winners Rudd and Kyle Petty, the last time Thunderbirds were listed as short-track winners was in 1959, when Tiger Tom Pistone and Cotton Owens swept the inaugural races at Richmond. Pistone later repeated at Martinsville.

If nothing else, Elliott had history and tradition against him on the short tracks.

He alluded to that when he spoke with Steve Waid of *Grand National Illustrated*.

He said, "I do think that running a Ford product was a little bit of a handicap for us at the end as far as running the short tracks, and I feel like that's one reason why our short-track program hasn't come together as it should. Look how many times Ford has won on a short track versus a GM car. I think that's where the actual statistics are misleading. It isn't only my record, it's Ford's. You've got to look at that."

Over the years, another mysterious problem had developed, the "September Sags," for want of a better description. Either physically or mentally, or a combination of both, the Coors/Melling team seemed to wear out in September,then catch its second wind for the stretch.

Consider. . .

In 1984, during September, the No. 9 T-Bird sputtered fifteenth at Darlington in the Southern 500, twenty-fourth at Richmond, thirty-second at Dover before recovering for a third at Martinsville and a furious finish that produced two wins, a second, a fourth and an eighth, setting the stage for the phenomenal 1985 campaign.

The next September was just as puzzling. Following the zenith of their career, winning the Southern 500 and the Winston Million, the tenth victory of the season, the Elliotts ran into all kinds of troubles. They were twelfth at Richmond, twentieth at Dover, seventeenth at Martinsville and thirtieth at North Wilkesboro. Since the Southern 500 came on the first day of the month, that September wasn't a total loss. This frustrating period enabled Darrell Waltrip to catch up and go ahead in the run for the points championship.

Waltrip attributed the stretch to a "natural letdown" on the part of the Elliotts, but the more practical Bill said it was a combination of mechanical failures and being in the wrong places at the wrong times.

The September of 1986 was no better, a ninth at Richmond, a twenty-seventh at Dover, an eleventh at Martinsville and a sixteenth at North Wilkesboro. Then the Coors Ford rolled two sevens, a third and a twenty-third.

Could it be that the Elliotts weren't approaching September with enough respect? Were his perfectionist ways, his very nature, taking their toll on Ernie Elliott, whose health had been somewhat less than robust? For whatever reason, September remained a real puzzle. Of the Coors team's first 23 victories, only one, the Winston Million Southern 500 of 1985, was won in the first month of fall.

Until 1987, fall presented a dismal picture, but then, in the midst of turmoil and controversy over the ill-defined duties of Ivan Baldwin and Ernie Elliott, something really positive happened. Bill Elliott had his most productive September ever.

Starting with his eighth-place finish at Darlington, he ran a consistent fourth at both Richmond and Dover before falling back to thirteenth due to ignition coil and spark plug wire problems in the Goody's 500 at Martinsville. By the time the Goody's 500 rolled around, Baldwin and the Elliotts had parted company, and Ernie was back turning the wrenches on both short and long tracks. The report was that Baldwin was considering moving on to Australia, a country that was heating up to the stock car game.

At Richmond, the Earnhardt express rolled on, claiming its eleventh win of the season and its sixth straight on the shorter tracks. Ricky Rudd, the short-timer in the Bud Moore T-Bird, was impressive in winning the Delaware 500 at Dover, and Martinsville provided a real surprise when Darrell Waltrip, in the Tide machine, beat out Earnhardt and Terry Labonte on the last lap of the controversial Goody's 500.

Running third with only a few hundred yards to go, Waltrip, anxious to break a streak of twenty-seven straight winless races, tangled with Labonte, who tangled with Earnhardt, and then Waltrip slipped down to the inside to beat both to the checkers.

"I shot into him [Labonte], he shot into Dale, they shot up the track and I shot into the lead," said Waltrip.

Labonte complained about the other two Chevy drivers. He said Earnhardt had tried to run him high in turn two and, "As we went into the third turn, Darrell never lifted. He ran over both of us."

Waltrip, on the other hand, said he did nothing wrong.

"For the first time in a long time, I was in the right place at the right time," he said.

He was asked about his intentions as the race wound down.

"Intent?" he repeated with a mischievous Waltrip grin, reflecting the mental games he likes to play. "I guess there will always be some question of intent."

The situation was awkward for Earnhardt, who found himself the victim of his own tactics. He was angry, mad — he'd dominated the race — but he knew that anything he said could be held against him in the future. As the long-time canary-eating cat, he was careful not to burp too loudly. So after the perfunctory meeting with the NASCAR review committee, which described the finish as a "racing incident," Earnhardt merely said, "The race is over."

As usual, the Elliotts were just happy to get out of Martinsville with their sheet metal intact. It is not one of Bill's and Ernie's favorite tracks. Starting eleventh and finishing thirteenth, Bill recorded just about his average finish over the layout that takes its toll on tires and brakes. Historically, his worst finishes have come at Martinsville.

"I remember in the early days we took a modified car up there that had those inner tubes, and the brakes got so hot they burst the tubes," says George Elliott. "The track was so hard on brakes that Holman and Moody used to pull their cars in at some point in the race and change the brake pads — and still remain competitive."

Admitting he'd "never been good at Martinsville," Elliott said he looked forward to North Wilkesboro and the Holly Farms 400, a track configuration more suited to his style. If he hadn't won a short-track race, he was gaining on it, and insiders predicted when he made his breakthrough it would be at North Wilkesboro. Not only had he won the pole in the spring First Union 400, his 116.003 miles an hour had shattered the existing record at the five-eighths-of-a-mile track. Of all the short tracks, he felt more comfortable at North Wilkesboro.

And in the fall Holly Farms 400 it showed.

The week started with another one of Hank Schoolfield's informative press gatherings, this time with points leader Earnhardt, who led Elliott by 568 and needed to gain only 24 points in the Holly Farms 400 to clinch the title. With the big payoff virtually in his back pocket, Earnhardt could afford to be mellow and magnanimous, and he was. Speaking of an appearance on NBC's *Today* show with Elliott, he said, "The host, Bryant Gumbel, tried to get us to go at one another,but it didn't work." He also said he'd been mad all week, not because Waltrip had victimized him and snapped his short-track winning streak at six but, rather, "because finishing second always makes us mad."

He added, "Everyone was gunning for the same hole, and that's what happens. All this talk of retaliation is bunk. I ain't tearing up Richard's car over somebody who's not worth it."

The Goody's 500 finish had one benefit, according to Earnhardt. "It will sell tickets for the race this week," he said.

He was right about that, but, historically, Winston Cup fans don't see what they expect. For example, Martinsville patrons always expect a wall-banging,metal-exchanging,temper-losing race, but, with exception of Waltrip's last-lap bumper-thumper, the 1987 Goody's 500 was a real yawner.

Hardly anyone anticipated Elliott's repeating his pole performance at North Wilkesboro.

He'd gone seven races, or since the Talladega 500, without a position on the inside front. This was a period in which the younger drivers, Labonte, Davey Allison and Alan Kulwicki, had dominated the qualifying with two poles apiece. The seventh went to veteran Geoff Bodine at Martinsville, and it was a very emotional day for him.

"Why does everything seem to go wrong for you one week, one year, and the next everything goes right?" he asked. "I don't know. All week we've questioned . . . why haven't you won poles, why haven't you won races . . . and we keep coming up with excuses. They've been valid, but the fans and media make them sound like excuses. We had eight poles last year, and we hadn't won one this year. This pole sort of gives us our self-esteem back and puts us in next year's Busch Clash.

"Last year we couldn't stay off the front row, and this year we hadn't been on the front row. I hadn't missed that since I've been in Winston Cup racing, and I'm proud of that and want to continue that streak."

Bodine's words underlined the importance of attaining some success and recognition in racing. A driver who has all minuses and no pluses finds himself on the outside looking in. The earliest winner of all time in Winston racing, Ron Bouchard, who captured the Talladega 500 in only his eleventh start, had been shut out ever since and was without a ride in 1987. The sponsors' bottom line is: What have you done for me lately?

Going into North Wilkesboro, many of the big names of racing were struggling. Harry Gant had gone fifty-seven races without a win and had failed to finish nineteen of twenty-four. His last victory had come in this very same Holly Farms race in 1985. The King, Richard Petty, had not won in ninety-five starts. Benny Parsons had sixty-seven winless races, Morgan Shepherd forty-seven, and Kenny Schrader had yet to visit the winner's circle in eighty-six tries.

Running under his own banner for the first time, Cale Yarborough didn't look at all like a three-time points champion.

Until Martinsville, Waltrip had had a horrendous year. The Goody's 500 provided him with a measure of success, and at North Wilkesboro he made a strong run for the pole with a reading of 115.001.

But there, just ahead of him with 115.196 miles an hour, recording his second pole on a short track, was Bill Elliott. With Baldwin gone, Ernie Elliott was back preparing the Coors Thunderbird, and he had it purring like a kitten.

"I felt the car would run very good here, but you never know," said Bill. "When you're talking about tenths of a second, a bobble here or there can cost you. A mistake in the corner can cost you.

"We're on the pole, that's what counts. The car ran good, now I just hope it holds up. At least we know what it can do for the race."

Completing the top five qualifiers, behind Waltrip, were Benny Parsons, Labonte and Kulwicki and sitting back in tenth was Earnhardt, who needed to gain twenty-five points on Elliott to wrap up the driver's championship.

As always, the North Wilkesboro favorite was Junior Johnson and his No. 11 Chevrolet, and seldom, if ever, does he disappoint the hometown fans. As a car owner and driver, he had won sixteen times (with fourteen poles) at the track just a few miles from his shop.

He is a legend in and out of the hills. Everyone knows of his old moonshining days and his presidential pardon from Ronald Reagan, but few are aware of Johnson's native business acumen. He was one of the major contributing founders of Holly Farms, and even today his chicken barns house almost a hundred thousand chicks. Additionally, he has a small herd of cattle, a pack of 'coon hounds and a favorite mule. Bob Latford, his able and knowledgeable public relations specialist, describes him thusly: "Junior Johnson still lives by the creed he learned as a farm boy: Work hard for what you want, treat others fairly and don't mess in others' affairs."

Sound familiar? It's the code of the hills, applying also to such environmental kinsmen as the Elliotts, Gants, Parsonses, Arringtons and Woods. Like all the others, however, Johnson does not hesitate to gain the edge on the field if he can do it and get by with it.

As the Winston caravan moved into North Wilkesboro, Johnson was in an unaccustomed position. His new driver, Labonte, though third in the points standings, 127 behind Elliott, was under tremendous pressure to make a move. He'd had four poles, runner-up finishes at Talladega and Watkins Glen and ten top-five places, but he lacked the most important ingredient — a win.

What more appropriate place for Johnson's car to win than at North Wilkesboro?

It did.

Whether by provincial inspiration or something else, NASCAR had a lot of appropriate winners in 1987. Earnhardt, driving the Mr. Goodwrench/Wrangler Chevrolet, prevailed in the Mr. Goodwrench 500 at Rockingham; Ricky Rudd, in the Motorcraft Thunderbird, swept the Motorcraft 500 at Atlanta; Davey Allison, the hometown driver, sped to the Winston 500 winner's circle; Tim Richmond, the free soul with the California personality, won at Riverside; Elliott was the class of the field at Michigan, home of car owner Harry Melling, and Earnhardt made a clean sweep of sponsors by claiming the Wrangler 400 at Richmond.

"Now's my time at bat, and I don't want to disappoint anyone," Labonte had said.

He didn't.

Despite an early argument with the wall, which, ironically remedied a toe-in handling problem, Labonte ran a strong race over the .625 mile and finished, under caution, ahead of runner-up Earnhardt. Elliott, intent on finishing, ran a conservative race and protected his third-place points position with a solid third, a lap down. He was smooth and consistent throughout the four hundred laps, the first thirty-nine of which he led. It was his best short-track finish of the season and prevented Earnhardt from clinching the Winston Cup title on that Sunday afternoon.

Though he'd won three races, more than a million dollars in prize moneys, becoming the first race driver in any division to win a million or more for three straight years, and had seven poles and five speed records to his credit, Elliott's season had been the subject of critical scrutiny by some writers. There was speculation that Bill and Ernie were about to part company, that the family connection would end and Bill would join another team, that the Georgia red-head was spending too much time on personal appearances, that no one was really in charge of the Coors team. The absence of car owner Harry Melling from most of the races tended to fuel the rumors.

Earlier, in a period of twenty-four hours, Elliott made personal appearances in no fewer than five states, an off-track schedule said to be a distraction even to the hardiest soul.

Pursuing the story, Mike Mulhern, motor sports editor of *The Winston-Salem* [North Carolina] *Journal*, asked Elliott if he'd leave the team and the car for another arrangement.

Replied Bill, "I can't forget that the car got me to where I'm at."

The whole situation was a paradox on the horns of a dilemma. Here was a guy who'd won a million, was the biggest draw on the Winston Cup circuit, the most popular driver since Richard Petty's heyday and except for an exceptional year by Earnhardt would have been on his way to the points championship. Yet his season was said to be subpar, incomplete.

"Rumors about the Elliotts are not new," says one knowledgeable racing man who has been around the garages for almost thirty years. "I hear them every year. Let me put it this way. There might be changes and the brothers might have their disagreements, but I don't think they'll ever leave each other."

There's another recurring theme in the story of the Elliotts. Just when they appear to be down, and almost counted out, just when they're challenged by outsiders, they circle the wagons and come back fighting as a family.

25

Rock Solid and Winning Big

A MONG OTHER CREDENTIALS in their portfolios, the Elliotts are keen and opportunistic businessmen, at their best for big-money races and new sponsors. History has proven that with each new sponsor, be it for one race or many seasons, Bill Elliott has followed with a superior performance.

Witness . . .

— In 1980, when he picked up a meager five hundred dollars from Harry Melling to plaster Mell-Pro on his car prior to the National 500 at Charlotte, he returned a sixth-place finish, to that point his best effort at CMS.

— The next year he opened Melling's twelve-race sponsorship package with another sixth and his biggest purse to date, $30,615, in the Daytona 500.

— Returning a year later, under Melling's full ownership, Bill bettered both Daytona marks, placing fifth and collecting $36,125.

— And in 1983, having just concluded his agreement with Coors at the shank end of the schedule, he went out and won his first Winston Cup race ever, the Winston Western 500 at Riverside.

Car builder Banjo Matthews had mentioned the Elliotts' uncanny ability at "'strategic planning." No one could approach their skill at targeting a specific goal. They knew where the money was, at Daytona and Charlotte, and were seldom caught unprepared. Bill had won more than twice as much at Daytona ($867,420), where he had only two race victories to his credit, than at Michigan

($406,890), where he was a six-time winner. At Charlotte, where he'd won only once prior to the fall of 1987, there was a lot of money lying around to be claimed, and he had banked $547,346 of it.

For Bill, Ernie and Dan, the grass was always greener where it was green, and frequently this had to come at the expense of preparation time for the less lucrative races, primarily the short tracks. However, several years ago, when RJR pumped $2 million into the points fund, the smaller arenas took on new importance, and the Coors team began to redefine its goals. First to realize the spoils in planning over the long range rather than shooting the works each Sunday was Waltrip, who won the driver's title and $400,000-plus with only three victory lane visits in 1985 and collected $225,000 for placing second to Earnhardt in 1986, also with an unglamorous three wins. Of course, a great deal of that credit belonged to his former car owner, Junior Johnson, who doesn't miss many tricks in racing.

As the 1987 season wound down and the Winston Cup caravan moved into Charlotte for the October 11 Oakwood Homes 500, the points championship was out of the question for Elliott. As he said, "My only chance is for someone to kidnap Earnhardt." Of more immediate concern were the rumors making the rounds about upheaval and turmoil in Dawsonville. Things weren't going well at all. Since his win at Talladega on July 26, Elliott had only a couple of fourths, at Richmond and Dover, and the third at North Wilkesboro.

Most of the Elliott people were talking about next year. The big news at Charlotte was the health problems of Tim Richmond, who had been dropped by the Hendrick team. There was talk that the mysterious case was drug-related, though Richmond denied it. To replace Richmond in the No. 25 Folger's Coffee Chevrolet, at least for one race, Hendrick selected Jimmy Means, a midpack regular, and that caused some excitement.

From the Elliotts, however, on October 8, Bill's thirty-second birthday, there was a surprise announcement, and an omen that wasn't picked up by the others. On the spot where seven years earlier, almost to the day, car owner Harry Melling had painted "Mell-Pro" on the car of a little-known driver from Georgia, Melling announced he was taking his name off the Coors Thunderbird and replacing it with Motorcraft, which had signed on as an associate sponsor effective with the 1988 season. Beginning with Speed Weeks at Daytona, No. 9 would be raced under the Coors/Motorcraft banner. All along Ernie Elliott had argued that everyone knew who the car owner was, and the space on the car could be better utilized for an associate sponsor.

In making the announcement, Melling said, "It is an extension of our long relationship with the Ford Motor Company, and the marriage of Motorcraft with Melling Racing, a division of the Melling Tool Company, is a natural alliance. It makes good business sense.

"Motorcraft and Melling both are involved in providing quality parts and equipment for the automotive aftermarket, and we look forward to this relationship . . . . Melling Racing looks forward to great success in the 1988 season with the continued support of the Adolph Coors Company and our new association with the Motorcraft Quality Parts."

There was no objection from Coors.

Said Cully Marshall, the company's field marketing manager, "We've thoroughly enjoyed our association with Bill Elliott and Harry Melling since we initially contracted with Melling Racing back in 1984, and we're anticipating the enhancement of this association now that Motorcraft has joined what we feel is the top racing team in the business.

"Bill Elliott has become the fastest and most popular driver in the most competitive series in motor sports, and we think our involvement with Bill in particular and stock car racing in general has helped introduce our quality products to millions of people at the same time we've been expanding our marketing efforts across the country.

"We think the addition of Motorcraft as an associate sponsor on Bill's car will provide us with opportunities to create an even greater awareness of our products."

Previously, Motorcraft had been the primary sponsor of the Bud Moore Thunderbird team, with Ricky Rudd as driver, but Rudd was leaving to be replaced by young Brett Bodine, and the Ford parts division made a decision to expand its support, in an associate's role, to several teams, including Moore's.

Elliott changes, it seems, were coming in bunches. At the same time it was announced that the Coors fortress in Dawsonville, the inner sanctum of racing engineering, would be opened to the public for the first time the week before the Winston Cup finale in Atlanta. Said Bill, "We have never before been in the position to invite all our fans to visit the race shops, and we're all looking forward to showing them where the work is done." That same weekend also marked the grand opening of Bill Elliott Ford in Dahlonega, a firm originally founded by George Elliott.

With all the news and press releases out of the way, Bill, Ernie and Dan were ready to go racing. Either Davey Allison, who had the fastest practice time (171.848), or Elliott was expected to win the pole. It didn't happen. Allison was tenth and Elliott seventh, his worst start at CMS since 1984.

Instead, the front was crowded with old-timers. Bobby Allison, recording a 171.636 two-lap average in his Buick, broke a 149-race poleless streak, and at forty-nine became the oldest driver ever to sit on the inside front in Winston Cup racing. Trailing him, in order, were forty-six-year-old Benny Parsons, thirty-eight-year-old Geoff Bodine, forty-seven-year-old Harry Gant and thirty-seven-year-old Jimmy Means, in the Tim Richmond Chevrolet, earning the best starting position of his career.

Earnhardt, hoping to wrap up the points title, grabbed the ninth starting slot.

One garage veteran hinted that the rubber setup had been designed to even up the odds for the old-timers. "I think they would have loved to see Richard Petty on the pole, but then he wrecked in practice," he said. "Davey Allison's was the first fast car to go out, and he looked like he was on ice."

Nonetheless, Bobby Allison was a popular figure at the head of the line and, as the race proved, his Buick was extremely strong.

The bottom line is this: One way or another, NASCAR has ways of staging an interesting, competitive show.

For the Elliotts, the return to Charlotte was like old times. Ivan Baldwin was gone, and once more there were Bill, Ernie and Dan against the field on their own turf, a super speedway. The announcement that Motorcraft was throwing its resources behind the team was an added incentive, an omen from the past, and a special time. The Dawsonville gang had always translated good news into good results.

There was even a show of harmony in the pits. Papa George Elliott donned his "Coors" outfit and nestled into his director's chair, and owner Harry Melling, absent from most of the races during the season, made it a point to make an appearance.

Prior to the race, Tim Richmond, the subject of much speculation, showed up in the garage area, decked out in all-black sultan trousers and a loose-fitting shirt, a gold neck chain and shades and sporting carefully coiffured locks. Surrounded by fans and friends, he chatted with his old crew chief Harry Hyde and signed autographs.

Now it was time for driver introductions and the Oakwood Homes 500.

Predictably, Elliott was greeted with thunderous cheers and Earnhardt with a mixture of boos and applause. One fan held a banner reading, "This bird's for you, Dale!"

What can't be predicted is the tone and direction a Winston Cup race will take.

For example, you expect Martinsville to sound like something out of Batman — Bam, Clash, Crash, Clang, Smash. The audio was mysteriously missing in the Goody's 500 and, instead, appeared on the Oakwood Homes 500 soundtrack. For whatever reason, cars were getting into each other.

Poor old Jimmy Means lasted only twenty-two laps before he mixed it up with Ken Schrader, Buddy Baker, Derrike Cope, Greg Sacks and Earnhardt. His No. 52 (25 transposed) was totaled. For Neil Bonnett, it must have been eerie *déjà vu,* lying in an ambulance on his way to Cabbarus County Hospital, just as he was during the World 600 in May. This time, however, his injuries were much more serious, a broken upper leg and perhaps hip.

And Geoff Bodine's greatest fear was realized on lap 127 when he crashed into his little brother, Brett, as part of an eight-car accident. There are so many kin, fathers and sons and brothers, on the Winston Cup circuit that family crashes are inevitable and often unavoidable, but unlike some of the more detached, Geoff Bodine said he was not yet completely comfortable with that situation.

He talked about it before the race.

"I dragged him down here; he was up racing modifieds in New York," said Geoff. "He said he didn't have a job, so I basically got him a job with Harry Hyde working on my race cars. Then he got the late model ride when I couldn't drive at Martinsville and he won the race. That got him started, got him rolling, opened the door for him.

"But he'll always be my brother, my little brother; I changed his diapers. He's ten years younger and I'll always think of him as my little brother and love him that way.

" It's hard for me to go and race with him. I've said this before. He's here now and I'm definitely going to have to learn to race with him. I'm going to have to get over that feeling when I see him coming that he's my brother and think of him as just another driver."

Naw.

Realizing he was trying to convince himself, Bodine added, "I'll never get it all out of my mind. He's my brother and I'll never be able to stop thinking of him that way."

Those words were recalled when the brothers had their first crisis and totaled their cars. Thankfully, however, they escaped sound and healthy. Meanwhile, Earnhardt, who needed only a third-place finish to nail down the Winston Series crown, and Elliott were having opposite afternoons. Earnhardt found the wrecks and lost his brakes along with seven laps. Using that sixth sense and those reflexes George Elliott talked about, Bill managed to dodge flying metal and keep his nose clean.

The early part of the race was a shakedown, cautious period, for the Dawsonville team. The most consistent leader was pole-sitter Bobby Allison, who was giving it his best shot. However, because of the seven cautions and the many pit stops, the race had such diverse leaders as Brad Teague, Rick Wilson, Trevor Boys, Ernie Irvan, Larry Pearson and A. J. Foyt.

But when it came down to the finish, Allison and Elliott diced it out. After biding his time behind Allison for some thirty-five laps, the Coors redhead moved to the front sixty-two laps from the checkers and looked back only once.

That was when the ominous blue-and-yellow No. 3, seven laps down, pulled up behind him and wanted to play. Earnhardt has this obsession about being out front, the fastest, and whether seven laps down or ahead, he feels he has something to prove. More than any other driver, he likes to play with Elliott because Bill is his chief rival, just as Ford is Chevrolet's chief rival. At this juncture of the race, Elliott had to be careful and not get so absorbed in Earnhardt that he forgot Allison.

After announcing his presence on Bill's bumper, Earnhardt moved around and unlapped himself. Just when he relaxed, here came Elliott again alongside the Wrangler Chevrolet, acting as if he was going to retaliate, but, deciding the better part of winning was discretion, Elliott dropped back and let Dale go. After all, Earnhardt was still six laps off the pace.

Asked later if Earnhardt was playing with him, Elliott replied, "Well, he had that grin on his face."

And was he playing with Earnhardt?

"We'll never know, but he outran me. He might have had the stronger car today, but it doesn't make any difference how strong you are when you're six laps down. With sixty laps to go, I felt I had everything going and would win if it didn't go away."

The No. 9 Thunderbird flashed across the finish line 2.2 seconds ahead of Bobby Allison with only one other car, Sterling Marlin's, in the lead lap. Cautions had held the winning speed to 128.443 miles an hour. By collecting $74,040, Elliott hiked his career winnings at Charlotte to $621,386 on only two wins, both in the fall. It also raised his lifetime Winston Cup earnings to $6,242,290, $1,488,806 of which had come at two tracks, Daytona and Charlotte.

No one better illustrates the current big moneys in racing than Elliott and Earnhardt, who through Charlotte had $6,313,401 on only thirty-one wins. Elliott, of course, recorded his twenty-first victory in the Oakwood Homes 500. As a contrast, Richard Petty had collected $6,542,857 on two hundred triumphs; all-time money winner Darrell Waltrip $7,761,921 on seventy-one victory lane visits; Bobby Allison $6,606,284 on eighty-three first places; and Cale Yarborough $4,934,256 on eighty-three wins.

Breaking it down into average winnings per career races, after the Oakwood Homes run, the list went like this:

Elliott, $27,259 on 229 races; Earnhardt, $23,296 on 271; Waltrip, $18,306 on 424; Yarborough, $13,793 on 358; Allison, $13,212 on 500, and Petty, $12,558 on 521. These figures are incredible considering that Elliott won his first Winston Cup race at the very end of the 1983 season. He was four years old when Petty won his first race at Columbia, South Carolina, in 1959.

Winning at Charlotte was justification of sorts, but it didn't change the points situation with Earnhardt, who finished twelfth. It only delayed the inevitable. All the Wrangler team, which led by 525 points, had to do was show up at Rockingham for the AC-Delco 500 and the $400,000 was theirs.

"We wanted to win it [the title] here at Charlotte," Wrangler team owner Richard Childress had said. "It would have been nice because this is Dale's home track. But Rockingham will be just fine."

From another perspective, the Elliotts were also looking forward to Rockingham. "We've had an up-and-down year," said Bill, "and we've finally got things on a roll."

Momentum and harmony had returned to the Coors team. With the Baldwin episode history, Ernie Elliott's heart was back in racing, and he was doing his thing. When he does that, it's bad news for garage rivals.

In midweek, before the AC-Delco 500, the Earnhardt team had an announcement more surprising than the Elliott disclosure about their new sponsor. Wrangler, which had been the primary sponsor for Earnhardt since 1980, was pulling out, to be replaced by Mr. Goodwrench, the General Motors parts division.

There was irony in the change.

With Elliott having Motorcraft as an associate sponsor, and Earnhardt going with Goodwrench, 1988 promised to instigate an all-out war between the parts divisions of the two major automobile companies. *En garde!* It's cam shafts at fifty paces!

Car owner Richard Childress admitted that Elliott would be a formidable opponent in 1988. "Bill and his team are consistently strong," he said. "Then, too, Junior Johnson's team is always up there. There are some other teams with potential."

It may come as a surprise to critics and fans, but Dale Earnhardt displayed a sentimental streak at the press conference. "I'm sorry to see the blue-and-yellow go," he said. "We've had some good years with Wrangler, and I'm going to miss the colors. Guess I'll have to get used to Goodwrench black at Daytona in '88."

With the Winston Series championship awaiting him at the starting line on Sunday, Earnhardt said Childress was taking no chances about his showing up.

He said, "I went hunting the other day, and as I was sitting in this blind I heard a rustling above me. I parted the brush and sitting there with a shotgun was Richard.

"Later, bedding down for the night, I crawled into the top bunk and he settled in the bottom bunk. He was going to be there to catch me if I fell. He really wants this championship.

"This has been a real good team and relationship. We started out together in 1984. As we went in '85 we didn't think we could do it, then in late '85 we started doing it. Then we won last year and went into this year — the best year I've ever had. The reason is the consistency of the team. They get me out of the pits so fast I hardly have time for a drink of water."

Bob Kelly of Winston, sponsor of the press conference, also introduced crew chief Kirk Shelmerdine and engine builder Lou LaRosa, majordomos on the Wrangler team.

Shelmerdine admitted the Fates had something to do with the exceptional season. "No one could have expected a year like we had," he said. "We've been lucky at some races — like Darlington in the spring when Bill Elliott ran out of gas on the last lap — or at Martinsville, where Geoff Bodine and Kyle Petty collided late in the race with Bodine headed for victory lane. Dale went past him while he was trying to get going again and won the race."

LaRosa, alluding to the report that other teams were trying to hire members of the Wrangler crew, said, "In this sport money talks, but everyone on our team wears hearing aids."

His engine-building philosophy, he said, concentrates more on staying power than horsepower.

On Saturday before the race the Wrangler crew gave the public an example of their efficiency by winning the Unocal Pit Crew Competition for an unprecedented third straight time. They changed four tires and added fuel from two separate cans in a world record time of 23.831 seconds, shattering their own old mark of 27.601.

"There are three or four different ways to go about a pit stop," said Shelmerdine. "We have a playbook like football or basketball.

"Instead of the gas man going over the wall right away, we held him back so the left-side tire man could go over the wall and get the left-side lug nuts loose. When the tire carrier came back over the wall, the gas man went out. This let us get a jump on getting the left-side lug nuts loose while still staying within the NASCAR rules of having only six men over the wall."

It is more than a cliché that races are won or lost in the pits. It's fact. A couple of seconds saved on a pit stop can mean the difference between winning and a fifth-place finish. Earlier in the season, Elliott's chances took a decided downturn on delays in the pits, prompting George Elliott to say, "I'm going to find out if someone is partying too much."

At Rockingham, Bill Elliott had three objectives, (1)win his eighth pole of the season and wrap up the thirty-thousand-dollar Busch Pole Award, (2)maintain a good distance between himself and Terry Labonte, who was third in the points standing, and (3)if given the opportunity, win the AC-Delco 500. Of these goals, the last was considered the most difficult, since the North Carolina Motor Speedway hadn't favored him in the past. Except for his win in the fall of 1984, his fourth-place finish in the spring Goodwrench 500 had matched his highest finish at NCMS.

On pole day the worst possible scenario unfolded. Young Davey Allison, his closest competitor for the Busch Pole Award, overcame team turmoil, the firing of his equally young crew chief, Joey Knuckles, and raced to his fifth inside front position of the season, his second straight at Rockingham, with a run of 145.609. He was followed by Earnhardt with 145.222 and Elliott with 144.774.

For Elliott, missing the pole was disappointing but not surprising. Of his twenty-eight career poles, none had come at NCMS. He had six at Talladega, five at Michigan, four at Daytona, three at Darlington and two each at Atlanta, Charlotte, Dover, Pocono and North Wilkesboro. His best start at Rockingham was the outside pole in the fall of 1984 when he won the Hodgdon American 500. Nonetheless, the challenge of Davey Allison only served to pump up Bill, Ernie, Dan and the Coors team for the race itself.

"Before Charlotte, the adjusted goals called for intensified efforts to win two of the last four races," said George Elliott. "It was figured that would end all that talk about what a bad year the team was having. Charlotte accomplished half of that plan."Rockingham completed the other.

On the day before the AC-Delco 500, Bill Elliott, age thirty-two, for the first time tried his hand at driving of another sort — golf.

He decided to tag along with motor sports announcer Barney Hall, David Pearson, Bud Moore and Earl Parker. Driving the cart and just kibitzing, he was invited to take a few whacks at the ball.

"Bud and David were giving him pointers on how to hit the ball," says Herman Hickman, veteran publicist of the North Carolina Motor Speedway. "Bill got to hitting the ball pretty good and ended up playing about fifteen holes.

"In fact, he was hitting the ball so good that Barney turned to Bud and David and said, 'Hey, you guys, quit talking to Bill.'"

As his snow-skiing buddy Joe Locke once said, Bill is a natural athlete who learns in a hurry and masters any sport he attempts. His exceptional hand-eye control applies to golf as well as racing, snow skiing, skating or water sports. He and many others refute the old argument that race drivers aren't athletes.

His golf lesson behind him, Bill returned to the driving he loves best, turning the wheel of the No. 9 Thunderbird.

October 25, 1987, broke with a cloud cover cooling the air and the track in the North Carolina sandhills, located in hinterlands reached only by winding roads from Ellerbe and Rockingham. It was a relaxed time for Winston Cup racing. All Earnhardt had to do was show up, and he had his second straight points championship. Heartened by their success at Charlotte, the Elliotts were reinvigorated and confident.

Coming out for the driver introductions, Bill was mobbed for autographs. His popularity, even in the garage area, is a modern phenomenon. He could hardly walk two steps before another program, piece of paper, hat or T-shirt was offered for a signature. He and Earnhardt exchanged good-natured pleasantries. The Charlotte confrontation seemed like ages in the past.

The responses to introductions remained unchanged: cheers for Elliott and a mixed bag for Earnhardt.

Usually, when Bill wins a race, it falls under one of two categories, strategic or dominant. The Oakwood Homes 500 was a strategic triumph. He laid back, avoided trouble and led only the last sixty-two laps.

The AC-Delco 500, on the other hand, was the flip side, domination. He led 234 of the 492 laps. In comparison, runner-up Earnhardt was out front for 121 laps. It was a stark contrast to the spring race, when Earnhardt ran away from the field, leading 299 laps, and Bill finished fourth, failing to get out front for a single lap, indeed a rarity.

Only once during the AC-Delco 500 was Elliott as far back as sixth. Running through the corners like he was on rails, he was out front 215 of the last 272 laps, with only two challengers, Earnhardt and Labonte. Pushing his Monte Carlo to catch the streaking Georgian, Earnhardt tagged the wall seventy-nine laps from the finish and fell back to seventh.

He eventually climbed back to second, finishing a full 5.25 seconds behind Elliott and just ahead of a surprising Waltrip, who edged Labonte at the end. Eight cautions for forty-six laps held the winning speed to 118.258 miles an hour, and this time NASCAR's "longest 500-mile race" lasted for four hours, thirteen minutes and fifty-two seconds. First place paid $50,025.

Though flushed and tired, Elliott was a relieved and happy race driver as he met the press. He had come from rumors of internal team squabbling to the pole and a third-place finish at North

Wilkesboro and back-to-back wins at Charlotte and Rockingham. He, Ernie and Dan were living their answers on the track.

True, the points race had been officially lost to Earnhardt, but they had long been resigned to that.

Asked if winning the race made the points standing easier to take, Bill replied, "Naw, it didn't make any difference. That was over and done with. Like I said earlier in the week, I'm just trying to hang on to second where Terry [Labonte] and I have a good race going."

There was a point in the race where Elliott didn't know if he'd make it or not. "It was just before the last caution," he said. "Rudd blew an engine and my windshield was covered with oil, and I couldn't see anything except the white line right on the bottom. It got where I couldn't see that either. I had to be within two or three car lengths before I could see those in front of me.

"I had a lot of trouble with slower cars because I couldn't judge getting by them and getting in that corner. As a result, I felt I could give up some time by just being careful rather than trying to over-drive the car. I was having an awful time."

When Earnhardt banged the wall and spun out, Elliott pitted, took on tires and got his windshield cleaned and came out third behind Labonte and Waltrip. He was too strong for either and soon left them.

The Elliotts were beginning to savor the familiar feeling of success.

"This season reminds me a lot of the 1984 season," said Bill. "Like in '84, we've won at Charlotte and Rockingham. Now what we want to do is run strong in the last two races — we feel like we're coming on strong — keep our act together and come on good in '88."

The finish was to be better than he had expected. Also more tragic than anyone had expected.

26

Riverside-Atlanta

R IVERSIDE, NOVEMBER 8, 1987, was a race to forget.
So was the entire first week of that November. Racing bad
news and tragedy, it seems, come in clusters.

Grand Prix racing lost Jim Fitzgerald, sixty-five, winningest
driver in Sports Car Club of America (SCCA) history and racing
partner to actor Paul Newman. The colorful, devil-may-care racer,
who spent his late years teaching at the Road Atlanta Drivers'
Training School and counted actor Tom Cruise among his pupils,
died of a broken neck following a crash in the St. Petersburg Grand
Prix.

In his eulogy at the funeral in Clemmons, North Carolina, Newman said, "I'm sure Fitz already has a good ride Up There."

The week also brought news of the death in Daytona Beach of
Houston A. Lawing, seventy-nine, vice-president of the International Speedway Corporation and NASCAR's first public relations
director, a dapper little man but a racing giant.

Next to Bill France, Sr., no one did more to publicize and popular-
ize stock car racing than the soft-spoken and courtly Lawing. In the
early days of racing he did it all, nailing posters to telephone poles,
visiting newspapers and selling skeptical editors on coverage, teaching young writers the difference between carburetors and cylinder
heads, writing press releases and heading the publications
department.

Lawing's work with France and NASCAR began in 1947 when the

sanctioning body's public relations office was in an upstairs office on South Elm Street in Greensboro, North Carolina. For many years his faithful and competent assistant was Bob Pope, and France, in real coups, added clout to the image of racing by hiring such popular retired national columnists as Henry McLemore and Oscar Fraley to assist Lawing. Crusty old-time journalist Pat Purcell also did a lot of advance work.

In recognition of his contribution to racing, Lawing was named to the National Motorsports Press Association Hall of Fame at Darlington in August of 1987, but, unfortunately, he had suffered a stroke two days earlier and was unable to be present.

"Houston Lawing made a vast contribution to racing," said Tim Sullivan, himself one of the sport's pioneer PR men.

The cold hand of fate was not through. It was to reach out and touch the Coors race team in the Winston Western 500 at Riverside.

The week started innocently enough.

In a slight surprise, Geoff Bodine, with a lap of 117.934, won his second pole of the season over favorites Ricky Rudd, Rusty Wallace and Terry Labonte, who ran second, third and fourth.

Elliott was sixth-fastest but clinched the thirty-thousand-dollar Busch Pole payoff when Davey Allison, who trailed seven-to-five, failed to win with only one race remaining, at Atlanta.

On race day the pit arrangement was not what Ernie Elliott would have selected if he'd had his choice. The Coors team was stationed in the second station from the mouth of pit road and surrounded on one side by the Darrell Waltrip crew and on the other by the Terry Labonte team.

Ernie had always been uneasy about being at the entrance of pit road. Too many things can happen, especially on most road courses, where space is limited.

On Sunday, November 8, his worst fears were confirmed.

It happened on the eighth lap of the 119-lap race after West Coast ace Hershel McGriff brought out a caution with a blown engine, sending most of the drivers into the pits for tires and fuel.

As Jim Robinson, another West Coast driver, barreled into the pits, he clipped the car of Michael Waltrip, sending it into a spin. What followed was the most serious incident an Elliott team had ever suffered.

Waltrip's out-of-control No. 30 slammed into outside-rear-tire-changer Chuck Hill, a four-year veteran of the crew, and hurling him into tire-carrier Butch Stevens, jack-man Steve Colwell and front-tire-changer Dan Elliott, leaving bodies sprawled all over the place, a heart-stopping and gruesome scene. The Coors Thunderbird, with its wheels off, was never touched and Bill Elliott sat there feeling helpless. Those were his friends, more like family, and his brother.

Obviously, Hill's condition was the most critical of all. He was motionless, with blood seeping from his mouth.

"They thought Chuck was dead," remembers George Elliott. "He was unconscious and bloody and not moving, and it looked real bad."

At home in Dawsonville, Mildred Elliott was watching the race on television, and her heart sank when the carnage scene was flashed on the screen. At times like that no one suffers more than a mother.

"I looked and saw Ernie, but I couldn't see Dan," she says, recalling that moment of horror. "The ambulance was there, and everyone was running around, and no one seemed to know exactly who was hurt and how bad. I can't tell you the relief when they brought Dan up and interviewed him about the accident."

Dan had been the last hit in the domino effect of the accident. All three of the others had landed on him, and he suffered a badly bruised shoulder. His crewmates weren't as lucky. Hill, rushed to a nearby hospital, suffered massive internal injuries, a broken hip and broken arm. A ruptured spleen was removed. He remained in intensive care for several weeks and faces a long rehabilitation program.

Though sustaining broken bones, Stevens and Colwell were more fortunate. Stevens had a broken leg, and Colwell a broken jaw and fractured knee.

Strapped in his car, Bill didn't know who was hurt or how badly. He thought about packing it in for the day, but Ernie relayed the message that the injured crew members wanted him to go on. Still, as he said, his heart wasn't in it.

Once the injured had been dispatched for medical attention, three volunteer members from Waltrip's pit crew jumped over the wall, completed changing tires and got Bill on the track again. Junior Johnson also offered some of his crew, even though he was in a close battle with the Coors team for second place in the points race.

Despite all the wrangling, arguing, fist-shaking and even fighting, racers and racing people make up a close-knit family, and just as wars bring differing citizens together, a common cause or tragedy unites all those in the cruelest sport of all.

For Bill Elliott, the disastrous events of the day had made the race only a chore to complete, and after finishing twenty-third he rushed to the hospital to be with his friends. The race was won by Rusty Wallace, his second road-course victory of the season.

It was not a pleasant trip home for the Coors team. Chuck Hill had to be left behind in the intensive care unit of the Riverside Community Hospital. Colwell, a paving contractor and a close friend of Bill's, had opted to return home to Emory Hospital in Atlanta for treatment. Stevens and Dan Elliott were all banged up and in casts and slings.

One more race remained, the *Atlanta Journal* 500, but with his crew decimated, Bill's chances remained remote at best.

Qualifying was no problem. You don't need a pit crew to run a lap or two; he was healthy and able to set up the car and drive, and Ernie was healthy and able to weave his magic on the working parts. Ford products had always been strong at AIR, winning twenty-three of the fifty-five races over the 1.522-mile almost circular track, where handling is as important as horsepower. Ford had prevailed in the spring with Ricky Rudd winning the Motorcraft 500, though Earnhardt sat on the pole with a record 175.497.

Because of wind gusts on the backstretch, neither Elliott nor Earnhardt approached the spring standard, but Bill was closest. His 174.341 lap, earning him the eighth pole of the season and the twenty-ninth of his career, was almost a mile per hour faster than his Chevrolet rival.

Winning the pole was fine, but was it a curse?

Not in twenty-seven years, or the second race ever run over AIR in 1960, when Fireball Roberts turned the trick, had the pole-sitter won an Atlanta race.

That was one of the reasons Elliott shouldn't have won. There were others. Except for his spectacular 1985 season, when he swept both races, he'd never won at his home track. And now he'd be asked to give it his best shot with not one but eight hands tied behind his back, the quick and agile hands of his injured crewmen. Chuck Hill was still in the intensive care ward of a California hospital, Colwell was recuperating at his Blairsville home, and Dan Elliott and Butch Stevens, though present, would be unable to perform.

For the first time in their racing lives the family- and team-oriented Elliotts had to depend on outsiders to help in a race. But, as the Fates would have it, they were able to obtain the pit services of the closest thing to family. It could not have been planned any better.

Joey Knuckles was out of work. So were the Ballard brothers, Danny, Clint and Stoney, and Freddie Wilson. Knuckles had been crew chief for Davey Allison and had played a major part in his rookie wins at Talladega and Dover. But he'd crossed swords with the team owners and been fired.

His presence in the Coors pit was important in another way. He and his friends were quite familiar with handling a Ford, a Thunderbird.

The way Ernie had prepared the car and the way he was driving, Bill needed only a relatively quick stop; he could do the rest.

The *Atlanta Journal* 500 was not just another race for the Elliotts; it was a mission. They had dedicated it to Chuck Hill and the injured crewmen.

In Atlanta, AIR ranks about fifth in sports interest, behind Georgia, Georgia Tech and Atlanta Falcons football and Atlanta Braves baseball, but the track hit it just right for the *Journal* 500. All three football teams were having average or atrocious seasons and, of course, the Braves were in hibernation. Unlike the dismal flop of the Winston in May of '86, when fewer than twelve thousand people paid their way into the arena, a record sixty-five thousand showed up under perfect November skies to witness the final Winston Cup race of the season.

In a way it was a historic occasion, the changing of the guard. As motor sports reporter Dr. Jerry Punch reminded a national TV audience, the field included ten drivers aged forty-six or older, including A. J. Foyt, fifty-two; Richard Petty, fifty; Bobby Allison, forty-nine; Harry Gant, forty-seven, and Benny Parsons, Buddy Baker, Morgan Shepherd and Cale Yarborough, all forty-six. Together they'd won 385 Winston Cup races and twelve championships.In 1987 this distinguished honor roll had a grand total of one victory, that coming when Allison slipped through to take the Firecracker 400 on the last lap.

Yarborough, who had indicated he would share his ride in the future with young Dale Jarrett, suggested that the *Atlanta Journal* 500 was the most important race of his career in terms of his future. As is customary at the shank of a season, the silly time was in full bloom, and drivers were jumping from ride to ride.

Parsons was driving his finale for Rick Hendrick, to be replaced by Kenny Schrader, and joining Junie Donlavey. Rudd was taking Shepherd's ride with Kenny Bernstein, to be replaced on the Bud Moore Ford team by Brett Bodine. Joe Ruttman, the designated relief driver for Richard Petty and Neil Bonnett, planned to return with his own team. And NASCAR was preparing to welcome Indianapolis driver Ed Pimm, who would compete in the Mike Curb Sunoco Buick, and Mark Martin, a real comer from Grand National racing who'd gotten solid support.

Odd man out, it seemed, was Tim Richmond, whose great potential was obscured by his perplexing ailment.

There could be no better illustration of the changing times than the start of the *Journal* 500.

A. J. Foyt, the most successful race driver of all time, considering his versatility, jumped the start and was penalized a lap. Soon thereafter he lost another lap to leader Elliott. By lap seventy-six, he was in the garage for his forty-fifth Did Not Finish in seventy-one NASCAR races.

From start to checkers, the strongest car on the track was the red-nosed T-Bird from Dawsonville. The only others who could challenge

Elliott were Davey Allison, in another Thunderbird, and the omnipresent Earnhardt, in that order.

The only question was whether the unfamiliar pit crew could work as a cohesive unit upon such short notice and very little practice.

That concern proved unfounded.

The first test came on lap thirty-three when Yarborough, his Oldsmobile ablaze, stalled on pit road, forcing him to dive out of the passenger-side window and call it a day. Pitting on the next caution lap, Elliott found himself blocked by Yarborough's car and an ambulance. That was to be his slowest stop of the race, as Earnhardt beat him out. Even then the Coors Ford was back on the track in 24.01 seconds, not bad.

Later Knuckles and the crew made four tire changes and added fuel in 23.31 seconds, super good.

Head-to-head, it was no race after Davey Allison went a lap down due to an untimely pit stop on green a lap before a caution. Having led three times for 85 laps, Elliott "turned up the wicks" 82 laps from the finish of the 328-lap race.

He whipped past Earnhardt and never looked back, beating his archrival to the checkers by a whopping 12.94 seconds, on an average speed of 139.047. Trailing Earnhardt on the lead lap were Rudd and Bobby Allison, while Davey Allison was fifth, a lap down.

Win number twenty-three was one of Bill's most satisfying efforts, and the first-place payoff of $74,200 was only a byproduct.

Referring to Chuck Hill and the mangled crewmen, he said, "Hey guys, this one's for you."

Bill, Ernie and Dan had overcome a great deal of adversity. "After all that's happened to us the last couple of weeks, this really means a lot for us to come out and win this race," Bill said. "I want to say hello to Chuck in California, and we hope he gets back home soon."

As always, Elliott did not gloat over beating Earnhardt.

"Dale's car got awful loose for some reason," he said. "There at one time he got away from me, and I thought, 'I ain't going to be able to do anything with him.' All of a sudden I got looser and looser, and it seems like my car got better and better, and I just put the pedal to the metal and here we are."

Indeed here he was, the first pole-sitter to win the *Atlanta Journal* 500 since Fireball Roberts in 1960, a six-time winner, a winner of three of the last four races and owner of a $1,263,650 season, with more to come at the NASCAR awards banquet.

Even Earnhardt, ol' One Tough Customer, was impressed.

He congratulated Bill and added, "After what happened in California, those boys needed that."

The season, for the Elliotts, had been like an Army obstacle course. They won at Daytona, had problems of all kinds, mechanical failures and internal differences, and they had closed in sensational fashion, winning five of the last thirteen races.

That's exactly how they wanted to go into 1988.

With momentum.

Still ahead for Bill, however, was another crisis — the most critical of his life.

With the season over, he looked forward to relaxing and getting away from racing at least for a while. One of his lifetime dreams had been to fly in a United States Air Force fighter jet and, through friends, a Fam (Familiarity) Flight had been arranged in an F-16 out of Dobbins Air Force Base in Marietta, Georgia. Later, Elliott would make a public service announcement for the Air Force.

On the Tuesday after the Atlanta race, an Air Force limousine pulled into the driveway of his lakeside Blairsville home at 6:30 in the morning and transported him to Dobbins, where he was introduced to Maj. Wayne F. Conroy, his pilot. It was explained that Elliott would be allowed to take the controls for some minor turns in the beginning and then Conroy would assume the stick for maneuvers with a couple of F-15s.

Trying his hand early, Bill executed a few uncomplicated turns and then turned the controls over to Conroy.

During the third set of maneuvers, Elliott's plane and one of the F-15s somehow collided head-on at five hundred miles an hour.

"Out of the corner of my eye, I saw the underside of the other plane," Elliott told Ed Hinton of *The Atlanta Journal-Constitution*. "But it happens so fast that by the time you comprehend that you've seen the other plane and that you're hit, it's all over and the other plane is gone. Like they say, dead before you know it."

The worst possible situation developed for Elliott thereafter. He lost radio contact with his pilot. Remember what George Elliott has said. The most important thing for Bill is control, knowing what is going on and what he can do. He had to sit there in a state of total helplessness, his catlike reflexes useless, at the mercy of the unknown. It was pure torture.

"It shook him up," says George Elliott. "He said it was the most helpless feeling he ever had in his life. He couldn't do anything, couldn't talk to anyone and had no control over the situation.

"They really didn't know what happened. It seemed the F-15 came up under the F-16. Bill said it felt like they just hit turbulence, one big jolt. Out of the window he saw fuel spewing everywhere. They circled and saw the other pilot [Lt. Col. Bruce MacLane] parachuting after ejecting from his crippled plane.

"Then they limped home while a third pilot and plane looked and checked where the parachuting pilot landed.

"A friend of mine called and told me about the accident a few minutes after it happened. He heard it on a scanner and called right away. I was still worried because I recall from my Navy days that often they'd put out this kind of propaganda until the families were notified."

After what seemed like an eternity, Major Conroy passed a handwritten note to Bill telling him he was going to test the landing gears at Dobbins and that if they lost control of the plane they'd eject. What followed was fifteen minutes of terror. Was it all going to end like this?

A guy thinks of those things. Elliott said he sized up each area below him as a possible landing site as the wounded plane yawed, shuddered and coughed. Never again, he vowed, would he worry about Dale Earnhardt or any other race driver.

The incident had a happy ending. Conroy brought the F-16 Fighter Falcon in for a perfect landing, and, instead of enjoying his day off, Elliott found himself involved in another huge press conference.

The popular racing radio program, *NASCAR Live*, with Eli Gold, was bombarded with phone calls from fans throughout the country inquiring about Bill. Finally, Martha Elliott was reached by phone, and she assured the listeners that Bill was just fine.

"I talked to him just a few minutes ago," she said, "and he said he was going to come home and quietly have a nervous breakdown."

Asked if he'd like to drive the limousine home to Blairsville, Bill declined.

"You'd better drive," he told his military escort. "I think I've used up all my luck today."

Though some won't admit it, most race drivers believe that everyone has a certain amount of luck, a quota, so to speak.

As Formula One driver Jacky Ickx says, "I am sure that a moment will come when you have a feeling that you have done enough, that your potential for luck has come to an end, because there is a certain amount of luck involved in motor racing. When you almost have an accident and escape without damage, you use some luck. When you have a bad accident and escape with minimal damage, you use some luck. Eventually, there is a moment when something in you says, 'My luck is used up. Now you have done enough.'"

Back in Dawsonville, George and Mildred Elliott, the brothers and Martha were relieved when Bill returned home.

"I asked him if he'd go back up and he said he would," says George. "For ten to fifteen years he's been trying to get a ride in a supersonic jet, but this was a tough way to do it. In the Navy we had this sign that read, 'I hate mid-airs, they spoil the day.'"

After this harrowing experience, Bill canceled some personal appearances and stayed around the shop for a few days to rest up for the last official racing function of 1987, the NASCAR Awards Banquet in New York City.

There, on the night of December 4, NASCAR president Bill France, Jr., announced the final points and money winnings standings, to wit: Earnhardt, 4,696 points, $2,069,243, only the second driver ever to top the two-million mark; Elliott, 4,207 points, $1,599,210, a million-dollar winner for the third straight year; Terry Labonte, 4,007, $825,369; Darrell Waltrip, 3,911, $511,768, and Rusty Wallace, 3,818, $690,652.

When motor sports announcer Mike Joy interviewed Elliott in the audience and said, "We're glad to have you here," a still-somber Bill Elliott replied, "I'm glad to be *anywhere*."

27

A Long Road
to Success

IF THE ATLANTA clouds had a silver lining on the morning of
March 20, 1988, it was not apparent to Bill Elliott from his room in
Crawford Long Hospital.

Just another day in the office turned out to be just another day in
the medical ward.

His Sunday at Atlanta International Raceway, in the Motorcraft
500, had gone about like the new Winston Cup season — dreadful
and luckless. The gremlins had struck again. It wasn't enough that
he was five laps down with ten to go, due to distributor problems; he
had to go and argue with the wall and lose. A blown tire had ended
his day with a thud and prompted real concern in his pit.

"After he hit, he didn't answer us (on the radio) for two or three
minutes," said brother Dan. "Finally, when he said, 'Man, that sure
rang my clock,' we were greatly relieved."

Result of the accident: a severely bruised right shoulder. That and
a head cold, a sore throat, and a low blood count sent Elliott to
Crawford Long for observation.

The last time he had raced at Atlanta International Raceway in
the fall of '87, he had sat in the winner's circle; this time his old archrival Dale Earnhardt sat there, and Bill was a lackluster nineteenth.

It had been that kind of start for the new season.

He had rolled two twelves and a six in races at Daytona, Richmond
and Rockingham.

At Daytona, where Bill is usually the marque attraction, the Coors team had fallen victim to NASCAR's restrictor plate rules. Heretofore Ernie Elliott had overcome every bit of legislation thrown at him, but the restrictor plates effectively shut off the secret of his power burst. Try as he might, his search for more speed proved futile.

Bill did all right in the preliminaries. He won the IROC and placed fifth in the Busch Clash, but trouble was evident in the 125-mile qualifier. He had hardly completed a lap when a serious transmission problem sent him to the garage, relegating him to the 31st starting position, his worst since a 38th his rookie year.

Realistically, the Elliotts didn't hold out much hope for the Daytona 500 and they were right. Lacking the power to challenge the fast cars, they had to settle for twelfth.

"Under the old rules, our combination was super quick," Bill said. "With the new rules, we have to start looking for new things to be quick. We haven't found it yet."

You know there's trouble in River City, or Daytona, when Bill Elliott doesn't lead a lap, and he led not a single lap of the '88 500.

As usual, Speed Weeks had more than its share of stories and speculation. Tim Richmond, who had blazed on the scene with seven wins in '86, was prevented from racing because of a flap over his medical records, and all kinds of rumors were flying. It appeared his stock car racing career was over. Soon thereafter NASCAR's top honcho, Bill France Jr., announced a drug-testing program, and most of the drivers said they were agreeable. No one wants a fuzzy-headed guy running around in circles at 200-plus miles an hour.

As for the race itself, it was a day for the old-timers. One 50-year old driver, Bobby Allison, won it, beating son Davey to the line, and another, Richard Petty, grabbed most of the attention on the 6 o'clock news and the talk shows with a terrifying, flipping, side-spinning crash reminiscent of Allison's fence-climbing incident at Talladega.

One way or another, Speed Weeks always leaves fans with something to talk about the whole season.

The trail from Daytona, one of the top jet tracks, leads to Richmond, a track of relaxed half-milers, and in the spring of '88 the Virginia track was to hold its last racing before major lengthening and renovations.

Elliott, beset with suspension problems, recorded another twelfth, and the others squabbled about who won.

Neil Bonnett, in a Pontiac, got the checkers, but runner-up Ricky Rudd said he won and Richard Petty said, "I think I did." Rudd and Petty claimed Bonnett was not on the lead lap, but NASCAR said otherwise.

Two weeks later, at Rockingham, the sleeping Elliott powertrain began to show signs of stirring. He was anxious for some success. So was Dale Earnhardt, now in a black and gold No. 3, rather than the old familiar blue and yellow Wrangler colors. His start, with two tens, wasn't much better than the Coors team and he was off to a rocky ride in search of a third straight Winston Cup championship.

Qualifying was more encouraging to Elliott than Earnhardt. The 32-year old Georgia redhead won the pole with a fast lap of 146.612 miles an hour. He was happy to be back on a track where he'd won in the fall of '87.

"It feels good to come back to a place where you did run good and then run good again," he said. "This way I feel like maybe everything isn't out to lunch."

Maybe not out to lunch, but then maybe not exactly right either.

The good news is that Bill finally led a race, and that had to be a morale-booster for a guy accustomed to leading all races. The fact is, he led 110 of the 492 Goodwrench 500 laps. The bad news is that the tires kept getting uneven on him and he couldn't make a run for the big prize.

He finished sixth, but it could have easily been first with a little luck and tire wear.

For all intents and purposes, Rockingham was the beginning of the Great Tire War in '88. Once more Neil Bonnett won the race and people began to notice that he was running tires from the new kid on the block, Hoosiers, a small independent, strictly-racing tire company headed by Bob Newton. Runner-up Lake Speed and third-place finisher Sterling Marlin also were on Hoosiers.

Said Elliott, "If all things had been equal, I'd have beaten everybody today. We had some great pit stops and outstanding tire changes. We were just putting on the wrong brand.

"We had everybody covered. There wasn't a car out there that should have run with us."

Bonnett came out of Rockingham leading Marlin by 58 points, Earnhardt by 87, and Rusty Wallace by 112. In sixth place was Bill Elliott, 121 points behind.

If Rockingham was a welcome sight, Atlanta was more so. That too had been a winning stop for the Coors team in its strong finish of '87. And it was Bill's home track and all the people from Dawsonville would be there and what more could you ask for?

As it turned out, Atlanta was lucky for Earnhardt, not Elliott. Old 'Iron Head' broke out of his slump and won and Elliott ended up in a room with a view at Crawford Long Hospital.

No doubt the Elliotts were beginning to wonder if someone, or something, was after them. True, they'd won three of the last four in '87, a replay of '84, but there were ominous warnings from the gods of disaster. It started with the horrifying suddenness of the pit accident at Riverside that seriously injured several crewmen and brought drastic changes in the personnel. Just when he'd begun to relax from the thoughts of Riverside, Bill found himself at thirty thousand feet in a crippled F-16 with no control over his life.

So far he'd had more close calls than James Bond.

There was more distressing news. Bill's close friend and skiing partner, Joe Locke, only 42, was terminally ill with cancer.

If there is one trait a race driver needs, it is the aura of indestructability. Once that is punctured, or threatened, a problem arises. The Elliotts had been tested under soul-searching conditions. Things weren't going good. Their quickness advantages at Daytona and Talladega had been stripped from them. There was much work to be done on the track and in the garage to overcome their eleventh place standings in the points race.

So on March 20, flat on his back and aching in his Crawford Long Hospital bed, it was difficult for Bill Elliott to make out a silver lining in all the dark clouds. Later, a writer was to quote him as saying racing was no longer fun, prompting some to speculate he was considering retirement.

There is a lesson to be learned here. Consider the Elliott career. He started out at the bottom, stayed there for many years, then moved up all the way to the peak of success, the zenith of racing, eleven wins and the Winston Million, and now here he was in a six-month run of personal crises. Being fatalists, most drivers expect both bad and good luck. They just hope the bad doesn't last long or neutralize the good.

There were some who thought the Elliott magic had disappeared. Understandably, it was not an up-time in the Coors camp, nor a time for bookmakers to slap the short odds on the No. 9 car.

But a great transformation was about to take place.

Like a phoenix rising out of ashes, the Coors team was to turn bad luck and a horrendous start into one of the greatest seasons ever on the Winston Cup circuit.

What was to follow was to change the face of Winston Cup racing. Elliott, who had lost the '85 points championship in the last race of the season at Riverside, was to come back and win his first Winston Cup in the last race at Atlanta. And surprisingly, the contender would not be 'Black Bart,' Dale Earnhardt the intimidator. Instead, out of the gray area of potential, will come riding Rusty Wallace and his white and green No. 27 Pontiac.

A St. Louis native who came south to race, Wallace had beat around the NASCAR circuit for seven years and was known more for his ability on road and half-milers before '88. His first win came at Bristol in '86 and his first super speedway success at Watkins Glen in '87. Prior to '88, his only other two victories were at Martinsville and Riverside.

Always, however, he'd been predicted as a future superstar. Considering his post-race fisticuffs with Kyle Petty after The Winston of '87, it appeared that the son of Missouri short-track ace Russ Wallace would become a boxer before succeeding as a racer. Certainly no one expected him to blossom with such explosive suddenness. There was a time during the '88 season that he seemed unbeatable. Three times he came from two laps down to win.

His emergence changed racing.

But on March 27, 1988, the week after Atlanta, Wallace was not considered a serious contender for the TranSouth 500 at Darlington. The pre-race big question was, would Elliott, sore shoulder and all, be able to drive and survive a grueling 500 miles?

He had no doubt.

"Nobody knows my car as well as I do," he said, declining to share No. 9 with a relief driver. "I'd rather try to go out and run all day than fool with trying to put somebody else in it. You forget about the pain when you get into that race car.

". . . I'll just run as hard as I can and see what happens. Earnhardt has already said he's going to make it a boring race."

The shoulder handicap was obvious during qualifying when the Georgia redhead was fourteen spots behind pole sitter Ken Schrader, earning his second inside front of the season. Schrader was one of the Young Lions, said to have the same potential as Wallace.

On race day, Elliott was a contender throughout. Doing well to dodge all the spinning cars and wrecks that were said to be a result of the Great Tire War, he picked up his first Top Five place of the year, a fourth. The race was notable in that it was won by 40-year old Lake Speed, his first Winston Cup success in eight seasons, and the first Oldsmobile in the Darlington victory lane since Cale Yarborough's in the 1978 Southern 500. Trailing in order were Alan Kulwicki, Davey Allison, Elliott and Sterling Marlin.

Speed, a deeply religious person who said prayer got him through the down periods of his racing career, paid a special tribute to Racing Hall of Famer Darel Dieringer, then 61 and critically ill with liver cancer. Dieringer had introduced the Jackson, Mississippi, native to Winston Cup racing in 1980.

The TranSouth was unlucky for points leader Bonnett who wrecked, finished nineteenth, and gave up the lead to defending champion Earnhardt. In sixth-place, 78 points back, was Elliott.

It was a good performance for the Coors bunch and the fun was returning to racing.

In two weeks, at Bristol, life was to become a downright laugh-in.

The date, April 10, 1988, was a milestone in the career of the Elliotts.

In their twelfth year, their 238th race, their 52nd on a short track, they scored the long-awaited breakthrough on a half-miler, sending an ominous signal to rival drivers who had considered the Elliotts vulnerable on the short tracks. That flaw in the racing ointment had played a major role in their loss of the 1985 Winston Cup championship. His short-track record hung like an albatross around Bill's neck. Of his 52 starts on the bullrings of NASCAR, he'd had 11 Top Five finishes and been as high as third only twice, at Martinsville in '84 and at North Wilkesboro in '87.

But as he said, "I haven't had Junior Johnson or Bud Moore to coach me. When the cars were downsized, they had a little harder time grasping it and we were all even again.

"At Martinsville three years ago I had no idea what to expect. Just ten races on the short tracks in five years doesn't tell you a lot. I learned by what little I ran in practice. It just takes time. Others have had more starts on the short tracks than I have and they have veteran people coaching them. For example, the first time I ever saw North Wilkesboro was in 1983.

"We've been trying to overcome the little things that have hurt us on the short tracks. I'm a whole lot more confident."

That confidence showed on April 10.

There was nothing flukey about the manner in which Elliott rang up No. 1 on a less-than-a-mile racing layout. Outside of Harry Gant's 121, he led the most laps, 116, and he showed another side of his character to come back and blow Geoff Bodine away after the No. 5 car got physical with him eight laps from the finish.

Whether by design or improvisation, 'Awesome Bill' from the Georgia hill always drives a strategic race. He likes to lie low until crunch time; then, like a tiger, spring on the field. Starting from the supposedly unlucky 13th position in the Valleydale Meats 500, he was inconspicuous until the 379th lap when Gant wrecked.

With one exception, he led the rest of the way.

The exception came on lap 492, with Bodine riding his bumper. It became clear there would be a challenge. And sure enough, in a few seconds Bodine went side by side in the third turn and the cars tangled, with the No. 9 T-Bird making a full spin in the dust and miraculously staying off the wall.

When the caution came out, Elliott executed a brilliant move. He ducked into the pits, got four fresh tires and fuel, and was back on the track in a heartbeat. Bodine chose to stay on the pavement.

Three laps from the 500-lap finish, the green came out and Elliott went after the No. 5 Chevrolet — aggressively, it might be added. A lap later he was door-to-door with Bodine on turn four and went by the tire-weary Chevy like it was standing still. Winston Cup newcomer Mark Martin jumped behind Elliott and whipped past Bodine to finish second.

To say that Elliott was pleased was to understate the occasion.

"To win here is the greatest feeling there will ever be," he said. "It just shows you, you can't give up no matter what happens or where you are."

About the collision, he said, "I think he got into me a lot more than I got into him. I gave him all the track I could, but he just spun me out."

Said Bodine, "It wasn't a big bump I gave Elliott in turn four, but it was enough to get him sideways. It was late in the race and you've got to hold your ground."

Actually, the Valleydale 500 marked two important steps in the Coors program. First, of course, it brought Coors its first short-track win. Secondly, it showed a more aggressive, tougher Elliott when the circumstances called for it. That trait came out several times during the season.

One driver who wasn't getting a lot of attention in those days was Rusty Wallace and, in retrospect, it is interesting to note that his short-track season was going in the other direction from Elliott's. He ran a relatively strong race in the Valleydale, but fell victim to a chain accident. Bobby Allison hit somebody and Wallace hit Bobby. As a result, Wallace went a lap down and finished fourth.

Wallace and Bristol were to have another damaging confrontation in the fall.

Bristol was more than just a breakthrough for the Coors team. It marked the first time a Ford had won over the .533-mile track since David Pearson, in the spring of 1971. And when Martin followed No. 9 across the line, it was the first 1-2 Ford finish since 1965.

One by one, the Elliotts were achieving the goals they had set. Winning a short-track race was one. The last, and biggest of all, was the Winston Cup championship. That had to be next.

The road to the Winston had both short and long stretches. Before they moved on to the long, or the super highways, they had two more short tests, the First Union at North Wilkesboro where Bill had always been very close to winning, and the Pannill 500 at Martinsville, where he was never comfortable.

First, however, there was another of Hank Schoolfield's press conferences prior to North Wilkesboro and, it seems, Elliott had always been on a roll when he came to Schoolfield's shindigs. This time he was relaxed and affable and he tackled the questions head-on.

On the Cup chase, Elliott said:

"I'd certainly like to win a championship and I'd like for it to be this year, but there is lots of racing left. In '85 I lost the championship in the last four or five races, so right now I'm not going to worry about points (he was fourth, 24 behind the leader, Earnhardt). I'm just going to worry about finishing races.

"Now I feel so good about our team. You need time to work on the car, deal with the media and deal with the fans. I may be sitting in the truck and look like I'm resting, but I'm thinking all the time about the car."

Elliott was asked, is racing no longer fun?

"If you do a job long enough, no matter how much fun it was to start with, the fun goes away. I'd rather be home working with the race car, but other things are expected to be done. I try to keep the appearances under control, but you can't say 'no' to your sponsors. That's part of it. If you need money from your sponsors down the road, it's (making appearances) something I've got to do."

Not only that, said Elliott, but the competition has gotten much fiercer.

He said, "When I first started in '76, drivers would come to Rockingham and just be concerned about getting in the field. Once they got in, they'd just ride around during the race because they knew they didn't have the money or equipment to compete. That's not the case now. There's so many good teams, they're going after it everywhere."

In addition to other problems, 1988 brought another major decision: which tire to use? It became a guessing game. Up until North Wilkesboro, the two companies had split six races. By and large, however, the Elliotts stuck to Goodyear except on rare occasions.

The return to North Wilkesboro proved to be only so-so. So did Martinsville. The Coors team finished tenth and eleventh and, oddly, climbed from fourth to third in the point standings but lost ground on the point deficit, going from minus 24 to minus 115. Terry Lebonte, to no one's surprise, won the First Union 400 and Earnhardt won the Pannill 500. A third-place finish at North Wilkesboro propelled the defending Winston Cup champion to his largest lead of the season, 77 points over runner-up Sterling Marlin.

Other than Bill's Bristol win, the first round at short tracks had been average — a twelfth at Richmond, a tenth at North Wilkesboro, an eleventh at Martinsville. During the second half of the season, he didn't score any wins, but improved his positions dramatically, with a second at Bristol, a seventh at Richmond, a sixth at Martinsville and a fifth at North Wilkesboro.

But that was to come later. Up until now, the best thing for the Coors team about Martinsville was that it led to the long road at Talladega. That was where Elliott was king of the Indian burial grounds.

But the restrictor plates had changed things, and an imaginary conversation could have gone something like this:

"Where you been, Bill?"

"Talladega."

"What happened?"

"Nothing much."

With a speed arm tied behind him, Elliott had to settle for an 11-7 quinella, eleventh starting position and seventh-place finish. Davey Allison won the pole with a 198.969 lap, some 14 mph slower than Elliott's world record. And Phil Parsons, younger brother of Benny, became the second first-time winner of the season by taking the Winston 500 in an Olds.

The oddity is that Bill never led a lap! So in his two patsy tracks, Daytona and Talladega, he had been shut out from the lead. In fact, in five of the first nine races he had failed to lead a lap and in another, at Darlington, he was out front on only one turn. For sure, it wasn't a typical Elliott start.

Charlotte was next and you know how Bruton Smith's and Humpy Wheeler's racing emporium is; things always happen at Charlotte. The big topic was the grudge match involving Elliott, Earnhardt and Bodine in The Winston, RJR's much ballyhooed sprint race.

The Charlotte program started on a sad note for Bill. On the Saturday before The Winston, a day set aside for fan appreciation, he had to leave for Murphy, N.C., where he attended the funeral of his friend and skiing partner Joe Locke, who succumbed to cancer. Only a few days earlier he had promised Locke he'd be one of the pallbearers.

The script for The Winston was one of those "it happens every time" stories. With no prodding, race drivers will pull all kinds of shennanigans on the track — bumping, threatening and complaining. But the minute that fans and the media put them on display and expect the worst, they bow their backs, become very clannish, and show off their halos.

Their attitude then is: "What, us fight each other?"

The third running of The Winston was almost Tide-clean, and Terry Labonte, reacting to car owner Junior Johnson's statement that he should be more aggressive, won it aggressively.

Two from the '87 incident, Earnhardt and Bodine, were not factors. Dale had trouble with the wall and tires and finished seventh; and Bodine parked his Chevy early due to a mechanical problem.

Following Labonte across the start-finish line, in order, were Sterling Marlin, Davey Allison and Elliott.

It was a piece of cake.

Then, as if to demonstrate there were no ill feelings from '87, Earnhardt and Elliott, all smiles and harmony, skipped off to Newton, N.C., the Tuesday after The Winston to sell Chevrolets at Dale's dealership. That's about as far as a man can walk in another's shoes. Solidarity forever . . . or until the next racing crunch.

Returning to the Charlotte Motor Speedway for qualifying the next day, the two got mixed results, perhaps due to the uncertainty over which tire to use. Winston Cup sophomore Davey Allison swept the pole with a record 173.594 (bettering Elliott's old mark of 171.712) to edge Geoff Bodine's 172.524. Elliott was sixth and Earnhardt was seventh.

Not one to spread himself thin by racing on Saturday and then again on Sunday, Bill made an exception for the Winn-Dixie 300 Grand National race to test his own V-6 Thunderbird, prepared in Ernie's research and development program. Despite some late problems, he posted a solid seventh.

Sunday and the Coca-Cola World 600 brought the most bizarre chapter of The Great Tire War.

Goodyear was having all kinds of trouble. Richard Petty and Ricky Rudd had injuries in tire-induced wrecks, and the firm's director of racing, Leo Mehl, was concerned.

"The safety of the drivers is what this is all about," he said.

After huddling with NASCAR and the Hoosier rivals, he was granted permission to substitute the tire for the Charlotte track with a harder, safer but slower compound used for Daytona.

Everyone started the big race on Hoosiers except veteran Dave Marcis, who, pointing out that Goodyear supplied him with free tires when he was struggling in the Sixties, refused to jump ship.

Marcis' loyalty was rewarded with only the second 'lifetime deal' offered by Goodyear. The other belongs to Indy racing tire pioneer A. J. Foyt, who helped the company in its development program.

Neither Elliott nor Earnhardt was a factor in the late stages of the 600. A blowout and an argument with the wall with less than 100 laps left effectively eliminated Bill from contention and Dale never recovered from a lap lost in the penalty box for bumping Geoff Bodine. Elliott finished 19th and Earnhardt 13th in a race won by veteran Darrell Waltrip.

In a manner of speaking, said Waltrip, the Hoosier tires were too good in that "they ran the wheels off the cars."

Point standings after Charlotte: Earnhardt led by 71 over Wallace, by 97 over Marlin, by 106 over Labonte and by 110 over Elliott.

The first ten races of the Winston Cup season had been less than scintillating for the Coors crew. Five times they'd been out of the Top Ten and placed only twice in the Top Five. They were on the bubble; the season could go either way. The upcoming Budweiser 500 at Dover would be a fair barometer.

Unbeknownst to all, the next two races were to set the table for the run at the Winston Cup.

At Dover, Bill was to dominate, shave 60 points off Earnhardt's lead and climb to third in the points race. A week later, at Riverside, a new name was to appear at the lead position of the Winston Cup race for the first time. After seven years, Rusty Wallace was making a move.

Dover was rewarding for Elliott but it wasn't easy.

He started on Goodyears, lost a lap because of an unscheduled pit stop and decided to switch to Hoosiers. It was like Clark Kent stepping into the phone booth. With more secure footing, he was the dominant Elliott of old, leading 192 of the 500 laps, including 124 of the last 135.

Only Morgan Shepherd and Wallace, in that order, were on the lead lap at the finish.

Elliott talked about his big crisis on lap 224.

"I felt a problem with the left front tire and I decided I needed to stop and replace it, even if it meant going a lap down," he said. "The car was working so well, especially after switching to Hoosiers, that once I made up the lap I was confident I could win the race."

Dover had been a big step forward, but, unfortunately, the next three races left the Georgia carrot-top with his largest point deficit of the year, 150.

At Riverside, Wallace won and he was 16th, a loss of 54 points, now 104 in arrears. The race was significant in two respects: it was the last race ever at Riverside, which was to be turned into a real estate development; and it was a return to the scene where the Coors team had suffered a real disaster in '87.

At Pocono, Wallace was third and Bill was 10th and now 140 points back. Big news here was the horrifying crash that sent Bobby Allison to the hospital in critical condition with head and internal injuries.

The ultimate in affronts came at Michigan, Bill's home away from home where he's always expected to lead the qualifying and win the races. Well, he did sit on the pole, with a record 172.687 mph, but he had to settle for a second by two car lengths behind winner Wallace.

"I could catch up to him but the air coming off his car in the corners was messing me up and I couldn't get there," said the lanky Georgian.

As the racing caravans moved into Daytona for the Firecracker 400, Wallace held the inside advantage for the RJR mid-season payoff of $150,000. It was unlikely that the Pontiac driver would lose more than 130 points to Earnhardt or 150 to Elliott. And Bill's best shot was to edge ahead of old No. 3 and collect $100,000 instead of the $75,000 that went to the third-place finisher after 15 races.

Bill, Ernie and Dan couldn't win the $150,000 jackpot, so they did the next best thing. They won the race ($63,500) and collected the third-place Winston Cup payoff ($75,000) for a day's work of $138,500

— not too shabby. And, in the process, Bill cut 53 points off Wallace's lead. Wallace finished twelfth, the first time in six races he'd been out of the Top Ten, and, in retrospect, the heavy point loss at Daytona was a vital minus at the end of the season.

Elliott's racing style can be likened to a catcher calling for different pitches. Sometimes he completely dominates; other times he waits for a late kick; still other times he plays cat-and-mouse. At Daytona, where he started 38th after failing to qualify during the first round for the first time since the '86 spring race at Martinsville, he used an entirely new ploy.

He and Olds driver Rick Wilson hooked up in a two-car draft and found they could make tracks on the entire field. They went that way for the final 60 miles before breaking away for a last-lap sprint, which Elliott won by a foot or so.

"If we hadn't helped each other, he would have never made it to second and I couldn't have worked my way to the lead," said Elliott.

Daytona was the start of a roll for the Coors/Motorcraft T-Bird.

Including the Firecracker, 'Awesome Bill' swept four of nine races during that important stretch of the Winston Cup schedule.

The Summer 500 at Pocono was No. 2.

Running what he described as his "most flawless" race since 1985, Elliott crossed the finish line a quarter-mile ahead of runner-up Ken Schrader. He led for 122 of the 200 laps around the triangular 2.5-mile track and picked up 94 more points on Wallace, who lost a transmission, spent 14 laps in repairs and finished 24th.

"I haven't had a race this easy in a long, long time," said Elliott. "You know, it sort of reminded me of what Dale did last year. You go out and run, you dominate and make no mistakes."

And take no prisoners.

The Pocono race marked Bill's fourth victory of the campaign and the 27th of his career. It was also the place where he moved into second, ahead of Earnhardt, only three points behind Wallace.

The win was important in that nothing went according to form during the next three races. At Talladega, Bill's track, Rusty gained eight points with a fifth to Coors' eighth; at Watkins Glen, Rusty's track, Bill stayed even with a third to Wallace's second, and at Michigan, Bill's favorite, Wallace gained 10 points with a second to Bill's third.

In Elliott's behalf, Michigan presented mitigating circumstances. He had won the pole with a record 174.940 and was the race pacesetter until a fire in an adjoining pit forced him to leave with two lug nuts untightened. As a result, he lost time to winner Davey Allison and Wallace.

When all the dissecting is done, it will be discovered that the next three races — Bristol, Darlington and Richmond — decided the 1988 Winston Cup championship.

Remember all that stuff about Bill's weaknesses on the short track and Wallace's superiority on the half-milers? Well, Bristol and Richmond rose up and bit the Kodiak Bear right on its exhaust pipe and Elliott flat outran him at Darlington.

It is a story of contrasts.

The short-track blues started for Wallace at Bristol.

During a practice run, he crashed into the wall, wrecked his car, and suffered a painful neck injury that required hospitalization.

He was given the green light to start the Busch 500 on Sunday, but the pain forced him to turn over the driving to young Larry Pearson, and the No. 27 Pontiac came in ninth, seven laps off the lead.

Meanwhile, Earnhardt and Elliott were staging a furious duel for the lead at the finish and the Chevy ace managed to hold off Dawsonville's most famous citizen for a 1-2 finish. For the first time in the long season, Bill moved into the Winston Cup lead, 16 points ahead of Wallace, never again to trail.

By Labor Day weekend and the Southern 500, pressure was beginning to build. Wallace said he was ready and wouldn't need a relief driver.

"We got behind (in points) because I wrecked at Bristol," he said. "If I hadn't, I felt like we had a car good enough to win the race."

With both Earnhardt and Wallace breathing on his neck, Elliott had a right to feel like he had double General Motors trouble.

He said, "The problem is, you don't have one guy to deal with. You've got two. I'm concerned about beating them. The championship is going to come down to the team with the least amount of bad luck."

If close buddies Earnhardt and Wallace had Elliott shaken, he didn't show it on qualifying day. He went out and snatched the pole with a run of 160.827 mph, a record for that race. Earnhardt, who seldom sits on the pole, earned the outside position and Wallace was in the No. 5 slot.

The Southern had its usual sellout crowd despite omnipresent rain clouds, and vice presidential candidate Dan Quayle showed up to be seen.

More than any other race, the Southern 500 personified the '88 season. The finish was a preview of the Winston Cup standings at the end: Elliott, Wallace and Earnhardt, in that order. Elliott led three times for 154 laps, Earnhardt five times for 81 and Wallace four times for 49.

This victory can be attributed to inspired pit work by Ernie and Dan Elliott and the Coors crew.

Up to the last pit stop, Bill had sort of laid low, letting Wallace and Earnhardt have their time at the front. Earnhardt was the leader when they all pitted on caution on lap 330.

Bill came out first.

The final 36 laps provided the most cliffhanging action of the racing year.

They went at it, Elliott and Wallace, all jets going, full bore, playing their daring game of chicken. Wherever Bill went, there was Rusty on his tail and at his side, wedging in and trying to pass, always threatening. Never was there a moment for Bill to breathe. Physically and mentally, those 36 laps took more out of him than most 500-mile races.

He won it. Won it by a scant .24-second, and at the finish he was one tired race driver.

"Bill had just enough to hold me off," said Wallace. "He pinched me off and I salute him."

Elliott said he felt secure racing with Wallace.

"I've raced a good bit with Rusty and I knew he wouldn't rub on me and wreck us," he said.

For all that effort all the Coors team gained at Darlington was ten points. Now it led by 26 over the car owned by the Blue Max Racing Team headed by Raymond Beadle.

Next was Richmond, reshaped into a tri-oval and lengthened to .750-mile, which was to decide the '88 Winston Cup championship.

Richmond was to Rusty Wallace what Waterloo was to Napoleon. Even four wins out of the last five Winston Cup races couldn't make up for the points lost in the Miller High Life 400.

And it happened early in the race.

Only eighteen laps from the green flag, Wallace and Geoff Bodine tangled. Wallace, unable to continue, was sentenced to 35th in the finishing order.

There were accusations from both sides.

Wallace threw around words like "conehead" and "brain fade," and said "if I lose the points championship, it'll be because of this." Bodine denied any wrong and said both guys were just racing hard.

Whatever and whomever was to blame, Rusty Wallace suffered a severe setback on the road to the Winston Cup. He lost 93 points to Elliott and fell to third behind Earnhardt. The points after the Bristol read: Elliott, 3,363; Earnhardt, 3,246; Wallace, 3,244.

Wallace's future didn't look that good. Many thought his best chance would be the final swing through Virginia and North Carolina with stops at Martinsville, Charlotte, North Wilkesboro and Rockingham.

But first there was the Delaware 500 at Dover and Elliott was the only one of the leading trio to have won there.

He said his mission was clear.

"We don't have any choice but to stay with our same strategy — one race at a time, try to win and figure the points will take care of themselves if we do," he said. "Sure, it's tough to win races out there these days; thirteen different drivers have already proven this year that they can win and there are plenty of others very capable of it. That's the bad news. The good news is that it's just as tough for everyone else."

As for Wallace, he said he had no choice but to "win races."

He didn't win at Dover. Elliott did.

In another one of those unerring performances, the Dawsonville Kid led 392 of 500 laps, to record the sixth victory of the season and the 29th of his career. The Southern 500 script was altered only slightly, this time Earnhardt beating Wallace for second.

Elliott was pleased.

"It was almost like 1985 again," he said. "If I keep doing my job, they gotta catch me."

With six races to go, Earnhardt trailed by 127, Wallace by 139.

Before the Martinsville race, all-time moneywinner Darrell Waltrip said he detected a change in Elliott.

"Bill has gotten tougher," he said. "He's quit driving the car like it belonged to Daddy and started driving it like it belonged to somebody else. He used to drive like Daddy told him, 'Boy, don't you tear up that car.' Like my brother Mike drives mine, you know.

"All along I've picked Bill to win the points championship and I stick by that. If he can get by the next couple of weeks, he'll be all right."

To prove he can race as well as talk, Waltrip went out and won the Goody's 500 at Martinsville. And Bill hung in there with a sixth to Wallace's third, losing only 15 points.

Rain and inclement weather postponed the Holly Farm 400 at North Wilkesboro for two weeks and thus the Oakwood Homes 500 at Charlotte came after Martinsville. One characteristic of CMS in the fall is that there are always as many press conferences and announcements as there are laps.

This week wasn't much different. Kyle Petty announced he was switching rides, Junior Johnson disclosed he would drop Chevrolet for a T-Bird, Cale Yarborough confirmed his retirement, and Peter Coors said he was happy to extend the sponsorship of the No. 9 Ford for three more years. Most teams were looking back and re-evaluating the first 25 races.

The rest of the season was to belong to a rampaging Wallace, who went through Charlotte, North Wilkesboro and Rockingham like Sherman through Atlanta. Each time he came from two or more laps down to win and each time, to his dismay, he looked in his rear-view mirror to find Elliott just a few paces back.

The Georgia redhead was fourth at Charlotte, fifth at North Wilkesboro and fourth at Rockingham, always within sight and never in a position where he'd lose a lot of points.

He had two priorities, to wit: (1) finish the race, (2) stay on the lead lap within sight of the winner. And, of course, if the opportunity presented itself, win.

Wallace, who had said he'd dog Elliott every step of the way, was himself showing some of the frustration after Rockingham when he said, "We've picked up 50 points on Bill in the last three races, but 50 points aren't going to be enough. We don't have a lot of choice, the way I see it. We have to go as hard as we can go and do everything we can to win each of the remaining races. If we do that and it's still not enough, then I'll be the first to shake Bill's hand."

The Kodiak team missed a good bet to pick up some points in the first-ever Checker 500 at Phoenix, a mile-track with no banking that replaced the Riverside spot on the schedule. He was fifth to Bill's fourth in a race highlighted by Alan Kulwicki's maiden if unorthodox trip to victory lane in a Winston Cup race. To celebrate, Kulwicki ran a victory lap backwards, or, as he called it, "a Polish lap."

Wallace came out of Phoenix like he'd gone in, 79 points back. He needed better than that.

The Winston Cup finale at Atlanta International Raceway, Bill's backyard track, was built up to be the ultimate in dramas. The shootout had narrowed to two drivers, Elliott and Wallace, with Earnhardt having been mathematically eliminated at Phoenix. His championship string had been snapped at two.

Both racing warriors were ready.

Said Elliott, "Now we're headed to the last race and they tell me 18th or better will clinch the Winston Cup championship. Well, Atlanta won't be any different than Phoenix was. It's going to be tough to win. We're going to have to stay with the strategy that's worked for us all year — run hard, try our best to win. Do that and the points will take care of themselves."

Said Wallace, "If there is a point where you give up on something like this, it doesn't come until that checkered flag falls on the last race."

Crunch time for Wallace meant he had to sit on the pole, lead all the laps, win the race and hope that Elliott blew sky high early.

Elliott's game plan was much simpler: finish 18th or better. What he needed to do and what Wallace wanted him to do were two different things. Naturally, Wallace preferred for the Coors driver to mix it up with him at the front and risk not being around at the finish, just as a boxer far behind on points prefers for his opponents to move in close and throw wild haymakers instead of jabbing and moving.

As expected, Wallace went full bore from qualifying day, when he swept to the pole. It did come as somewhat of a surprise that Elliott failed to qualify in the first round and then stood on his speed for a 30th starting position. He was moved up to 29th when one of the cars fell out.

Wallace did all he had to do. He won and he led the most laps. And Elliott did all he needed to do. He placed 11th and won his first Winston Cup points championship, a prize said to be worth at least $2 million in monies, endorsements and other benefits. The final margin was 24 points.

In doing it his way, he took some heat, especially from the Atlanta media, and, in the emotion of the finish, Wallace tossed a few barbs.

He said, "There was nothing I could do but just drive my car's wheels off and hope. And here he (Elliott) was just staying ninth and tenth. I think I would have tried to have won the race in a conservative way or at least not get lapped and put a show on for the fans."

In reply, Elliott said he did what he had to do to win the Winston Cup, but he didn't necessarily enjoy it.

"It was hard not to try and win that race in front of our hometown fans," he said. "I hope they understand, and that winning the Winston Cup for them made up for our not trying to win the race. I wasn't about to throw it away. We could have raced for the win and ended up in the wall, losing the championship.

"It wasn't easy to be conservative. All my life I have tried to win races — not just finish in a certain position. It was against my nature, but it was the smart thing to do. If others want to criticize me, that's okay.

"The bottom line is that the Winston Cup is in Dawsonville and Georgia. There is no guarantee we'll ever win it again."

Few could argue with that logic.

Somehow, in all the excitement of the Atlanta Journal 500, it slipped everyone's mind that the date, November 20, marked the fifth anniversary of Bill's first Winston Cup win, at Riverside. In those five years the Coors/Motorcraft team has won $7,362,784, an incredible amount for such a short period of time, or a grand total of only 146 races. For his 29 wins in that span of time, Elliott has averaged an unbelievable $50,430.03 per outing.

The '88 season and the Winston Cup spoils totaled $1,554,639, making Elliott a million dollar winner for a record fourth straight year. It also raised his career earnings to $8,300,519 and elevated him to third place among all race drivers behind leader Darrell Waltrip, $8,679,217, and runners-up Earnhardt, $8,308,848. Star-crossed Bobby Allison ($7,215,554) fell to fourth, ahead of Richard Petty ($6,850,859) and Al Unser and A. J. Foyt from the Indy circuit.

For sure, at age 33, the reserved North Georgia hill boy had become a genuine racing phenomenon, the king of speed on the fastest tracks. Once again he collected the $30,000 awarded to the Busch pole winner — he had six to Kulwicki's four — and ran his career total to 35, ranking him fifth in the modern era. However, with the retirement of Cale Yarborough, Elliott becomes the undisputed active king of super speedway qualifying with 33 poles.

Only long-retired David Pearson (64) and Yarborough (48) are ahead of 'Awesome Bill' in super raceway poles.

Unlike other years, Bill and his brothers relished their trip to New York in December to receive their spoils at the annual NASCAR Winston Cup Awards banquet in the Grand Ball Room of the Waldorf Astoria Hotel.

For the once-struggling racing family, that in 1981 had already decided to fold its tent and call it quits before Harry Melling stepped in to rescue it, New York was a visit to the money tree.

Dolph von Arx, Gerald Long's successor at RJR, handed Bill a check for $500,364 and described him as "old moneybags." The Coors team also picked up $25,000 from Unocal, $12,000 from each STP and Champion Spark Plug, $30,000 from Busch, $25,000 from True Value, $20,000 from Gatorade and $5,000 from Sears.

The country boys from Dawsonville had struck it rich.

Proudest of all were the parents, George and Mildred Elliott, who saw a dream fullfilled in the success of their brood, the kids who used to drive the forklifts at the building supply company.

Bill Elliott did not forget.

"It's been a long road," he told Tom Higgins of *The Charlotte Observer,* dean of Winston Cup writers. "Lordly, who would ever have thought it would come to this. Certainly not me. Not during the time from '76 to '80 and '81 when we were trying to break into racin' and usin' the ol' Riverview Elementary School in Dahlonega as a shop.

"We had dreams when we kept our cars at that old school that Daddy lined up as a shop. But for us to think about coming to New York in this capacity, why, we might as well have thought about going to Mars.

"It seemed like light years away for us."

At the Waldorf-Astoria, Ernie, who doesn't say much at the tracks, gave an eloquent acceptance speech and Bill thanked the 75 crewmen, workers and friends who had made the trip from Dawsonville. He cited his wife Martha, Winston, Harry Melling, Coors, Motorcraft, Ford, crewmen, friends, Melvin and Janie Turner, his brothers and their families, his mother and father, his secretary Becky McCord, and Alexis Leras, the Melling PR representative.

And Melling had to be pleased with himself.

His original $500 investment had returned more than $8 million.

Though 1988 was the Year of The Elliotts, it was also the year of change in NASCAR and the Winston Cup. Things were never going to be the same again. Cale Yarborough and Benny Parsons, who had four Winston Cup trophies and more than $10 million in winnings, announced their retirement. Yarborough would tend to his many business interests and own a car driven by Dale Jarrett, and Parsons would join the electronic media and do other promotional work.

The futures of Bobby Allison and Buddy Baker, both seriously injured in wrecks, were in doubt. Allison had not recovered from a first-lap wreck at Pocono in June and Baker had undergone surgery to remove pressure from his brain following an accident at CMS in May.

Altogether, the four veteran drivers represented 206 Winston Cup wins.

The only active drivers remaining from the pioneer era were Richard Petty, winless since '84; Dave Marcis, one win in 12 years; Harry Gant, on a long losing streak; Morgan Shepherd, a sometimes contender, and A. J. Foyt, an occasional participant in stocks. Buddy Arrington, G. C. Spencer and J. D. McDuffie were still around to fill out the field.

Winston Cup had welcomed four first-time winners in '88: Lake Speed at Darlington, Phil Parsons and Ken Schrader at Talladega, and Kulwicki at Phoenix. Since Elliott and Wallace had six wins apiece, that totals up to 16 of the 29 races. Of the rest, Earnhardt won three; Neil Bonnett, Davey Allison and Darrell Waltrip two apiece, and Terry Labonte, Bobby Allison, Geoff Bodine and Ricky Rudd, one apiece.

There were definite signs of the changing of the guard. Moving up to replace the departing drivers were the Elliotts, Wallace, Earnhardt, Davey Allison, Rudd, Labonte, Phil Parsons, Schrader and Kulwicki. And lurking just behind them, ready to spring, were Mark Martin, Dale Jarrett, Greg Sacks, Michael Waltrip, Rick Wilson, Bobby Hillin, Sterling Marlin, Brett Bodine, and Ken Bouchard (rookie of the year).

In the middle group, contenders from time to time, were Darrell Waltrip, Geoff Bodine, Neil Bonnett, Richard Petty, Joe Ruttman and those in the middle-age group. Guys like Kyle Petty, Harry Gant, Morgan Shepherd and Marlin had switched rides and were question marks.

There were other major changes. Junior Johnson had decided to drop Chevrolet for Thunderbird for his driver, Labonte, and master engine builder Lou Larose left Earnhardt for Rudd's team.

Mike Alexander, who replaced Bobby Allison in the No. 12 Buick, was critically injured in a non-Winston Cup race during the off-season and his physical condition for '89 was in doubt.

No one knew just how they would fill out the Winston Cup puzzle in '89. On the other hand, no one expected Rusty Wallace to make his move in '88.

The beauty of the sport is its unpredictability.

A year ago Bill Elliott attended the NASCAR banquet at the Waldorf Astoria, fresh from a near-fatal flight in an F-16. Nine months ago he lay in Crawford Long Hospital wondering about the inequities of fate. But now he was a millionaire many times over, king of the hills and Most Popular Driver for the fifth year in a row. An example of how things change is that Most Popular runner-up was Darrell Waltrip, formerly the most hated.

For the moment, at least, the boys from No. 9 were on Cloud Nine. Four days later they'd be at Daytona testing, and the racing carousel would start all over again.

There were more and better goals to shoot for.

R. J. Reynolds and Unocal had sweetened the pots.

RJR's von Arx disclosed that, in the future, Winston would pay the points champion not $400,000, but a million big ones, a cool mil. The increased $2.5 million payoff will benefit all top finishers.

And Unocal will honor those who win both the qualifying poles and the subsequent races on Sunday. That will pay more than $7,000, and will roll over. For example, if it happens after the first 10 races of the season, the payoff is $70,000.

Just when the Elliotts had thought they'd seen it all, and won it all, here came those racing people with more challenges and more bait.

Appendix:
By The Numbers

BILL ELLIOTT'S WINS
(Through 1988)

Date	Track (Length)	Start	Miles	Runner-up	Margin	Earnings
1983 (1)						
Nov 20	Riverside (2.62)	10	311.78	B. Parsons	Caution	$26,380
1984 (3)						
Jun 17	Michigan (2.0)	1	400	Yarborough	2.0	$41,600
Oct. 7	Charlotte (1.5)	2	500	B. Parsons	14.5	$52,633
Oct 21	Rockingham (1.017)	2	500	Gant	12"	$30,400
1985 (11)						
Feb 17	Daytona (2.5)	1	500	Speed	.94	$185,500
Mar 17	Atlanta (1.522)	3	500	Bodine	2.64	$59,800
Apr 14	Darlington (1.366)	1	500	Waltrip	2.5	$42,900
May 5	Talladega (2.66)	1	500	K. Petty	2.0	$60,500
May 19	Dover (1.0)	4	500	Gant	29.0	$44,500
Jun 9	Pocono (2.5)	1	500	Gant	.02	$44,525
Jun 16	Michigan (2.0)	1a	400	Waltrip	13.0	$48,600
Jul 21	Pocono (2.5)	2b	500	Bonnett	5.0	$44,025
Aug 11	Michigan (2.0)	1	400	Waltrip	4.0	$57,600
Sep 1	Darlington (1.366)	1	500	Yarborough	2.0	$53,725
Nov 3	Atlanta (1.522)	3	500	Yarborough	4.25	$57,650
1986 (2)						
Jun 15	Michigan (2.0)	8	400	Gant	2CL	$56,900
Aug 27	Michigan (2.0)	3	400	Richmond	1.45	$55,950
1987 (6)						
Feb 15	Daytona (2.5)	1	500	B. Parsons	3CL	$204,150
Jul 26	Talladega (2.66)	1	500	D. Allison	.15	$70,920
Aug 16	Michigan (2.0)	3	400	Earnhardt	.76	$52,875
Oct 11	Charlotte (1.5)	7	500	B. Allison	1.5	$74,040
Oct 25	Rockingham (1.017)	3	500	Earnhardt	5.26	$50,025
Nov 22	Atlanta (1.522)	1	500	Earnhardt	12.94	$74,200
1988 (6)						
Apr 10	Bristol (.533)	13	266.5	M. Martin	2CL	$45,750
Jun 5	Dover (1.0)	17	500	M. Shepherd	21	$53,000
Jul 2	Daytona (2.5)	28	400	Wilson	18"	$63,500
Jul 24	Pocono (2.5)	2	500	Schrader	8.27	$53,200
Sept 4	Darlington (1.366)	1	500	Wallace	.24	$75,800
Sept 18	Dover (1.0)	3	500	Earnhardt	1.48	$56,400

a - qualifying rained out, started via owner's points.
b - awarded pole when original winner was disqualified.

ELLIOTT POLES
(Through 1988)

Date	Race	Track	Length	Finish	Speed
1981 (1)					
Apr 8	CRC Rebel 500	Darlington	1.366	4	153.896
1982 (1)					
Aug 22	Champion 400	Michigan	2.0	27	162.995
1984 (4)					
Jun 27	Miller 400	Michigan	2.0	1	*164.339**
Jul 22	Like Cola 500	Pocono	2.5	3	152.184
Aug 12	Champion 400	Michigan	2.0	3	165.217
Nov 11	Journal 500	Atlanta	1.522	2	170.198
1985 (11)					
Feb 17	Daytona 500	Daytona	2.5	1	*205.114**
Apr 14	TranSouth 500	Darlington	1.366	1	157.454
May 5	Winston 500	Talladega	2.66	1	*209.398**
May 26	Coca-Cola 600	Charlotte	1.5	18	164.703
Jun 9	Van Scoy 500	Pocono	2.5	1	152.563
Jul 4	Firecracker 400	Daytona	2.5	2	201.523
Jul 21	Summer 500	Pocono	2.5	1	151.973
Jul 28	Talladega 500	Talladega	2.66	4	207.578
Aug 11	Champion 400	Michigan	2.0	1	165.479
Sep 1	Southern 500	Darlington	1.366	1	156.641
Sep 15	Delaware 500	Dover	1.0	20	141.543
1986 (4)					
Feb 16	Daytona 500	Daytona	2.5	13	205.039
May 4	Winston 500	Talladega	2.66	24	*212.229**
Jul 27	Talladega 500	Talladega	2.66	27	209.005
Nov 2	Journal 500	Atlanta	1.522	3	*172.905**
1987 (8)					
Feb 15	Daytona 500	Daytona	2.5	1	*210.364**
Apr 4	First Union 400	North Wilkesboro	.625	10	*116.003**
May 3	Winston 500	Talladega	2.66	22	*212.809***
May 24	Coca-Cola 600	Charlotte	1.5	23	*170.901**
May 31	Budweiser 500	Dover	1.0	2	145.056
Jul 26	Talladega 500	Talladega	2.66	1	203.827
Oct 4	Holly Farms 400	North Wilkesboro	.625	3	115.196
Nov 11	Journal 500	Atlanta	1.522	1	174.341
1988 (6)					
Mar 6	Goodwrench 400	Rockingham	1.017	6	146.612
Jun 26	Miller 400	Michigan	2.0	2	*172.687**
Aug 21	Champion 400	Michigan	2.0	3	*174.940**
Sept 4	Southern 500	Darlington	1.366	1	*160.827**
Oct 16	Holly Farms 400	North Wilkesboro	.625	5	116.901
Oct. 23	AC Delco 500	Rockingham	1.017	4	*148.359**

Poles by Tracks: Talladega 6, Michigan 6, Daytona 4, Darlington 4, Atlanta 3, Pocono 3, North Wilkesboro 3, Charlotte 2, Dover 2, Rockingham 2.

Fastest: 212.809, Talladega, '87; Slowest: 115.196, North Wilkesboro, '87.

Poles By Track Length: Two miles or over, 19; two and a half miles or over, 13; mile and a half or over, 23; under a mile and a half, 11; under a mile, 3.

*Italics indicate track-record speed, and
**indicates world stock car racing record (to date).

WINNING CARS BY ERAS

1949-51
Winning Make: Olds, 35 victories
Others: Hudson 12, Plymouth 7, Mercury 4, Lincoln 4, Studebaker 3, Ford 1, Chrysler 1, Nash 1

1952-54
Winning Make: Hudson Hornet, 66 victories
Others: Olds 23, Chrysler 8, Plymouth 3

1955-56
Winning Make: Chrysler Hemi, 49 victories
Others: Ford 16, Dodge 12, Olds 11, Chevy 5, Mercury 5, Buick 2, Hudson Hornet 1

1957-60
Winning Make: (Tie) Ford and Chevy, each 68 victories
Others: Olds 16, Plymouth 15, Pontiac 13, Thunderbird 6, Dodge 1

1961-62
Winning Make: Pontiac, 52 victories
Others: Chevy 25, Ford 13, Chrysler 1

1963-69
Winning Make: Ford, 167 victories
Others: Plymouth 100, Dodge 66, Mercury 20, Chevrolet 16, Pontiac 4

1970-71
Winning Make: Plymouth, 43 victories
Others: Dodge 25, Mercury 15, Ford 10, Chevy 3

1972-75
Winning Make: Chevrolet, 35 victories
Others: Mercury 30, Dodge 23, Plymouth 8, Matador 4, Ford 4

1976-80
Winning Make: Chevrolet, 84 victories
Others: Mercury 19, Olds 18, Ford 14, Dodge 13

1981-82
Winning Make: Buick, 47 victories
Others: Ford 9, Chevrolet 4, Pontiac 1

1983-84
Winning Make: Chevrolet, 36 victories
Others: Pontiac, Ford and Buick, 8 each

1985-88
Winning Make: Chevrolet, 55 victories
Others: Ford 39, Pontiac 12, Buick 6, Olds 3
* * *

Total wins 1949-1988: Ford 349, Chevrolet 331, Plymouth 190, Dodge 162, Olds 107, Mercury 93, Pontiac 90, Hudson 79, Buick 63, Chrysler 59, Matador 5, Lincoln 4, Studebaker 3, Nash 1.

Highest number of wins in single year: 48, by Ford in 1965.

BILL ELLIOTT RECORD
(1976 through 1988)

SUPERSPEEDWAYS

Year	Races	Won	2nd	3rd	4th	5th	6th-10th	11th-31st	DNF	Poles	Outside Poles	Money Won
1988	27	5	1	2	4	0	4	4	1	5	2	$ 655,925
1987	21	6	3	0	2	1	1	3	5	6	3	861,890
1986	21	2	0	2	1	2	6	3	5	4	1	506,310
1985	20	11	2	0	2	0	1	3	1	11	0	943,203
1984	20	3	1	3	3	1	5	2	2	4	6	417,893
1983	20	1	4	1	1	2	7	2	2	0	4	277,880
1982	18	0	3	3	1	1	1	4	5	1	0	197,295
1981	13	0	0	0	1	0	6	1	5	1	0	68,570
1980	11	0	0	0	0	0	4	3	4	0	1	42,545
1979	11	0	1	0	0	0	3	5	2	0	0	51,640
1978	10	0	0	0	0	0	5	2	3	0	0	42,065
1977	10	0	0	0	0	0	2	3	5	0	0	19,925
1976	7	0	0	0	0	0	0	1	6	0	0	10,320
TOTALS	203	28	15	11	15	7	45	36	46	32	17	$4,095,461

ALL WINSTON CUP RACES

Year	Races	Won	2nd	3rd	4th	5th	6th-10th	11th-31st	DNF	Poles	Outside Poles	Money Won
1988	29	6	2	2	4	1	7	6	1	6	4	$1,554,639
1987	29	6	3	1	5	1	4	4	5	8	3	1,599,210
1986	29	2	0	2	1	3	8	7	6	4	2	1,069,142
1985	28	11	2	0	2	1	2	7	3	11	0	2,433,187
1984	30	3	1	4	4	1	11	4	2	4	7	660,226
1983	30	1	4	1	3	3	10	4	4	0	4	479,965
1982	21	0	3	3	1	1	1	6	6	1	0	226,780
1981	13	0	0	0	1	0	6	1	5	1	0	70,320
1980	11	0	0	0	0	0	4	3	4	0	1	42,545
1979	13	0	1	0	0	0	4	6	2	0	0	57,330
1978	10	0	0	0	0	0	5	2	3	0	0	42,065
1977	10	0	0	0	0	0	2	3	5	0	0	19,925
1976	8	0	0	0	0	0	0	2	6	0	0	11,635
TOTALS	261	29	16	13	21	11	64	55	51	35	21	$8,266,969

ELLIOTT 1988 STORY

Chapter-By-Chapter

Date	Race	Laps/Led	Points/ Position	Start/ Finish	Money
Feb 14	Daytona 500	200/0	127/12th	31-12	$31,015*
		(200)			
Feb 21	Pontiac 400	399/0	127/12th	16-12	10,595
	(Richmond)	(400)			
Mar 6	Goodwrench 500	491/110	155/6th	1-6	17,910
	(Rockingham)	(492)			
Mar 20	Motorcraft 500	312/0	106/11th	3-19	11,940
	(Atlanta)	(328)			
Mar 27	TranSouth 500	366/1	160/6th	15-4	19,260
	(Darlington)	(367)			
Apr 10	Valleydale 500	500/115	180/4th	13-1	45,750
	(Bristol)	(500)			
Apr 17	First Union 400	397/18	139/3rd	2-10	12,010
	(N. Wilkesboro)	(400)			
Apr 24	Pannill 500	493/0	130/3rd	15-11	10,470
	(Martinsville)	(500)			
May 1	Winston 500	188/0	146/3rd	11-7	21,375
	(Talladega)	(188)			
May 22	The Winston	135/18	—	5-4	50,000
	(Charlotte)	(135)			
May 29	Coca-Cola 500	340/15	111/5th	6-19	17,200
	(Charlotte)	(400)			
Jun 5	Budweiser 500	500/198	185/3rd	17-1	53,000
	(Dover)	(500)			
Jun 12	Budweiser 400	94/0	115/4th	8-16	11,000
	(Riverside)	(95)			
Jun 19	Miller 500	200/0	134/3rd	4-10	15,460
	(Pocono)	(200)			
Jun 26	Miller 400	200/23	175/3rd	1-2	42,875
	(Michigan)	(200)			
Jul 2	Firecracker 400	160/22	180/3rd	38-1	63,500
	(Daytona)	(160)			
Jul 24	AC Spark Plug 500	200/116	180/2nd	2-1	53,200
	(Pocono)	(200)			
Jul 31	Talladega 500	188/1	147/2nd	8-8	16,220
	(Talladega)	(188)			
Aug 14	Bud On The Glen	90/17	175/2nd	3-3	26,640
	(Watkins Glen)	(90)			
Aug 21	Champion 400	200/34	170/2nd	1-3	31,775
	(Michigan)	(200)			
Aug 27	Busch 500	500/3	175/1st	6-2	29,150
	(Bristol)	(500)			

*Won $12,000 by placing fifth in earlier Busch clash.

ELLIOTT 1988 STORY
Chapter-By-Chapter

Date	Race	Laps/Led	Points/ Position	Start/ Finish	Money
Sep 4	Southern 500 (Darlington)	367/154 (367)	185/1st	1-1	75,800
Sep 11	Miller 400 (Richmond)	399/1 (400)	151/1st	20-7	11,600
Sep 18	Delaware 500 (Dover)	500/392 (500)	185/1st	3-1	56,400
Sep 25	Goody's 500 (Martinsville)	499/88 (500)	155/1st	2-6	15,650
Oct. 9	Oakwood Homes 500 (Charlotte)	334/4 (334)	165/1st	2-4	35,900
Oct 16	Holly Farms 400 (North Wilkesboro)	400/45 (400)	160/1st	1-5	21,625
Oct 23	AC Delco 500 (Rockingham)	491/204 (492)	170/1st	1-4	23,480
Nov 6	Checker 500 (Phoenix)	312/0 (312)	160/1st	6-4	19,475
Nov 20	Journal 500 (Atlanta)	327/0 (328)	130/winner	29-11	12,500

THE POINTS BATTLE
Week-By-Week

Daytona 2/14
Points Leader: Bobby
Allison
Elliott: 12th, -58

Richmond 2/21
Leader: Neil Bonnett
Elliott: 12th, -89

Rockingham 3/6
Leader: Neil Bonnett
Elliott: 6th, -121

Atlanta 3/20
Leader: Neil Bonnett
Elliott: 11th, -117

Darlington 3/27
Leader: Dale Earnhardt
Elliott: 6th, -78

Bristol 4/10
Leader: Dale Earnhardt
Elliott: 4th, -24

North Wilkesboro 4/17
Leader: Dale Earnhardt
Elliott: 3rd, -60

Martinsville 4/24
Leader: Dale Earnhardt
Elliott: 3rd, -115

Talladega 5/1
Leader: Dale Earnhardt
Elliott: 3rd, -107

Charlotte 5/29
Leader: Dale Earnhardt
Elliott: 5th, -110

Dover 6/5
Leader: Dale Earnhardt
Elliott: 3rd, -50

Riverside 6/12
Leader: Rusty Wallace
Elliott: 4th, -104

Pocono 6/19
Leader: Rusty Wallace
Elliott: 3rd, -140

Michigan 6/26
Leader: Rusty Wallace
Elliott: 3rd, -150

Daytona 7/2
Leader: Rusty Wallace
Elliott: 3rd, -97

Pocono 7/24
Leader: Rusty Wallace
Elliott: 2nd, -3

Talladega 7/31
Leader: Rusty Wallace
Elliott: 2nd, -11

Watkins Glen 8/14
Leader: Rusty Wallace
Elliott: 2nd, -11

Michigan 8/21
Leader: Rusty Wallace
Elliott: 2nd, -21

Bristol 8/27
Leader: Elliott
Runner-up: Wallace, -16

Darlington 9/4
Leader: Elliott
Runner-up: Wallace, -26

Richmond 9/11
Leader: Elliott
Runner-up: Earnhardt,
-117
Third: Wallace, -119

Dover 9/18
Leader: Elliott
Runner-up: Earnhardt,
-127
Third: Wallace, -139

Martinsville 9/25
Leader: Elliott
Runner-up: Wallace, -124
Third: Earnhardt, -140

Charlotte 10/9
Leader: Elliott
Runner-up: Wallace, -109
Third: Earnhardt, -183

North Wilkesboro 10/17
Leader: Elliott
Runner-up: Wallace, -89
Third: Earnhardt, -188

Rockingham 10/23
Leader: Elliott
Runner-up: Wallace, -79
Third: Earnhardt, -198

Phoenix 11/6
Leader: Elliott
Runner-up: Wallace, -79
Third: Earnhardt, -231
(Earnhardt eliminated)

Atlanta 11/20
Winner: Elliott
Runner-up: Wallace, -24
Third: Earnhardt, -234
Fourth: Terry Labonte,
-481
Fifth: Ken Schrader, -630

HOW THEY FINISHED
IN '88 WINSTON CUP

The final top 18 finishers in 1988 Winston Cup series, with name, hometown, type of car, total points and total bonus money won, including first-half payoff:

1. Bill Elliott, Dawsonville, Ga., Ford Thunderbird, 4,488, $475,000.
2. Rusty Wallace, Charlotte, N.C., Pontiac, Grand Prix, 4,464, $375,000.
3. Dale Earnhardt, Doolie, N.C., Chevrolet Monte Carlo, 4,254, $245,000.
4. Terry Labonte, Trinity, N.C., Chevrolet Monte Carlo, 4,007, $155,000.
5. Ken Schrader, Concord, N.C., Chevrolet Monte Carlo, 3,858, $120,000.
6. Geoff Bodine, Julian, N.C., Chevrolet Monte Carlo, 3,799, $95,000.
7. Darrell Waltrip, Franklin, Tenn., Chevrolet Monte Carlo, 3,764, $80,000.
8. Davey Allison, Hueytown, Ala., Ford Thunderbird, 3,631, $45,000.
9. Phil Parsons, Denver, N.C., Oldsmobile Cutlass, 3,630, $71,000.
10. Sterling Marlin, Columbia, Tenn., Oldsmobile Cutlass, 3,621, $52,000.
11. Ricky Rudd, Chesapeake, Va., Buick Regal, 3,547, $35,000.
12. Bobby Hillin Jr., Harrisburg, N.C., Buick Regal, 3,446, $43,000.
13. Kyle Petty, High Point, N.C., Ford Thunderbird, 3,296, $31,000.
14. Alan Kulwicki, Concord, N.C., Ford Thunderbird, 3,176, $30,000.
15. Mark Martin, Batesville, Ark., Ford Thunderbird, 3,142, $28,000.
16. Neil Bonnett, Bessemer, Ala., Pontiac Grand Prix, 3,035, $27,000.
17. Lake Speed, Jackson, Miss., Oldsmobile Cutlass, 2,984, $26,000.
18. Michael Waltrip, Huntersville, N.C., Pontiac Grand Prix, 2,949, $25,000.

ELLIOTT RECORD
Track By Track, Through 1988

Talladega

Race	No.	Won	Top 5	Top 10	Poles	Total Money
Winston 500	12	1	2	6	3	$196,145
Talladega 500	12	1	2	7	3	175,750
Totals	24	2	4	13	6	$371,895

Bristol

Race	No.	Won	Top 5	Top 10	Poles	Total Money
Valleydale 500	6	1	3	5	0	$ 90,320
Busch 500	7	0	2	5	0	71,420
Totals	13	1	5	10	0	$161,740

Darlington

Race	No.	Won	Top 5	Top 10	Poles	Total Money
TranSouth 500	10	1	7	10	2	$158,580
Southern 500	12	2	6	10	2	250,825
Totals	22	3	13	20	4	$409,405

Daytona

Race	No.	Won	Top 5	Top 10	Poles	Total Money
Daytona 500	10	2	5	7	3	$692,925
Firecracker 400	12	1	3	6	1	194,010
Totals	22	3	8	13	4	$886,935

Dover

Race	No.	Won	Top 5	Top 10	Poles	Total Money
Budweiser 500	6	2	5	6	1	$169,780
Delaware 500	7	1	3	4	1	120,990
Totals	13	3	8	10	2	$290,770

Charlotte

Race	No.	Won	Top 5	Top 10	Poles	Total Money
Coca-Cola 600	13	0	1	2	2	$252,478
Oakwood Homes 500	12	2	5	10	0	311,858
Totals	25	2	6	12	2	$564,336

Martinsville

Race	No.	Won	Top 5	Top 10	Poles	Total Money
Pannill 500	6	0	0	2	0	$ 51,055
Goody's 500	6	0	1	2	0	63,310
Totals	12	0	1	4	0	$114,365

Michigan

Race	No.	Won	Top 5	Top 10	Poles	Total Money
Miller 400	12	3	5	6	2	$227,255
Champion 400	11	3	6	8	4	254,285
Totals	23	6	11	14	6	$481,540

ELLIOTT RECORD
Track By Track, Through 1988

Pocono

Race	No.	Won	Top 5	Top 10	Poles	Total Money
Miller 500	7	1	4	6	1	$136,840
AC Spark Plug 500	7	2	3	4	2	153,850
Totals	14	3	7	10	3	$290,690

Richmond

Race	No.	Won	Top 5	Top 10	Poles	Total Money
Pontiac 400	7	0	2	3	0	$ 61,120
Miller 400	7	0	2	3	0	60,350
Totals	14	0	4	6	0	$121,470

Riverside

Race	No.	Won	Top 5	Top 10	Poles	Total Money
Budweiser 400	6	0	2	4	0	$ 71,605
Winston West. 500	6	1	2	2	0	74,640
Totals	12	1	4	6	0	$146,245

Watkins Glen

Race	No.	Won	Top 5	Top 10	Poles	Total Money
Bud on The Glen	3	0	2	2	0	$ 57,590
Totals	3	0	2	2	0	$57,590

Nashville

Race	No.	Won	Top 5	Top 10	Poles	Total Money
Coors 420	3	0	1	1	0	$ 12,875
Pepsi 420	4	0	0	2	0	13,945
Totals	7	0	1	3	0	$26,820

North Wilkesboro

Race	No.	Won	Top 5	Top 10	Poles	Total Money
First Union 400	6	0	0	5	1	$ 58,650
Holly Farms 400	6	0	3	4	2	79,165
Totals	12	0	3	9	3	$137,815

Rockingham

Race	No.	Won	Top 5	Top 10	Poles	Total Money
Goodwrench 500	9	0	2	5	1	$ 89,780
AC Delco 500	9	2	4	6	1	143,845
Totals	18	2	6	11	2	$233,625

Phoenix

Race	No.	Won	Top 5	Top 10	Poles	Total Money
Checker 500	1	0	1	1	0	$ 19,475
Totals	1	0	1	1	0	$19,475

Atlanta

Race	No.	Won	Top 5	Top 10	Poles	Total Money
Motorcraft 500	13	1	2	3	0	$123,180
Journal 500	11	2	4	6	3	218,635
Totals	24	3	6	9	3	$341,815

WINNINGS BY TRACKS

1. Daytona, $886,935
2. Charlotte, $564,336
3. Michigan, $481,540
4. Darlington, $409,405
5. Talladega, $371,895
6. Atlanta, $341,815
7. Dover, $290,770
8. Pocono, $290,690
9. Rockingham, $233,625

10. Bristol, $161,740
11. Riverside, $146,245
12. North Wilkesboro, $137,815
13. Richmond, $121,470
14. Martinsville, $114,365
15. Watkins Glen, $57,590
16. Nashville, $26,820
17. Phoenix, $19,475

WINSTON POLE WINNERS
(1971-88)

1. David Pearson	59	6. Richard Petty	32
2. Darrell Waltrip	57	7. Buddy Baker	31
3. Cale Yarborough	51	8. Geoff Bodine	22
4. Bobby Allison	44	9. Neil Bonnett	20
5. BILL ELLIOTT	35	10. Benny Parsons and	19
		Terry Labonte	

SUPERSPEEDWAY WINNERS
(1950-88)

1. Richard Petty	55	6. BILL ELLIOTT	28
2. Bobby Allison	52	7. Buddy Baker	17
3. David Pearson	51	8. Dale Earnhardt	16
4. Cale Yarborough	50	9. Neil Bonnett	15
5. Darrell Waltrip	31	10. Benny Parsons	13

SUPERSPEEDWAY POLE WINNERS
(1950-88)

1. David Pearson	64	4. Buddy Baker	29
2. Cale Yarborough	48	5. Richard Petty	26
3. BILL ELLIOTT	32	6. Bobby Allison	23

Al Thomy, who spent more than 20 years as a member of *The Atlanta Journal and Constitution* sports staff, is uniquely qualified to write of stock car racing in the South. He was there when Bill France promoted races at The Fairgrounds in Greensboro, N.C., and, as the first full-time racing editor of *The Atlanta Constitution*, he was there when the gates were opened at the Daytona, Darlington, Charlotte and Atlanta tracks. He has written profiles from the Flock brothers and Curtis Turner to Bill Elliott and Dale Earnhardt. This is his third book. Others were *Ramblin' Wreck* (Strode) and *Pepper* (Doubleday).